The Quality of Life in Latin American Cities

The Quality of Life in Latin American Cities

MARKETS AND PERCEPTION

Edited by
Eduardo Lora
Andrew Powell
Bernard M.S. van Praag
Pablo Sanguinetti

A COPUBLICATION OF THE INTER-AMERICAN
DEVELOPMENT BANK AND THE WORLD BANK

© 2010 The Inter-American Development Bank
1300 New York Avenue NW
Washington DC 20577
Telephone: 202-263-1000
Internet: www.iadb.org
E-mail: res@iadb.org

1 2 3 4 13 12 11 10

A copublication of the Inter-American Development Bank and the World Bank.

The Inter-American Development Bank	The World Bank
1300 New York Avenue NW	1800 H Street NW
Washington DC 20577	Washington DC 20433

ISBN: 978-0-8213-7837-3
eISBN: 978-0-8213-8213-4
DOI: 10.1596/978-0-8213-7837-3

Library of Congress Cataloging-in-Publication Data
The quality of life in Latin American cities : markets and perception / edited by Eduardo Lora ... [et al.].

   p. cm.—(Latin American development forum series)
"A Copublication of the Inter-American Development Bank and the World Bank."
Includes bibliographical references and index.
ISBN 978-0-8213-7837-3—ISBN 978-0-8213-8213-4 (electronic)

   1. Quality of life—Latin America. 2. Cities and towns—Latin America. 3. Latin America—Social conditions. 4. Latin America—Economic conditions. I. Lora, Eduardo. II. World Bank.

   HN110.5.A8Q33 2010
   306.09728'091732—dc22

                                      2010002327

Cover: Ultra Designs.

Latin American Development Forum Series

This series was created in 2003 to promote debate, disseminate information and analysis, and convey the excitement and complexity of the most topical issues in economic and social development in Latin America and the Caribbean. It is sponsored by the Inter-American Development Bank, the United Nations Economic Commission for Latin America and the Caribbean, and the World Bank. The manuscripts chosen for publication represent the highest quality in each institution's research and activity output and have been selected for their relevance to the academic community, policy makers, researchers, and interested readers.

Advisory Committee Members

Alicia Bárcena Ibarra, Executive Secretary, Economic Commission for Latin America and the Caribbean, United Nations

Inés Bustillo, Director, Washington Office, Economic Commission for Latin America and the Caribbean, United Nations

José Luis Guasch, Senior Adviser, Latin America and the Caribbean Region, World Bank; and Professor of Economics, University of California, San Diego

Santiago Levy, Vice President for Sectors and Knowledge, Inter-American Development Bank

Eduardo Lora, Chief Economist (a.i.) and General Manager, Research Department, Inter-American Development Bank

Luis Servén, Research Manager, Development Economics Vice Presidency, World Bank

Augusto de la Torre, Chief Economist, Latin America and the Caribbean Region, World Bank

Titles in the Latin American Development Forum Series

The Quality of Life in Latin American Cities: Markets and Perception (2010) by Eduardo Lora, Andrew Powell, Bernard M.S. van Praag, Pablo Sanguinetti, editors

Discrimination in Latin America: An Economic Perspective (2010) by Hugo Ñopo, Alberto Chong, and Andrea Moro, editors

The Promise of Early Childhood Development in Latin America and the Caribbean (2010) by Emiliana Vegas and Lucrecia Santibáñez

Job Creation in Latin America and the Caribbean: Trends and Policy Challenges (2009) by Carmen Pagés, Gaëlle Pierre, and Stefano Scarpetta

China's and India's Challenge to Latin America: Opportunity or Threat? (2009) by Daniel Lederman, Marcelo Olarreaga, and Guillermo E. Perry, editors

Does the Investment Climate Matter? Microeconomic Foundations of Growth in Latin America (2009) by Pablo Fajnzylber, José Luis Guasch, and J. Humberto López, editors

Measuring Inequality of Opportunities in Latin America and the Caribbean (2009) by Ricardo de Paes Barros, Francisco H. G. Ferreira, José R. Molinas Vega, and Jaime Saavedra Chanduvi

The Impact of Private Sector Participation in Infrastructure: Lights, Shadows, and the Road Ahead (2008) by Luis Andres, José Luis Guasch, Thomas Haven, and Vivien Foster

Remittances and Development: Lessons from Latin America (2008) by Pablo Fajnzylber and J. Humberto López, editors

Fiscal Policy, Stabilization, and Growth: Prudence or Abstinence? (2007) by Guillermo Perry, Luis Servén, and Rodrigo Suescún, editors

Raising Student Learning in Latin America: Challenges for the 21st Century (2007) by Emiliana Vegas and Jenny Petrow

Investor Protection and Corporate Governance: Firm-Level Evidence Across Latin America (2007) by Alberto Chong and Florencio López-de-Silanes, editors

Natural Resources: Neither Curse nor Destiny (2007) by Daniel Lederman and William F. Maloney, editors

The State of State Reform in Latin America (2006) by Eduardo Lora, editor

Emerging Capital Markets and Globalization: The Latin American Experience (2006) by Augusto de la Torre and Sergio L. Schmukler

Beyond Survival: Protecting Households from Health Shocks in Latin America (2006) by Cristian C. Baeza and Truman G. Packard

Beyond Reforms: Structural Dynamics and Macroeconomic Vulnerability (2005) by José Antonio Ocampo, editor

Privatization in Latin America: Myths and Reality (2005) by Alberto Chong and Florencio López-de-Silanes, editors

Keeping the Promise of Social Security in Latin America (2004) by Indermit S. Gill, Truman G. Packard, and Juan Yermo

Lessons from NAFTA: For Latin America and the Caribbean (2004) by Daniel Lederman, William F. Maloney, and Luis Servén

The Limits of Stabilization: Infrastructure, Public Deficits, and Growth in Latin America (2003) by William Easterly and Luis Servén, editors

Globalization and Development: A Latin American and Caribbean Perspective (2003) by José Antonio Ocampo and Juan Martin, editors

Is Geography Destiny? Lessons from Latin America (2003) by John Luke Gallup, Alejandro Gaviria, and Eduardo Lora

About the Editors

Eduardo Lora is the chief economist (a.i.) and general manager of the Research Department at the Inter-American Development Bank (IDB). He received his master of science degree from the London School of Economics and was a visiting researcher at Oxford University in 1989. Before joining the Bank in 1996, he served five years as executive director of Fedesarrollo in Bogotá, Colombia. He has written several textbooks, edited more than a dozen books on economic and social policy issues, and served as academic coordinator of six editions of the IDB's flagship annual publication. He writes a column in the Colombian magazine *Dinero* and has published numerous academic articles.

Andrew Powell is regional economic adviser of the Caribbean Country Department of the Inter-American Development Bank and was previously lead research economist of the IDB's Research Department. Awarded a doctorate from the University of Oxford, he has served as chief economist of the Central Bank of Argentina and as a consultant to the IDB, International Monetary Fund (IMF), the World Bank, and several governments. His recent papers in academic journals include work on the Argentine crisis, the role of the IMF, the behavior of international banks, dollarization, and Basel II and emerging countries. He has also published work on commodity price behavior, regulation, and banking.

Bernard M.S. van Praag is Emeritus University Professor of Economics at the University of Amsterdam. He has published numerous papers and several monographs on the measurement of happiness, econometric methods, poverty, social security, and health. He is also coauthor, with Ada Ferrer-i-Carbonell, of *Happiness Quantified* (Oxford University Press, 2004), already a standard reference in its field. Founding president of the European Society for Population Economics (ESPE) and former coeditor of the *Journal of Population Economics*, he has also served as associate editor of the *Journal of Health Economics* and as a consultant to the Dutch government.

Pablo Sanguinetti is research director of the Corporación Andina de Fomento (CAF) and professor of economics at Universidad Torcuato Di Tella in Buenos Aires, Argentina. He received his Ph.D in economics from the University of California, Los Angeles. His varied research includes economic reform in Latin American countries, the economic and political determinants of fiscal federalism, development and trade, political economy of regional integration, and Mercosur. His papers have appeared in journals in Latin America and other regions, and he has contributed chapters to several books. He has served as a consultant to the IDB, the World Bank, and Comisión Económica para América Latina y el Caribe (CEPAL).

About the Contributors

Lorena Alcázar is affiliated with the Grupo de Análisis para el Desarollo (GRADE) in Lima, Peru.

Raúl Andrade is affiliated with the Grupo de Análisis para el Desarollo (GRADE) in Lima, Peru.

Guillermo Cruces is affiliated with the Centro de Estudios Distributivos, Laborales y Sociales (CEDLAS) of the Facultad de Ciencias Económicas (School of Economic Sciences) of the Universidad Nacional de La Plata, La Plata, Argentina.

Zuleika Ferre is affiliated with the Economics Department of the Universidad de la República, Montevideo, Uruguay.

Ada Ferrer-i-Carbonell is affiliated with the Institute for Economic Analysis (IAE-CSIC) in Barcelona, Spain.

Néstor Gandelman is affiliated with the Universidad ORT Uruguay.

Luis J. Hall is affiliated with the Universidad de Alicante, Spain.

Andrés Ham is affiliated with the Centro de Estudios Distributivos, Laborales y Sociales (CEDLAS) of the Facultad de Ciencias Económicas (School of Economic Sciences) of the Universidad Nacional de La Plata, La Plata, Argentina.

Róger Madrigal is affiliated with the Centro Agronómico Tropical de Investigación y Enseñanza (CATIE) of Cartago, Costa Rica.

Carlos Medina is affiliated with the Banco de la República de Colombia.

Leonardo Morales is affiliated with the Banco de la República de Colombia.

Jairo Núñez is affiliated with the Department of Economics of the Universidad Javeriana, Bogotá, Colombia.

Giorgina Piani is affiliated with the Economics Department of the Universidad de la República, Montevideo, Uruguay.

Juan Robalino is affiliated with the Centro Agronómico Tropical de Investigación y Enseñanza (CATIE) of Cartago, Costa Rica.

Martín Tetaz is affiliated with the Centro de Estudios Distributivos, Laborales y Sociales (CEDLAS) of the Facultad de Ciencias Económicas (School of Economic Sciences) of the Universidad Nacional de La Plata, La Plata, Argentina.

Contents

Preface   xix

Acknowledgments   xxv

Abbreviations   xxvii

1   LATIN AMERICAN CITIES: THEIR ORIGINS, ACHIEVEMENTS,
AND PROBLEMS   1
    Eduardo Lora

2   MEASURING QUALITY OF LIFE IN LATIN AMERICA'S URBAN
NEIGHBORHOODS: A SUMMARY OF RESULTS FROM THE
CITY CASE STUDIES   31
    Andrew Powell and Pablo Sanguinetti

3   TOWARD AN URBAN QUALITY OF LIFE INDEX:
BASIC THEORY AND ECONOMETRIC METHODS   65
    Bernard M.S. van Praag and Ada Ferrer-i-Carbonell

4   WELL-BEING AT THE SUBCITY LEVEL: THE BUENOS
AIRES NEIGHBORHOOD QUALITY OF LIFE SURVEY   91
    Guillermo Cruces, Andrés Ham, and Martín Tetaz

5   QUALITY OF LIFE IN URBAN NEIGHBORHOODS OF
BOGOTÁ AND MEDELLÍN, COLOMBIA   117
    Carlos Medina, Leonardo Morales, and Jairo Núñez

6   PRICING AMENITIES IN URBAN NEIGHBORHOODS
OF COSTA RICA   161
    Luis J. Hall, Juan Robalino, and Róger Madrigal

7   INFLUENCE OF INDIVIDUAL, URBAN, AND CIVIL SOCIETY
    SPHERES ON QUALITY OF LIFE IN METROPOLITAN
    LIMA, PERU   187
    Lorena Alcázar and Raúl Andrade

8   HOUSING AND NEIGHBORHOOD SATISFACTION IN
    MONTEVIDEO, URUGUAY   223
    Zuleika Ferre, Néstor Gandelman, and Giorgina Piani

Index   255

FIGURES

1.1   Urban Population, by Continent   3
1.2   Homeowners in the Lowest Two Income Quintiles
      Holding Title Deeds, Selected Countries, 2007   7
1.3   Home Ownership, by Income Decile, Selected Cities,
      2000 or Latest Available Year   11
1.4   Substandard Home Construction, by Income Decile,
      Selected Cities, 2000 or Latest Available Year   11
1.5   Households Lacking Any Public Service, by Income
      Decile, Selected Cities, 2000 or Latest Available Year   12
1.6   Percent of People Who Feel Safe Walking Alone at
      Night, Selected Countries, 2007   22
1.7   Percentage of People Who Have Confidence in Local
      Police Force, Selected Countries, 2007   23
1.8   Percentage of People Whose Money Was Stolen
      in Preceding 12 Months, by Region and Income
      Level, 2007   24
1.9   Percentage of People Who Feel Safe Walking Alone at
      Night in Their City, by Region and Income Level, 2007   24
1.10 Perceived Importance of Selected Urban
      Problems, 2007   26
3.1   Satisfaction Indifference Curves   72
3.2   Two-Layer Model of Domain and Life Satisfaction   81
4.1   Distributor of QoL   111
5.1   Distribution of the ICV Index in *Localidades* of
      Bogotá (2003) and *Comunas* of Medellín (2006)   119
5.2   Life Satisfaction and Welfare, Bogotá, 1997 and 2003   136
5.3   Life Satisfaction and Welfare, Medellín, 2006   142
5.4   Distribution of QoL Indexes, by Household, Bogotá
      (2003) and Medellín (2006)   146

5.5   Distribution of QoL Indexes, by Census Sector,
       Bogotá (2003) and Medellín (2006)   147
5.6   Quintiles of Hedonic, LS, and Atheoretical QoL
       Indexes and Average Per Capita Income, Bogotá
       and Medellín   153
6.1   Distribution of the Subjective Valuation of
       Life Satisfaction   180
7.1   Distribution of Population, by Socioeconomic Level,
       Metropolitan Lima   190
7.2   Self-Reported Satisfaction with QoL, by District,
       Mean, and Distribution   196
7.3   Self-Reported Satisfaction with Overall QoL, by
       Socioeconomic Level   197
7.4   Shares of Individual, Urban, and Civil Society/Trust
       Spheres in the QoL Index   218
7.5   Shares of Individual, Urban, and Civil Society/Trust
       Spheres in the QoL Index, by District   218
7.6   Shares of Individual, Urban, and Civil Society/Trust
       Spheres in the QOL Index, by Socioeconomic Level   219
8.1   Stratum Composition of Montevideo
       Neighborhoods   225
8.2   Overall Happiness, by Census Tract   232
8.3   Satisfaction with Housing, by Census Tract   233
8.4   Satisfaction with Neighborhood, by Census Tract   234

TABLES
1.1   Rates of Home Ownership, Selected Years, 1947–2002   5
1.2   Rates of Urban Home Ownership, by Income Level   6
1.3   Public Services Coverage and Gaps in Urban Areas,
       Various Years   9
1.4   Quantitative and Qualitative Housing Deficits and
       the Costs of Eliminating Them, Selected Cities,
       2000 or Latest Available Year   14
1.5   Levels of Satisfaction with Homes and Cities, 2007   16
1.6   Correlations of Home and City Satisfaction with
       Selected National-Level Variables   17
1.7   Factors Contributing to Housing Satisfaction, 2007   19
1.8   Satisfaction with Various Urban Factors and
       Perceived Level of Public Safety, by Region, 2007   21
2.1   Overall LS Regressions for the Six Case Cities:
       Summary of Results and Significant Factors   39

2.2   Values of Neighborhood Characteristics, Selected
      Buenos Aires Neighborhoods   42
2.3   House and Neighborhood Characteristics Revealed in
      House Prices, Case Cities   46
2.4   Hedonic Estimation of Implicit Prices for Housing
      and Neighborhood Characteristics, Metropolitan
      Area of San José, Costa Rica   49
2.5   Ranking of Districts by Housing and Neighborhood
      Characteristics, Using Hedonic Prices to Construct
      a QoL Index, Metropolitan San José, Costa Rica   51
2.6   Using Hedonic Prices to Construct a QoL Index, by
      Neighborhood, City of Buenos Aires, Argentina   52
4.1   Summary Statistics: Household, Respondent,
      and Dwelling Characteristics   95
4.2   General Life Satisfaction and Satisfaction
      with Life Domains   97
4.3   Subjective Evaluation of Neighborhood
      Characteristics   98
4.4   Neighborhood Characteristics Indicators   99
4.5   Neighborhood Characteristics per Block,
      Household Survey, NQLS Geographic Module   100
4.6   Augmented Hedonic Price Regressions for
      Monthly Rent   102
4.7   QoL Index and Implicit Price Differences
      for NQLS Neighborhoods   104
4.8   Neighborhood Satisfaction Regressions,
      OLS and 3SLS   107
4.9   General LS and Neighborhood Satisfaction
      Regressions, OLS and 3SLS   108
4.10 Monetized Value of LS-Based Neighborhood
      QoL Index   110
4.11 Correlation between Hedonic and LS Indexes   112
5.1   Hedonic Regressions for Bogotá, 2003   122
5.2   Hedonic Regressions for Medellín, 2006   129
5.3   LS Regressions for Bogotá, 2003   137
5.4   LS Regressions for Medellín, 2006   143
5.5   Hedonic-Weighted QoL Index for Localities
      in Bogotá, 2003   149
5.6   LS-Weighted QoL Index for Localities
      in Bogotá, 2003   150
5.7   Hedonic-Weighted QoL Index for Localities
      in Medellín, 2006   151

5.8	LS-Weighted QoL Index for Localities in Medellín, 2006	152
6.1	Urban Characteristics	164
6.2	Rent Regression with Selection Correction for AMSJO	169
6.3	Ranking of Districts by Housing and Neighborhood Characteristics	173
6.4	Regression Results and Price Amenities with Selection Decision for AMSJO and GAM	176
6.5	Regression Results and Price Amenities with Selection Decision	177
6.6	Descriptive Statistics of the Subjective Valuation of QoL, by County	181
6.7	LS Regression Explained by Other Subjective Valuations, Model COLS	182
6.8	LS Regression Explained by Predicted Subjective Valuations, Model COLS	182
6.9	LS Regression Explained by Objective Variables, Model COLS	183
7.1	Socioeconomic Levels of Populations in Districts under Analysis, 2005	191
7.2	Indicators for Districts under Analysis	191
7.3	Characteristics of the Sample	193
7.4	Self-Reported Satisfaction with Income	198
7.5	Self-Reported Satisfaction with House Infrastructure	199
7.6	Self-Reported Satisfaction with Health	200
7.7	Self-Reported Satisfaction with Quality of Education	201
7.8	Self-Reported Satisfaction with Neighborhood Safety Conditions	202
7.9	Self-Reported Satisfaction with Cleaning Conditions of the Streets	203
7.10	Self-Reported Satisfaction with Parks and Green Areas	204
7.11	Self-Reported Satisfaction with Transportation System	205
7.12	Self-Reported Satisfaction with Recreational Activities	206
7.13	Self-Reported Satisfaction with Civil Society/Trust	207
7.14	Descriptive Statistics for Objective Indicators and Control Variables	208

7.15   Self-Reported QoL with Objective Indicators   209
7.16   Self-Reported QoL with Predicted Satisfaction,
       by Dimension   213
7.17   QoL Indexes under Different Specifications   215
7.18   QoL Indexes under Different Specifications,
       by District   216
7.19   QoL Indexes under Different Specifications,
       by Socioeconomic Level   217
8.1   Stratum Composition of Neighborhoods and
       Number of Households Surveyed   226
8.2   Objective Individual Characteristics:
       Summary Statistics   228
8.3   Happiness and Satisfaction: Summary Statistics   231
8.4   Housing Characteristics: Summary Statistics   235
8.5   Neighborhood Variables: Summary Statistics   237
8.6   Housing and Neighborhood Regressions   242
8.7   Overall Satisfaction, by Employment Status   248

Preface

Vienna (Austria) has surpassed Zurich (Switzerland) as the world city with the best quality of life (QoL), according to the Mercer 2009 Quality of Living survey. That survey is one of many city rankings produced worldwide and consulted extensively by multinational firms and organizations. According to this ranking, which covers 215 cities around the world, Zurich, Geneva (Switzerland), and several other European cities also have excellent conditions for attracting international executives. Those conditions span more than 10 categories, from a stable political and social environment to the availability of housing, consumer goods, recreational opportunities, and a long list of public services that, according to Mercer, are important for international employees' QoL.[1]

The stated intention of the Mercer ranking is to "help governments and major companies place employees on international assignments." Other systems of urban monitoring have similar objectives, such as evaluating cities' economic competitiveness or measuring their attractiveness to global business. For example, according to the Global Cities Index (produced by *Foreign Policy* magazine, in conjunction with A.T. Kearney and the Chicago Council on Global Affairs), the most global city in the world is New York, followed closely by London, Paris, and Tokyo. These cities excel in business activity, human capital, information exchange, cultural experience, and political engagement—all of which make them the most interconnected cities and allow them to set global agendas and to serve as hubs of global integration, according to the institutions that produce the index.[2]

For residents of cities, however, or for the mayors and city councils who need to promote their citizens' well-being, these monitoring systems are useful but clearly incomplete. What purpose is served by improvement in international rankings if a city cannot meet its residents' most basic needs? The mayor of Santiago de Chile, the Latin American city with the best infrastructure according to the Mercer survey, would be ill-advised to make decisions on public expenditures according to the tastes and needs of international business people stationed there, even when their influence and economic weight may be substantial. In certain aspects, the interests and needs of the inhabitants of Santiago may coincide with those of the foreign population, but the immediate responsibility of the local government is to its citizenry, at least for the basic reason that foreigners do not vote.

In recent decades, many cities, regions, and countries have established systems for monitoring the quality of urban life that take into account the interests and needs of cities' residents. The system with the widest coverage is found in Europe: the Urban Audit system of Eurostat, which uses more than 300 indicators to monitor QoL in 357 cities. This system has the explicit (and ambitious) intention to shed light on "most aspects of quality of life, e.g. demography, housing, health, crime, labour market, income disparity, local administration, educational qualifications, environment, climate, travel patterns, information society and cultural infrastructure" (Feldmann 2008, 2).

Efforts in other world regions have less geographic coverage but are equally ambitious. The QoL report covering 12 of New Zealand's cities encompasses 186 individual measures across 11 domain areas (Quality of Life Project 2009). In the developing world, initiatives in several cities of Brazil and Colombia stand out. Although less structured than their counterparts in Europe and New Zealand, some of those monitoring systems have greater flexibility in exploring issues of immediate interest to citizens. The Bogotá Cómo Vamos system, for instance, is a veritable barometer of public opinion on the principal aspects of the city's conditions.[3]

All of these systems share two interesting but problematic traits. First, in contrast to the indexes for executives or international businesses, which are based exclusively on objective data, systems for monitoring the QoL of the population at large combine objective information with opinions (in varying proportions). Whereas New Zealand's Quality of Life Project attempts to strike a balance between objective and subjective indicators, Bogotá Cómo Vamos has gradually moved from its origin as an opinion survey in the late 1990s to a mix of subjective and objective indicators. A remarkable feature of both systems, however, is the lack of interconnection between the objective and subjective indicators. In the New Zealand system, for instance, the most comprehensive measures of subjective well-being are reported as part of the health indicators, with no attempt to understand their relationship with the objective indicators in that or other domains. The same concerns apply to other systems that mix objective and subjective indicators (Santons and Martins 2007). It is hard to argue that the urban QoL can be satisfactorily monitored with the exclusive use of either objective or subjective indicators. Many important aspects of people's lives do not lend themselves to objective measure, such as the beauty of the urban environment (or the lack of it), feelings of insecurity, or the quality of the relationships among neighbors. But subjective measures may be misleading as well, because of a lack of public information, cultural biases, habituation, or aspiration factors. Partially for these reasons, international monitoring systems (including Eurostat's Urban Audit) avoid subjective variables as much as possible, believing that they limit international comparability. This limitation, however, amounts to throwing out the baby with the bathwater. An alternative solution is to understand the relationship between objective and subjective indicators and to exploit it in a complementary manner that enriches the interpretation of both.

The second problematic feature is the inclusion of a large number of topics. Because the very essence of urban life is the meeting of diverse individuals who undertake a variety of activities and may have greatly differing interests and tastes, it may seem necessary for a monitoring system to cover many dimensions of a city's services and amenities and of the ways in which residents use and value them. Although Urban Audit's more than 300 indicators address the interests of many different users, that very breadth may hinder rather than facilitate the policy-making process because it does not provide any ranking of needs or priorities. Moreover, the development of a universal set of indicators that would enable national or even worldwide comparisons among cities is a futile undertaking: huge differences exist in geographic, economic, and sociocultural contexts; and many aspects of QoL are qualitative in nature. One possible solution is to use participatory approaches to elicit residents' degrees of concern with different dimensions or their relative importance (see Fahy 2009). Another possible approach is to employ objective and subjective information jointly, using statistical methods to deduce which (and to what degree) dimensions and aspects of urban conditions are important, according to different criteria.

With these issues in mind, the contributors to this book explore a new method of monitoring the quality of urban life. This method attempts to resolve the problems that result from using a combination of objective and subjective information, and to cover multiple issues of potential importance for residents' QoL. To combine objective and subjective information in a coherent manner and to focus on the most relevant dimensions of the QoL in a city or neighborhood, the contributors use two conceptually basic criteria: the market price of housing and the individual's life satisfaction.

The sale or rental prices of housing in a city are a synthesis of how the market values certain characteristics or attributes—not only those of a house itself but also those of its surroundings. Housing prices therefore are a good synthetic measure of the quality of urban life that residents may enjoy, provided that those prices reflect all of the city's characteristics that have an effect on well-being. Here is where life satisfaction comes into play. Although life satisfaction cannot be measured with the same precision as the price of a house, it can be fairly well approximated by means of a very simple question that is often included in QoL surveys. Life satisfaction is, in turn, a synthetic measure of the recognition that individuals give to all aspects of their lives, including the home and city where they live. Just as housing prices may not reflect all aspects of a city that affect well-being, an individual's life satisfaction may not depend on some of the same variables that affect housing prices. Satisfaction may depend, instead, on other conditions of the city, along with numerous individual factors ranging from friendships and religious beliefs to one's state of health and temperament.

Therefore, these two approaches to measuring the factors that affect the quality of urban life—the hedonic price approach and the life satisfaction approach—can be used in a complementary manner to answer such questions as the following:

- What urban problems have the greatest impact on people's opinion of city management?
- Of those problems, which have the most widespread effects?
- Is the city improving or growing worse in areas that matter to people?
- Do perceptions of the severity of problems match objective indicators?
- Do gaps between perception and reality differ among various parts of the city, especially between high- and low-income areas?
- In what parts of the city is it most feasible for homebuilders to seek solutions to urban problems, such as inadequate road infrastructure, a lack of recreation areas, or poor safety conditions?
- Which of the city's problems should be addressed first by government authorities in light of their impact on the well-being of various groups of individuals and in light of the ability of private initiatives to respond?
- Which homeowners derive the greatest economic benefits from the public provision of infrastructure or services?
- When can or should property taxes be used to finance the provision of certain services—or the solution of certain urban problems?

Of course, there are other questions that cannot be answered by the method proposed in this book. In particular, the method does not permit comparison of the QoL in different cities nor, consequently, can it provide city rankings. The reason is quite simple: if residents of London value the excitement and diversity of their city and residents of Oslo consider order and homogeneity essential, there is no point in including both variables in the same index for purposes of comparison. A more abstract concept could be found that encompasses both qualities, but doing so would not greatly facilitate decisions on what should be done to improve either city.

Although the method proposed does not permit cross-city comparisons, it does permit the comparison of problems within a city and, thus, a ranking of their importance from the perspectives of the market and of both individuals and social groups. It also enables a valuation of public goods according to both criteria—a factor that is essential for making informed decisions on public spending.

The precision with which these questions can be answered depends, of course, on the quality and the level of detail of the objective and subjective data obtained. In the monitoring systems that already exist in some cities, most of the necessary information is available. Paradoxically, however, some cities do not gather information on the two key variables: sales/rental prices of housing and satisfaction with life (or, at least, with the city).

Nonetheless, the principal information-gathering effort involved in establishing a sound QoL monitoring system—such as the one proposed in this book—should take place during the system's preparatory phase rather than during its regular functioning. The power of a monitoring system resides not in trying to cover every type of topic, but in covering key issues on the basis of a careful exploration of the determinants of housing prices and of individuals' satisfaction with life or with the city.

This book suggests how that exploration should be undertaken, and how a monitoring system that has a solid conceptual basis and is both easy to operate and reasonable in cost can then be put into practice. Long the ideal of many scholars and observers of urban problems, such a system may now be close to realization.

In this book, examples of Latin American cities are used as case studies. As argued in the first chapter, there are good reasons to concentrate on Latin America: it is the world region with the most rapid urban development and is the most urbanized region in the developing world. In contrast to residents of cities in poorer regions, Latin Americans have managed to democratize homeownership and to extend basic services to the majority of households. That means that improving the QoL in Latin American cities is no longer primarily a matter of bricks and mortar. But the challenges are as large as they are diverse. They include inadequate public spaces and recreational facilities, deficient transportation systems, and the marginalizing of millions of poor people in segregated zones with little access to health and education services.

The cities chosen for the case studies were Buenos Aires (Argentina), Bogotá and Medellín (Colombia), San José (Costa Rica), Lima (Peru), and Montevideo (Uruguay). Although they are not a representative sample of the region, they are sufficiently diverse to illustrate the variation in problems among cities and the possibilities offered by the proposed method of analysis. Chapter 2 introduces the reader to the hedonic price and the life satisfaction approaches and presents a comparative summary of the conclusions of the six case studies. This chapter, like the first, is essential for the policy maker or activist in urban affairs who wants to understand the possibilities of the new systems for monitoring the quality of urban life. Chapter 3 is a concise and self-contained introduction to the economic theory on which the hedonic pricing and life satisfaction approaches are based and which forms the backbone of this book. Chapters 4–8 then summarize the most notable findings of the case studies, each emphasizing a different topic and focus.

This book does not pretend to solve all the problems that must be addressed to establish a system for monitoring the quality of urban life. It does aspire, however, to serve as a means by which local governments, analysts of urban problems, and communities themselves may take advantage of a new generation of urban QoL monitoring strategies that have significant potential for contributing to public decision-making processes.

Notes

1. See Mercer, "Quality of Living Global City Rankings 2009—Mercer Survey," http://www.mercer.com/qualityoflivingpr.
2. See *Foreign Policy*, "The 2008 Global Cities Index," http://www.foreign policy.com/articles/2008/10/15/the_2008_global_cities_index.
3. See Bogotá Cómo Vamos, http://www.bogotacomovamos.org/scripts/home .php.

References

Fahy, Frances. 2009. "Deriving Quality of Life Indicators in Urban Areas. A Practitioner's Guide." Department of Geography, National University of Ireland, Galway. http://www.epa.ie/downloads/pubs/research/econ/galway21_fahy _guide.pdf.

Feldmann, Berthold. 2008. "The Urban Audit—Measuring the Quality of Life in European Cities." Eurostat, Statistics in Focus, 82/2008. http://epp.eurostat .ec.europa.eu/cache/ITY_OFFPUB/KS-SF-08-082/EN/KS-SF-08-082-EN.PDF.

Quality of Life Project. 2009. *Quality of Life '07 in Twelve of New Zealand's Cities.* http://www.bigcities.govt.nz/pdfs/2007/Quality_of_Life_2007.pdf.

Santons, Luis Delfin, and Isabel Martins. 2007. "Monitoring the Urban Quality of Life: The Porto Experience." *Social Indicators Research* 80: 411–25.

Acknowledgments

This book is the result of a project carried out under the auspices of the Inter-American Development Bank's Latin American and Caribbean Research Network and was part of a research program on quality of life in Latin America and the Caribbean conducted on the occasion of the IDB's 50th anniversary. Andrew Powell, Bernard M.S. van Praag, and Pablo Sanguinetti were the academic advisers to this project, and Eduardo Lora was the director of the research program.

The following research teams participated in the project:

- Argentina: Centro de Estudios Distributivos, Laborales y Sociales (CEDLAS), Universidad Nacional de La Plata (UNLP). Guillermo Cruces, Andrés Ham, and Martín Tetaz.
- Colombia: Universidad EAFIT and Centro Nacional de Consultoría. Carlos Medina, Jairo Núñez, and Leonardo Morales.
- Costa Rica: Environment for Development Initiative at Centro Agronómico Tropical de Investigacíon y Enseñanza (CATIE). Juan A. Robalino, Róger Madrigal, and Luis J. Hall.
- Peru: Grupo de Análisis para el Desarrollo (GRADE). Lorena Alcázar and Raúl Andrade.
- Uruguay: Universidad de la República and Universidad ORT. Giorgina Piani, Néstor Gandelman, and Zuleika Ferre.

The case studies included in this volume are abridged versions of the complete reports, which are available upon request from the authors. Marcela Cristini and Ramiro Moya prepared additional background material for chapter 1.

The coeditors also wish to acknowledge the invaluable comments of two anonymous referees and the support received from the administrative staff of the IDB Research Department. For their editorial efforts, the coeditors are most grateful to the team led by Janice Tuten of the World Bank Office of the Publisher under the direction of Santiago Pombo, and also to Rita Funaro, John Smith, and Myriam Escobar Genes at the IDB, for their support in this area.

Abbreviations

3SLS	three-stage least squares
AMBA	metropolitan area of Buenos Aires
AMSJO	metropolitan area of San José
COLS	cardinal ordinary least squares
GAM	greater metropolitan area of San José
GDP	gross domestic product
LS	life satisfaction
NQLS	Neighborhood Quality of Life Survey
OLS	ordinary least squares
POLS	probit-adapted ordinary least squares
QoL	quality of life
SD	standard deviation
SEL	socioeconomic level
SISBEN	System for the Selection of Beneficiaries of Social Programs

All amounts are presented in U.S. dollars unless otherwise indicated.

1

Latin American Cities: Their Origins, Achievements, and Problems

Eduardo Lora

Latin America is the only region in the developing world where the majority of the population lives in urban areas. Whereas less than 40 percent of the population in Africa and Asia resides in cities or towns, 77 percent of the population in Latin America and the Caribbean is urban, according to United Nations calculations for 2005 (UN 2006, 3). Large urban areas imply many positive externalities and some negative ones. Indeed, the very existence of these areas of dense population suggests that the benefits of agglomeration outweigh the costs. However, this presumption provides no criteria for prioritizing policy actions to improve the quality of life (QoL) in the fast-growing cities of the region.

The process of urbanization has been accompanied by a very substantial improvement in the quality of housing infrastructure. Though much remains to be done to solve the persistent deficit in dwellings of reasonable quality, many other problems—from insecurity to traffic congestion, and from lack of public spaces to severe socioeconomic segregation—affect Latin American cities.[1] As an introduction to the rest of the book, this

The author acknowledges the valuable research assistance of Lucas Higuera and María Victoria Rodríguez and the useful comments offered by many colleagues, including Juan Camilo Chaparro, Rita Funaro, Andrew Powell, Bernard M.S. van Praag, and two anonymous referees. This chapter draws partly from work commissioned by the Inter-American Development Bank Research Department and produced by FIEL (Fundación de Investigaciones Económicas Latinoamericanas, Buenos Aires, Argentina), as reported in Cristini and Moya (2008).

chapter tries to present a panorama of the urbanization process and to describe some of the challenges facing Latin American cities, as seen both through the lens of the traditional indicators used in the region and through a new lens—that of people's own opinions.

The chapter starts by describing briefly the most salient features of the great urban expansion that has taken place in Latin America since the middle of the 20th century. The next section discusses persistent deficits in services (especially sanitation) and the inadequacies in building materials and standards that exist in various countries and cities, despite the region's success in democratizing property and providing basic services to most homes. The third section quantifies the cost of addressing those deficits. Solving these problems is a challenge not only because of the cost involved, but also because the amount that families should pay and the financing mechanisms that should be used are matters not yet clarified. Furthermore, as the rest of the chapter shows, improving the QoL in cities involves far more than bricks and mortar. Through extensive use of subjective data, the chapter compares Latin America with other regions in a host of dimensions, exploring how both objective and subjective factors influence satisfaction with housing and with cities in Latin America. Although this approach gives a sense of the relative importance of each of the dimensions considered, it cannot provide a basis for more practical decisions. The chapter concludes that many aspects of cities—such as transportation and the quality of public spaces or recreation services—fall outside of generalizations because diversity is the essence of urban life: different people look for different things in the same city, and cities and neighborhoods can respond differently to the diversity of their inhabitants' interests and needs. This fact calls for an approach that takes into account both objective and subjective variables—an approach that focuses on specific cities or even neighborhoods, and one that considers variations in tastes, needs, and interests.

The Great Urban Expansion

Since the mid-1900s, the urbanization process in Latin America has progressed more rapidly than in any other region (see figure 1.1). Squalid living conditions in the countryside, arising from the concentration of land ownership in the hands of a few families and the low labor productivity of the *campesinos* and tenant farmers, sparked a process of migration from rural areas to the city that continues in many countries. Driving the great expansions of Bogotá (Colombia), Caracas (República Bolivariana de Venezuela), Mexico City (Mexico), and Lima (Peru) since the 1960s has been rural migration, intensified by still-high fertility rates as well as lower (and rapidly falling) urban infant mortality rates. In the 1960s and 1970s, some large cities—such as São Paulo (Brazil)—also received great

Figure 1.1 Urban Population, by Continent

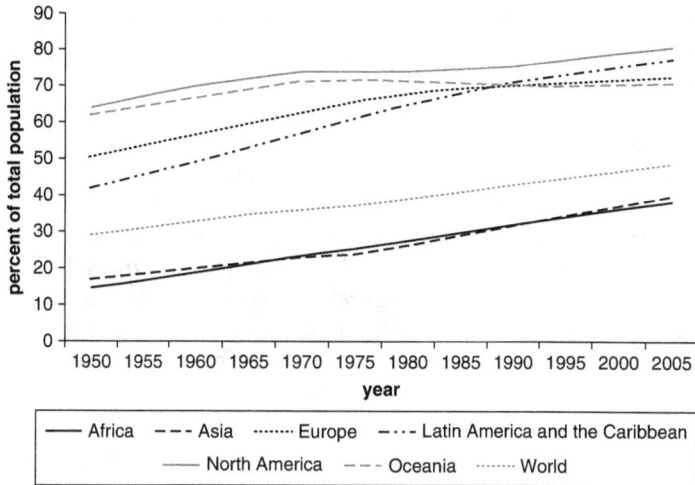

Source: Cristini and Moya (2008), based on World Urbanization Prospects: The 2005 Revision Population Database.

numbers of foreigners, who were more educated and had more capital than did the destitute *campesinos* and rural workers. This influx, however, was the exception. Urban expansion was driven mostly by internal migration, and the new city dwellers tended to have little or no education or capital. Moreover, guerrillas and armed conflicts in rural areas in Peru in the 1980s; in Guatemala, El Salvador, and Nicaragua for several decades; and even now in Colombia have sped up this migratory process.

Internal migration thus has led to the urbanizing of poverty because the number of poor people is larger in urban areas, although the poverty rate is higher in the countryside. Of the 209 million poor Latin Americans in 2007 (or 40 percent of the total population), an estimated 138 million (about 66 percent of those in poverty) lived in urban areas (ECLAC 2006). Because large cities are dominant in Latin America, the ability of the urban poor to escape poverty and improve their QoL depends critically on the opportunities and conditions offered by and in large cities.

Latin America has 4 of the world's 20 cities with more than 10 million inhabitants, and 55 of the world's 414 cities with more than 1 million people. Those 55 cities are home to 183 million people, one-third of all Latin Americans (Cristini and Moya 2008, 8–9). Although big cities are more important in Latin America than in the rest of the developing world, the largest cities no longer are the fastest-growing ones. In Argentina,

Brazil, Chile, and Mexico (which urbanized more rapidly and are more advanced in the demographic transition process than are most of the other countries), mega-cities are growing more slowly and are losing importance relative to intermediate-size cities. As expected, the cities that are growing most rapidly at present are in countries where population growth is still high and urbanization rates are low. As a consequence, the region's urban population increasingly consists of residents of intermediate-size rather than large cities.[2]

Instability, both political and economic, also seems to have had an impact on urban growth patterns in recent decades. Migration processes are triggered not only by conflicts in the countryside, but also by irregular changes of power in the cities. Although specific explanations vary, proximity to power may encourage relocation to large cities when regular mechanisms of public resource allocation weaken. The fact that economic instability—not only economic growth—contributes to accelerating the growth of the large cities suggests that those cities offer better opportunities for improving income and for coping with economic risks.[3]

Home Ownership and Services

The expansion of Latin American cities in the second half of the 20th century produced a democratization of home ownership at unprecedented rates in the region, and possibly in the world. Around 1950, roughly one in four families in Buenos Aires, Mexico City, or Santiago (Chile) owned its own home (see table 1.1); now, however, approximately two-thirds of families in those cities are homeowners. Nevertheless, according to recent statistics, home ownership in Colombia has stabilized at lower levels and has even fallen slightly. The most recent surveys of urban areas in 22 Latin American and Caribbean countries show average ownership rates of 68.4 percent (table 1.2; Cristini and Moya 2008). This rate is higher than that of other developing countries; and it is very close to that of the United States (69 percent), which has very developed mortgage markets and a long tradition of incentives for home ownership (Fay and Wellenstein 2005). In the region as a whole, the urban home ownership rate is higher among families with higher incomes (71 percent versus 64 percent), but the average difference of 7 percent hides some more marked cases. In Uruguay, for example, home ownership is greater than 75 percent for higher-income families and just 44 percent for lower-income families. In countries with larger rural populations, however, home ownership among the poor may be higher than among higher-income families because home ownership tends to be higher in rural areas (which also tend to be poorer) (Cristini and Moya 2008, 42).

The democratization of housing in cities undergoing rapid expansion in the second half of the 20th century occurred spontaneously, largely

Table 1.1 Rates of Home Ownership, Selected Years, 1947–2002
Percent of families

City	1947–52	1970–73	1990–93	1998–2002
Bogotá, Colombia	43	42	54	52
Buenos Aires, Argentina	27	61	72	75
Guadalajara, Mexico	29	43	68	62
Medellín, Colombia	51	57	63	56
Mexico City, Mexico	25	43	70	76
Río de Janeiro, Brazil	33	54	63	75
Santiago, Chile	26	57	71	73

Sources: Gilbert (2001); UN-HABITAT (2003); for Colombia, 1990–93 and 1998–2002, Departamento Administrativo Nacional de Estadística Surveys.

as a result of irregular acquisition of land by rural immigrants and the poor urban classes. Methods of acquisition ranged from the purchase of suburban land without subdivision permits to de facto occupation of privately or officially owned land. Most settlements of poor families in Peru, for instance, originated through land occupations. The district of San Juan de Lurigancho, whose 830,000 inhabitants now represent more than 10 percent of Lima's population, began in the 1960s as an irregular settlement area—like most districts in the three "cones" extending toward the desert to the north, east, and south of Lima (Reid 2008). Occasionally, occupations have been permitted by the government, as was true in some Brazilian and Mexican cities in the 1970s and 1980s, in Santiago before 1973, and in Lima during the administration of President Manuel A. Odría (1948–50).

Not all irregular settlements originated from illegal occupations, however. Currently, much illegality is formal only in its not being compliant with planning regulations or in the absence of relevant title deeds to confirm voluntary transfers of ownership. Many governments have implemented ownership title programs to solve this problem. As part of its strategy to regularize market functioning and reduce the size of the state, the military government in Chile handed over more than half a million title deeds between 1979 and 1989; and the two democratic governments that followed distributed another 150,000 title deeds up to 1998 (Rugiero Pérez 1998). In Peru, the Commission for Formalization of Informal Ownership recorded more than 1 million titles between 1996 and 2000 (Calderón 2001). But, even today, about half of homeowners at low socioeconomic levels lack deeds; and, in some countries, that percentage is higher (see figure 1.2).[4] The lack of titles has contributed to disorderly development of home building in large Latin American cities.

Table 1.2 Rates of Urban Home Ownership, by Income Level
Percent of families

Country	Low income	High income	Average home ownership
Argentina	58.4	70.6	66.0
Bahamas	51.9	61.8	57.7
Bolivia	55.4	55.0	53.9
Brazil	65.3	73.0	69.9
Chile	59.8	69.2	65.9
Colombia	57.8	64.1	60.0
Costa Rica	69.1	74.2	72.2
Dominican Republic	59.3	58.3	59.3
Ecuador	70.6	69.5	69.4
El Salvador	56.3	71.0	66.0
Guatemala	71.1	70.0	70.0
Guyana	31.3	42.9	40.6
Haiti	47.3	45.2	46.0
Honduras	57.2	62.0	59.2
Jamaica	57.2	48.5	52.5
Mexico	67.3	71.8	69.5
Nicaragua	67.6	79.6	76.6
Paraguay	75.6	74.2	74.4
Peru	55.1	70.0	65.7
Suriname	65.4	67.1	63.7
Uruguay	43.9	75.5	64.0
Venezuela, R.B. de	77.2	74.3	75.3
Latin America and the Caribbean[a]	63.6	71.3	68.4

Source: Cristini and Moya (2008), based on the Socio-Economic Database for Latin America and the Caribbean.

Note: "Low income" corresponds to the lowest two quintiles, and "high income" corresponds to the highest two quintiles. The data come from household surveys and may differ from census data.

a. These are weighted averages.

Figure 1.2 Homeowners in the Lowest Two Income
Quintiles Holding Title Deeds, Selected Countries, 2007

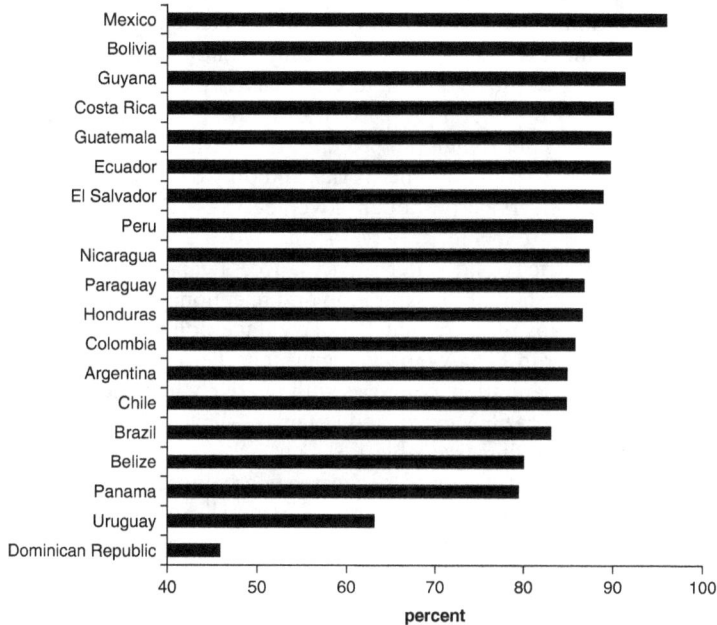

Source: Gallup 2007.

For example, 60 percent of the population of Mexico City in 1990 lived in self-built houses, with similar conditions in Caracas (42 percent) and Lima (38 percent) (Calderón 2001).

Nonetheless, a relatively high percentage of homes now complies with acceptable standards of construction and access to basic services. For several decades, what does and does not constitute an acceptable home has been the subject of intense debate among economists, architects, urban planners, and sociologists in Latin America. All agree that no universal standard can be defined because basic requirements depend on climate, building methods, customs, and ultimately on individual needs and tastes. A simple standard, based on available information rather than conceptual rigor, defines as unfit any housing built with low-quality materials, according to the standards of the country in which it is built. Using this criterion for 65 cities in the region that account for more than half the urban population, an average of 18 percent of homes are unfit. However, this average hides a distribution with rates ranging from 5 percent to almost 20 percent of housing in 17 of the region's 22 largest cities. The rates are particularly alarming in the intermediate cities of Bolivia, Brazil, and Mexico (Cristini and Moya 2008).

Apart from the quality of building materials, access to the essential services of sanitation, water, electricity, and (debatably) telephone is considered a basic requirement for good-quality housing. Although there are notable disparities among countries, access to electricity is practically universal in the urban areas of the region (95 percent of homes have this service), and access to running water is high (86 percent). In contrast, only 57 percent of homes have access to sanitation networks, and only 61 percent have access to fixed telephone service (although coverage rises to 87 percent when mobile telephones are included) (Cristini and Moya 2008, 51).[5] Although moderate for electricity and water services, access gaps by socioeconomic group are quite substantial for sanitation and telephone services. However, there are access gaps of more than 20 percentage points for electricity in Haiti and for water in El Salvador, Paraguay, and Peru (Cristini and Moya 2008, 52–53). For sanitation, countries with relatively high income levels— such as Argentina, Brazil, Mexico, and Uruguay—have access gaps of more than 30 percentage points (see table 1.3).

Democratization of access to services has advanced at a much more modest rate than has democratization of ownership or improvement in home building materials. Among the five cities graphed in figures 1.3, 1.4, and 1.5, Caracas is the city where access to public services is most extensive and equal at all income levels. However, one out of three homes in the three lowest-income deciles suffers basic deficiencies in building materials. In Buenos Aires and São Paulo, few homes are considered unfit by official standards; but in Buenos Aires, four out of five homes in the lowest decile lack sanitation, water, or telephone; and in São Paulo, less than half of the families in the three lowest deciles own their homes. In Lima and Mexico City, home ownership rates (all relatively low) do not vary greatly between rich and poor families. Although both cities have made an enormous effort to provide basic services to all homes, 15 percent of homes in the poorest decile in Mexico City and 33 percent in Lima remain without at least one service. Those two cities additionally display pronounced housing quality gaps: 35 percentage points separate the highest and lowest deciles' rates of substandard housing in Mexico City, and 27 points separate them in Lima (Cristini and Moya 2008).

Housing Deficits and the Costs of Fixing Them

How far are Latin American cities from solving the most basic deficiencies in home construction and the provision of water, sanitation, and electricity services? This ongoing question usually is addressed by calculations of "quantitative" and "qualitative" housing deficits. The former

Table 1.3 Public Services Coverage and Gaps in Urban Areas, Various Years

Country	Year	Sanitation		Water		Electricity		Telephone		Telephone/cell phone	
		Coverage (% of population)	Gap (%)	Coverage (% of population)	Gap (%)	Coverage (% of population)	Gap (%)	Coverage (% of population)	Gap (%)	Coverage (% of population)	Gap (%)
Argentina	2003	60.4	39.2	98.4	4.0	99.5	1.2	64.8	39.5	93.0	11.1
Bahamas	2001	12.8	-0.1	86.7	12.4	96.1	5.7	—	—	—	—
Belize	1999	—	—	—	—	—	—	62.7	38.9	93.3	—
Bolivia	2003–04	61.2	-3.2	90.2	9.7	92.5	6.1	45.5	27.0	86.6	11.0
Brazil	2005	65.5	30.2	95.6	9.9	99.6	0.9	95.7	7.0	98.0	4.0
Chile	2003	91.8	11.2	99.3	1.3	99.7	0.6	69.8	24.9	93.1	13.0
Colombia	2004	87.6	10.4	89.9	5.2	90.4	4.6	76.2	13.7	94.9	4.8
Costa Rica	2005	43.4	5.8	98.9	0.6	99.9	0.2	74.1	15.0	87.8	14.2
Dominican Republic	2006	32.3	14.6	80.6	18.9	94.4	4.7	40.6	43.8	84.9	20.1
Ecuador	2003	67.4	28.7	91.1	9.7	99.3	1.2	49.3	39.2	77.9	31.5
El Salvador	2004	50.6	30.7	73.7	23.8	90.7	14.4	59.0	19.2	87.2	8.9
Guatemala	2004	66.7	23.9	77.9	0.8	96.0	11.0	42.9	25.1	84.3	14.0
Guyana	1992–93	1.6	-3.3	88.7	7.3	91.0	14.6	83.3	1.6	95.2	0.4
Haiti	2001	—	—	23.2	11.1	61.9	28.7	—	—	—	—

(continued)

Table 1.3 Public Services Coverage and Gaps in Urban Areas, Various Years (continued)

Country	Year	Sanitation Coverage (% of population)	Gap (%)	Water Coverage (% of population)	Gap (%)	Electricity Coverage (% of population)	Gap (%)	Telephone Coverage (% of population)	Gap (%)	Telephone/cell phone Coverage (% of population)	Gap (%)
Honduras	2006	63.8	31.1	—	—	97.0	10.1	51.3	5.8	70.5	6.7
Jamaica	2002	32.9	1.3	65.3	12.0	92.3	6.3	—	—	—	—
Mexico	2005	69.5	37.1	94.9	8.9	99.6	1.0	68.4	20.3	81.4	23.3
Nicaragua	2005	36.4	23.8	89.5	13.4	95.5	12.8	37.1	32.4	79.5	18.8
Paraguay	2005	15.0	14.7	89.7	20.1	98.4	3.8	40.1	48.0	82.6	28.9
Peru	2006	77.6	34.3	83.4	23.8	96.3	12.6	58.2	50.5	82.2	29.1
Suriname	1999	97.8	0.1	87.3	7.4	99.3	0.2	—	—	—	—
Uruguay	2005	66.2	38.3	98.8	1.5	99.3	1.9	71.9	42.1	90.1	21.4
Venezuela, R.B. de	2002	95.1	5.7	93.9	6.7	99.1	0.9	69.2	24.5	89.8	12.6
Average		56.9	17.8	85.6	9.9	94.9	6.5	61.1	27.3	87.0	15.2

Sources: Cristini and Moya (2008), based on the Socio-Economic Database for Latin America and the Caribbean; for telephone coverage, Gallup (2007).

Note: — = not available. The gap is the difference in coverage between households in the highest two income quintiles and the lowest two income quintiles.

Figure 1.3 Home Ownership, by Income Decile, Selected Cities, 2000 or Latest Available Year

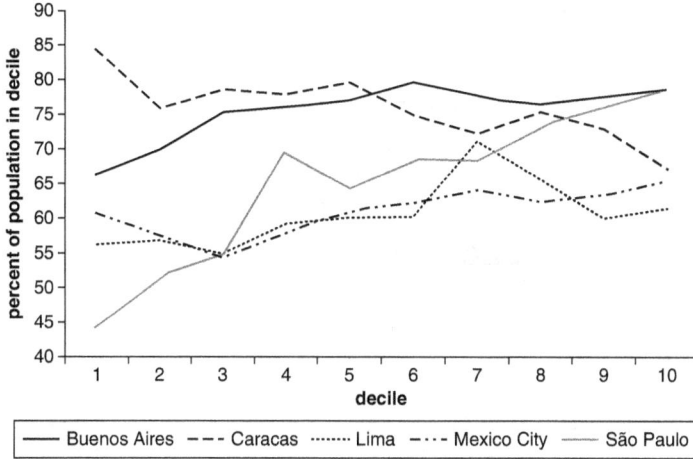

Source: Cristini and Moya 2008.

Figure 1.4 Substandard Home Construction, by Income Decile, Selected Cities, 2000 or Latest Available Year

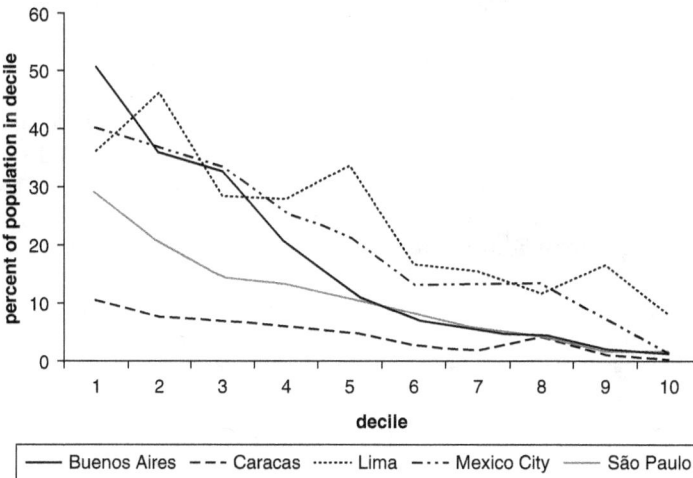

Source: Cristini and Moya 2008.

Figure 1.5 Households Lacking Any Public Service, by Income Decile, Selected Cities, 2000 or Latest Available Year

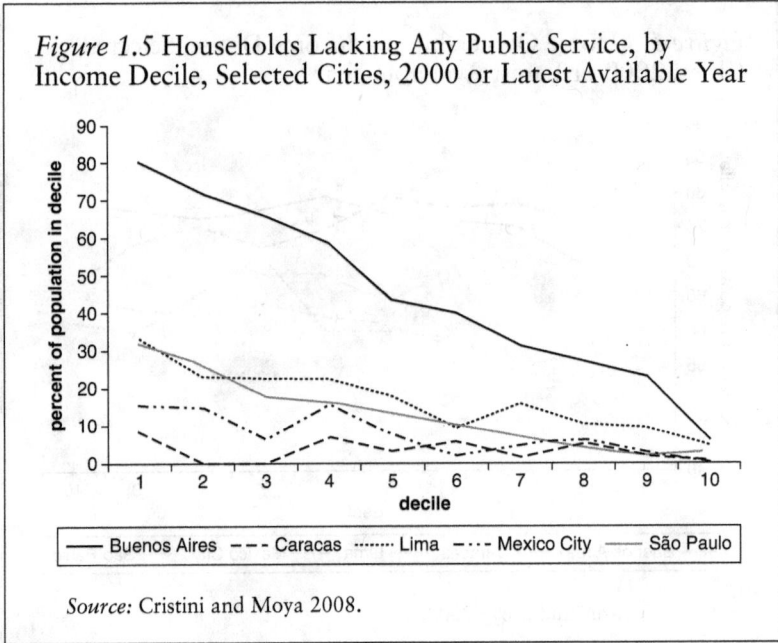

Source: Cristini and Moya 2008.

is the difference between the number of households and the number of homes; and the latter is some measure of housing quality, based on the quality of the building materials used, access to services, or other criteria. In 1995, the United Nations Economic Commission for Latin America and the Caribbean and the Latin American Demographic Center estimated that the total (quantitative plus qualitative) deficit in all Latin American and Caribbean countries was 53 million homes, or 54 percent of the housing stock. The quantitative deficit was calculated at 28 million homes, and the qualitative deficit was calculated at 25 million (defined simply as lack of connection to running water) (ECLAC 1996). The most recent estimates, based on more refined criteria, reveal alarming total deficits: 64 percent of total housing stock in Bolivia, and between 27 percent and 40 percent in Chile, Colombia, and Uruguay (Szalachman 2000, 35). Housing deficit calculations such as these are limited, however, by their imposition of homogeneous criteria—across countries, across rural and urban areas, and among cities—based on a very small number of variables. From a policy perspective, it can be more informative and useful to analyze each city separately, based on the best information available.

Another crucial limitation is that the deficit expressed as a number (or percentage) of homes does not convey the seriousness of the deficiencies or the costs of fixing them. A recent study by Cristini and Moya (2008) is a step in that direction. For 64 cities, they calculated quantitative deficits with

the traditional definition (households minus homes), and calculated qualitative deficits according to the quality of materials (based on local standards)
and access to water and sanitation services. The authors also calculated the
costs of eliminating the deficits in each city, taking into account housing
prices at low stock levels (implicit in the value of rentals), the possibility of
recovering existing homes (using predominant materials), and the cost of
connecting to services. Table 1.4 summarizes the results for 17 of the largest cities in their study. Eliminating the basic deficits of housing, water and
sanitation would cost an average of 8 percent of the gross domestic product
(GDP) of the cities considered.[6] About half of this cost involves improving
homes built with deficient materials. Several Brazilian cities have considerable challenges in this area, with estimated costs exceeding 10 percent
of city GDP for Fortaleza and Recife. However, in other large cities (for
example, Greater Buenos Aires, Mexico City, or São Paulo), that cost represents no more than 4 percent of local GDP. Correcting quantitative housing
deficits would cost more than 7 percent of local GDP in Bogotá and Recife.
In other cities, the costs would represent, on average, only 3.3 percent of
GDP. The average fixed cost of the investment in infrastructure needed to
provide universal access to water and sanitation services would be equivalent to only 1 percent of cities' GDPs (exceptions are Greater Buenos Aires
at 2.5 percent of GDP and Fortaleza and Recife at more than 5.0 percent).
As previous studies have concluded, these costs are modest.[7]

However refined they may be, calculations of housing deficits and the
costs of eliminating them are no more than illustrative exercises because
they do not take into account the demand side. Who would be willing to
pay for such improvements or connections to services? If families cannot
afford to pay these costs, would payment by national or local governments
be justified? Moreover, if not all deficits can be addressed at the same time,
which deficits should get priority?

Another limitation of using housing deficits to guide policy is that
they are based on only some aspects of housing; they ignore an array of
other factors that affect the quality of urban life. Depending on individual
conditions and tastes, the provision of public spaces, the quality of public
transportation, and the level of public safety may be of equal or greater
importance to people seeking housing.

Latin Americans' Satisfaction with Their Homes and Cities: Results from a Cross-Country Analysis

An alternative to calculating deficits is asking people's opinions about
their homes and urban living conditions to identify the most important
constraints on improving their QoL. The 2007 wave of the Gallup World
Poll (Gallup 2007) interviewed representative samples of 1,000 individuals
per country in 130 countries (20 countries from Latin America), and

Table 1.4 Quantitative and Qualitative Housing Deficits and the Costs of Eliminating Them, Selected Cities, 2000 or Latest Available Year

| | | Quantitative deficits | | Qualitative deficits | | | |
| | | | | Substandard housing | | Housing without sanitation or water | |
Country	City	Households (%)	Cost (% of city GDP)	Households (%)	Cost (% of city GDP)	Households (%)	Cost (% of city GDP)
Mexico	Mexico City	3.6	1.7	15.8	3.6	6.2	0.3
Brazil	São Paulo	4.8	3.0	12.4	2.5	13.7	0.7
Argentina	Gran Buenos Aires	3.7	2.6	13.5	4.0	41.2	2.5
Brazil	Río de Janeiro	6.1	6.2	12.7	5.5	9.4	0.8
Colombia	Santa Fe de Bogotá	12.1	7.5	—	—	—	—
Peru	Greater Lima	4.8	2.2	17.3	3.4	15.8	1.7
Brazil	Belo Horizonte	6.5	4.6	19.2	5.0	14.4	1.0
Mexico	Guadalajara	5.4	2.2	10.5	2.0	4.5	0.3
Brazil	Pôrto Alegre	5.3	4.6	10.9	3.5	15.3	1.3

Mexico	Monterrey	4.5	2.6	9.3	0.4	0.9	0.0
Brazil	Recife	10.3	8.7	50.6	18.5	56.0	5.2
Brazil	Brasilia	3.3	1.5	10.3	2.0	17.1	1.0
Brazil	Salvador	9.2	6.3	20.5	6.0	14.6	1.0
Brazil	Fortaleza	10.2	6.6	41.7	11.6	49.2	5.1
Colombia	Medellín	4.1	2.8	—	—	—	—
Venezuela, R.B. de	Caracas	—	—	5.6	1.6	4.2	0.3
Brazil	Curitiba	4.9	3.8	17.6	5.8	20.5	1.3

Source: Cristini and Moya (2008), based on household surveys and national census data.
Note: — = not available.

the results indicate that the great majority of Latin Americans claim to be satisfied with their homes and their cities.[8] The percentages are almost identical, on average, for both questions (79.7 and 79.5 percent) and close to the results obtained from other regions of the developed or developing world (with the exception of Sub-Saharan Africa, where the percentage is significantly lower) (table 1.5). In Latin America, the highest satisfaction rates for both home and city were in Guatemala (90.6 percent and 92.5 percent, respectively). The lowest levels of satisfaction with homes were found in Haiti and Trinidad and Tobago (57 percent and 66 percent, respectively), and the lowest levels of city satisfaction were found in Haiti and Peru (49 percent and 70 percent, respectively).

Opinions were more critical and rather more diverse on the question, "Would you say that the city/area where you live is improving or worsening as a place to live?"[9] Only 52.9 percent of Latin Americans answered positively in 2007, with results ranging from a low 36.4 percent in Uruguay to 66.3 percent in Ecuador. Nonetheless, Latin Americans were not substantially different from the rest of the world: the most favorable opinions were in the Middle East and North Africa (72.4 percent), and the most pessimistic responses were in Western Europe (50.2 percent) (Gallup 2007).

An analysis of overall satisfaction with home and city reveals that satisfaction generally does not correlate with objective conditions. Economic conditions in each country affect perceptions in ways that are not fully consistent with predictions of conventional economics. Although higher levels of income per capita are associated with higher levels of home and city satisfaction (table 1.6), the growth rate of income per capita is

Table 1.5 Levels of Satisfaction with Homes and Cities, 2007
Percent of poll respondents

Region	Satisfaction with their homes	Satisfaction with their cities	City is improving
East Asia and the Pacific	82.1	87.2	68.6
Europe and Central Asia	75.2	79.7	60.5
Latin America and the Caribbean	79.7	79.5	52.9
Middle East and North Africa	80.0	79.4	72.4
North America	0.0	88.0	57.9
South Asia	87.6	87.4	67.3
Sub-Saharan Africa	62.2	69.7	55.2
Western Europe	89.9	92.4	50.2

Source: Gallup 2007.

Table 1.6 Correlations of Home and City Satisfaction with Selected National-Level Variables

	Dependent variables					
Independent variables	Satisfaction with their homes		Satisfaction with their cities		City is improving	
Natural logarithm, GDP per capita, 2005	0.054***	0.047***	0.057***	0.056***	0.036*	0.032
Real annual average GDP per capita growth 2000–05	–0.008**	–0.009*	0.000	–0.001	0.018**	0.017*
Urban population growth 1950–2000	0.001	0.005	0.017*	0.020*	0.047***	0.025
Constant	0.350***	0.445**	0.276*	0.258	0.091	0.223
Regional dummies	Yes	No	Yes	No	Yes	No
Observations (n)	91	91	76	76	68	68
Pseudo R^2	0.436	0.554	0.280	0.408	0.237	0.359

Source: Author's calculations, based on Gallup (2007).

Note: The table presents probabilities calculated from regression coefficients estimated by probit analysis. Standard errors are clustered by region. Where no asterisk appears, the coefficient does not differ from zero with statistical significance.

*$p < .10$ **$p < .05$ ***$p < .01$.

inversely associated with home satisfaction. This surprising relationship has been called the "paradox of unhappy growth." The paradox suggests that satisfaction is influenced by aspirations, which increase with economic growth as individuals contrast their own consumption with that of others (Lora and Chaparro 2008).

As will be shown in chapter 3, home and city satisfaction are two of many dimensions that people implicitly may take into account when they evaluate their overall QoL. This fact will be central in the methodological approach adopted in this book because the value of nonmarket urban amenities may be inferred through their (direct or indirect) influence on life satisfaction.

Factors That Influence Satisfaction with Housing: Results from an Analysis across Individuals

Individual data often are more informative than country-level data when describing satisfaction with housing or any other life dimension. Although some authors (for example, Deaton 2007) suggest that using cross-country regressions may be valid because averaging at the country level reduces potential individual biases, such averaging may omit revealing differences when conditions within a country are considered. Because housing quality and the provision of neighborhood services vary greatly within countries, individual opinions in this area appear to be an interesting and complementary (if not superior) avenue for research.

Results across individuals can be used, for example, to determine which characteristics of homes are necessary for satisfaction with housing. Access to services is found to be very important, and that finding justifies its use as a criterion for defining qualitative housing deficits. All else being equal, access to running water increases the probability of satisfaction by 5.9 percentage points; and telephone service increases it by 2.9 percentage points (see the list of control variables in table 1.7).

Possession of title deeds also is associated closely with home satisfaction, increasing satisfaction by 7.9 percentage points when all else is equal (including home ownership, which in itself is less important).[10] This finding is relevant because, although home ownership rates are high even among families in the two poorest urban quintiles, approximately 42 percent of the homes owned by these families lack title deeds (Gallup 2007).

De Soto (2000) has emphasized the importance of title deeds in facilitating access to credit and releasing the productive potential of poor people's capital. However, empirical studies do not support his hypothesis, possibly because access to credit for the poor may be restricted for other reasons. For instance, creditors may be hard pressed to take possession and recover the homes offered as guarantee when debtors default on their obligations (IDB 2005). An interesting study compared the behavior of Buenos Aires families who had obtained title deeds with that of statistically identical families without title deeds. Families with deeds tended to invest more in improving their homes and had fewer nonfamily individuals living with them, possibly because they felt less need to maintain ties of solidarity as a precaution against the risk of being left homeless (Galiani and Schargrodsky 2007). Consequently, the increased home satisfaction of those with title deeds may be reflected in physical improvements in the home and in the space available for family members. Such satisfaction also may reflect a greater sense of security.

Many other characteristics may influence satisfaction. Obviously, families with higher incomes can have homes more to their taste. An individual in the richest quintile, for example, has a 9.2 percent higher probability of feeling satisfied with his or her home than does a comparable person in the poorest quintile (Gallup 2007). But, as discussed above, although income level contributes to satisfaction with housing, aspirations decrease satisfaction. Using the same data set, Lora and Chaparro (2008) find that satisfaction with housing is a material dimension of life (along with personal economic situation and job satisfaction) in which peer comparisons exert a

Table 1.7 Factors Contributing to Housing Satisfaction, 2007

Variable	Effect on probability of satisfaction
House characteristics	
House has water	0.059***
Someone in the house has a telephone	0.029**
House has electricity	−0.002
Family is owner	0.036*
Family has a title deed	0.079***
Personal characteristics	
Woman	0.009
Age	−0.007***
Age squared	0.000***
Family characteristics	
Family has children at school	−0.007
Number of household members	0.062***
Number of children at home	−0.070***
Income quintile 2	0.031**
Income quintile 3	0.047***
Income quintile 4	0.059***
Income quintile 5	0.092***
Regional statistics	
Country fixed effects	Yes
Observations (n)	6,471
R^2	0.058

Source: Author's calculations, based on Gallup (2007).

Note: Estimates are made from logit regression. Standard errors are clustered by country. Where no asterisk appears, the coefficient does not differ from zero with statistical significance. Although the urban samples of the 18 countries included in this regression ad up to 10,734 individuals, many observations were lost because of a lack of data on income quintile, house, or family characteristics.

*p < .10 **p < .05 ***p < .01.

strong influence. In housing satisfaction, the negative effect of other people's incomes counteracts the positive effect of an individual's own income. Thus, the probability of satisfaction does not depend on personal income, but on the gap between that income and the average income of one's reference group.[11] This comparison effect means that what is valid for the individual is not necessarily valid for the social group as a whole. A rich body of empirical literature, spearheaded by Richard Easterlin (1974), has studied this phenomenon. (Also see Ball and Chernova 2008, Luttmer 2005, and van Praag and Ferrer-i-Carbonell 2004.)

Factors That Influence Satisfaction with City of Residence

Whereas satisfaction with the home is an important element of overall life satisfaction, satisfaction with the urban area where that home is located is relevant as well. Subsequent chapters of this book will analyze satisfaction with the home and its location at a more detailed neighborhood level, so this section provides background to that analysis by considering more generally how Latin Americans perceive various aspects of their cities.

Gallup (2007) World Poll results permit comparison of Latin American urban areas with those of other regions along several dimensions (table 1.8). Public safety apparently is the weakest point of Latin American urban life, because only 41.6 percent of Latin Americans surveyed in 2007 felt safe walking alone at night in their cities or residential areas. Although not far from the corresponding percentage in the former communist countries of Europe and Asia or the countries of Sub-Saharan Africa, this percentage is substantially lower than in other regions of the world. Latin Americans additionally report one of the world's highest rates of victimization (having money stolen and being mugged) during the 12 months preceding the survey, second only to the rates in Sub-Saharan Africa.[12]

In fact, no Latin American country has managed to create a climate of real urban security. As illustrated in figures 1.6 and 1.7, perceptions of safety and confidence in police are low. Brazil, Chile, Argentina, and Bolivia are at the bottom in safety perceptions, although confidence in police is high in some of the countries most affected by fears of insecurity (such as Chile). This contrast prompts a question about the extent to which perceptions are shaped by objective reality.[13] Perceptions may underestimate or overestimate the real risks that people face: some of the countries where the population feels most safe have very high homicide rates, even by regional standards.[14]

The relationship among crime, safety, and income is not straightforward. In line with the findings that Gaviria and Pagés (2002) report, using Latinobarómetro data, the Gallup (2007) World Poll data reveal substantially higher reporting of crime victimization among people with higher incomes in Latin America—a feature that is much less pronounced in other regions, except South Asia (figure 1.8). Consistent with those findings, Latin America and South Asia are the only regions where the populations with higher incomes have the worst perceptions of insecurity (figure 1.9).

Table 1.8 Satisfaction with Various Urban Factors and Perceived Level of Public Safety, by Region, 2007
Percent of poll respondents

Region	Level of satisfaction with urban factor							People who feel safe walking at night
	Public transportation	Roads	Education	Health quality	Quality and price of available housing	Air quality	Water quality	
East Asia and the Pacific	76.2	75.5	79.6	80.9	71.1	72.1	82.4	70.5
Europe and Central Asia	66.4	42.6	57.6	41.4	37.6	45.7	53.1	44.8
Latin America and the Caribbean	59.4	54.1	68.0	59.1	48.8	68.7	74.1	41.6
Middle East and North Africa	65.6	61.0	63.4	62.5	46.8	53.6	59.1	69.7
North America	67.3	61.1	66.9	72.7	49.4	70.7	85.3	72.2
South Asia	78.1	69.6	83.0	75.2	52.6	76.2	72.7	69.8
Sub-Saharan Africa	47.2	40.1	58.2	49.0	43.5	63.4	60.8	47.5
Western Europe	75.5	75.8	81.3	81.2	39.8	70.2	87.8	68.2
Is Latin America and the Caribbean above or below the world pattern?	4.6	1.5	1.6	0.7	-1.5	2.2	6.8**	-17.4**

Source: Gallup 2007.

Note: The table shows simple averages of data by region. In the last row, each of the values is the coefficient of a dummy variable for Latin American and Caribbean countries in a country-level regression where the dependent variable is the rate of satisfaction and the explanatory variables are income per capita and the dummy variable. Where no asterisk appears, the coefficient does not differ from zero with statistical significance.

**$p < .05$.

Figure 1.6 Percent of People Who Feel Safe Walking Alone at Night, Selected Countries, 2007

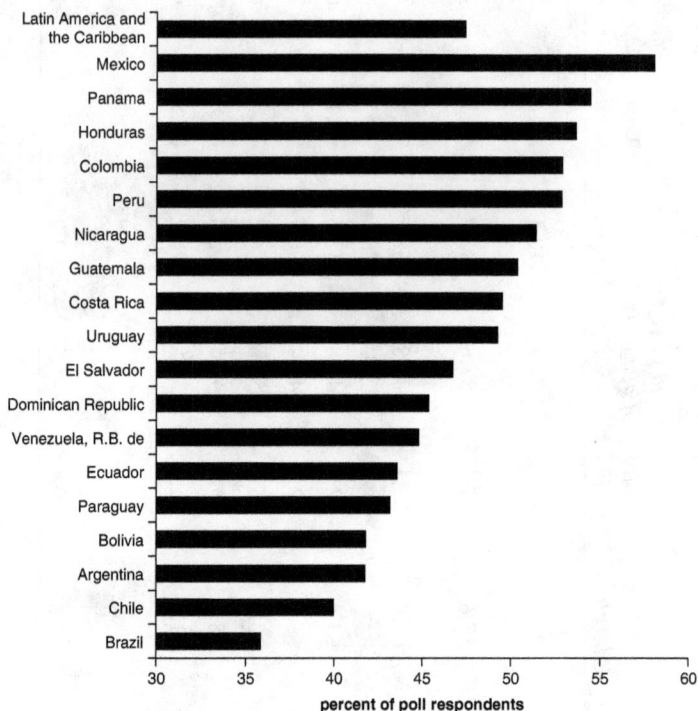

Source: Gallup 2007.

Among the aspects of urban life considered in the Gallup polls, only water quality gives Latin Americans significantly more satisfaction than would be expected for the income levels of the countries (see table 1.8). Three out of four Latin Americans say they are satisfied with this public service, with no appreciable differences by socioeconomic level. However, there are differences by country: in Guyana, Haiti, and the Dominican Republic, less than 60 percent of the population is satisfied with the quality of the service (Gallup 2007). In the other dimensions, Latin America does not differ significantly from the world pattern associated with levels of income per capita.

Respondents' opinions on various aspects of their cities can be used to deduce the priorities that people would assign to each of those aspects in order to feel better about their cities. Although there may be great

Figure 1.7 Percentage of People Who Have Confidence in Local Police Force, Selected Countries, 2007

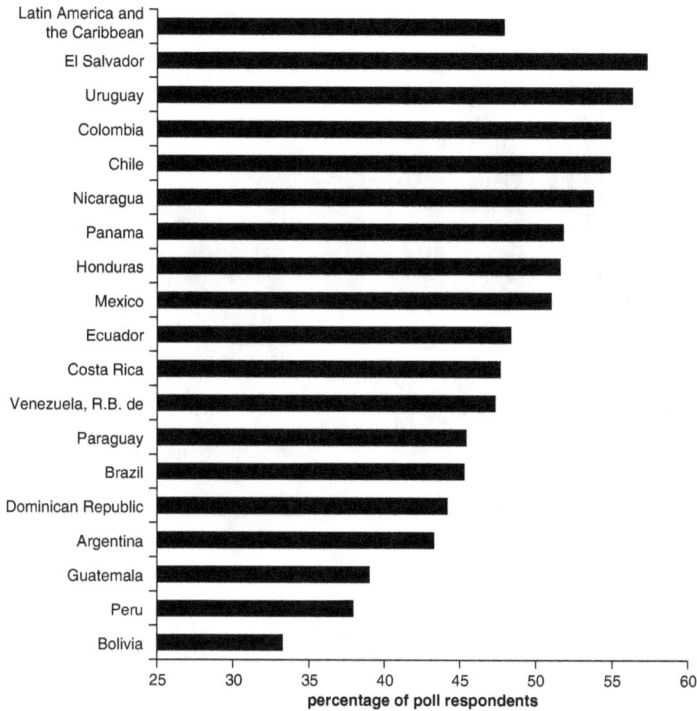

Source: Gallup 2007.

dissatisfaction with a specific aspect of a city, such a problem should not necessarily be assigned a high priority. For instance, only 52 percent of Latin Americans say they are satisfied with the state of sidewalks or pedestrian walks; and only 55 percent are satisfied with the availability of parks, plazas, and green areas (Gallup 2007). At the same time, 75 percent consider water quality to be satisfactory (a very high proportion, by world standards). But the problem of water could remain a higher priority for one of three reasons: (1) because water quality may be more important for individual satisfaction (with the city or, more generally, with personal QoL), (2) because water quality results in benefits for individuals and society that people may not consider in their subjective judgments, or (3) because solving the problem of water may be less costly than addressing other problems. This section presents a ranking of problems based entirely on individual satisfaction (the first criterion). However, the other

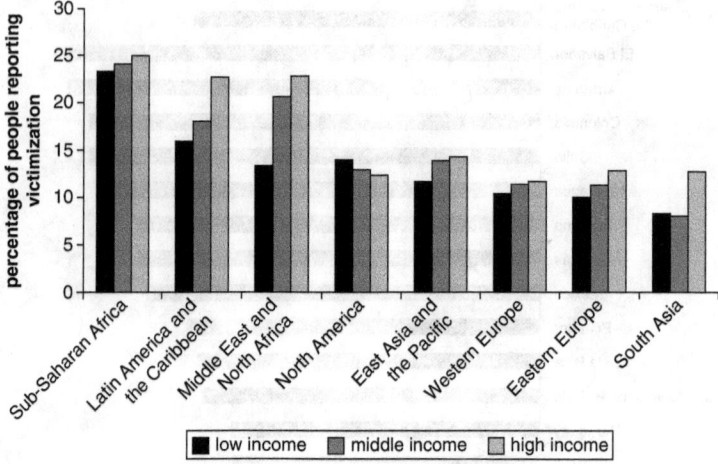

Figure 1.8 Percentage of People Whose Money Was Stolen in Preceding 12 Months, by Region and Income Level, 2007

Source: Di Tella, MacCulloch, and Ñopo (2008), based on Gallup (2007).

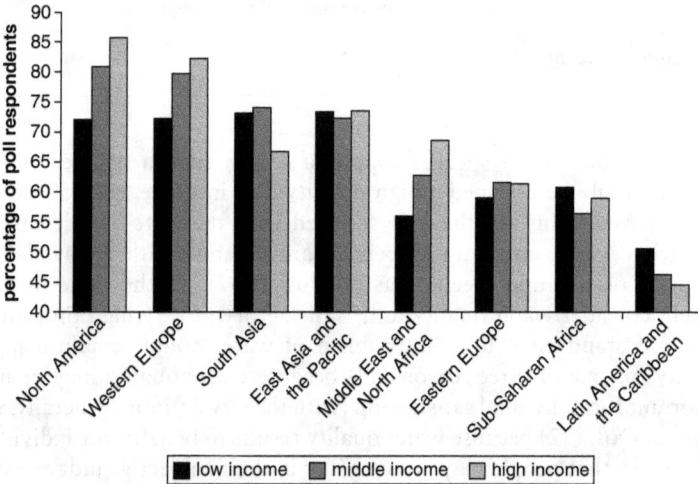

Figure 1.9 Percentage of People Who Feel Safe Walking Alone at Night in Their City, by Region and Income Level, 2007

Source: Di Tella, MacCulloch, and Ñopo (2008), based on Gallup (2007).

two criteria should be borne in mind when trying to draw policy implications from the analysis that follows.

With a focus on individual satisfaction with respondents' cities of residence, figure 1.10 shows the relative importance of several aspects of urban life covered by the Gallup polls. Both the percentage of people affected by the problems enumerated and the problems' impact on satisfaction with the city are considered. To establish the impact on individual satisfaction, an econometric analysis is used to identify which aspects of the city are most predictive of a respondent's satisfaction or dissatisfaction. The econometric analysis also considers the fact that satisfaction with the city may depend on an individual's own circumstances and possibilities (gender, age, employment status, socioeconomic level), satisfaction with his or her home, and cultural and other common country factors. Some of these controls are quite important—particularly, satisfaction with the home. A person who says he is satisfied with his home is 19 percent more likely to say he is satisfied with his city[15] than is a comparable individual who is not satisfied with his home (Gallup 2007).

Problems of safety are very frequent and high percentages of Latin Americans say that they feel unsafe walking alone at night or that there are gangs or illegal drug trafficking in their residential areas. These three expressions of a lack of safety also have a statistically significant impact on satisfaction with the city. The combination of high frequency and impact suggests that safety is the problem that most affects the QoL in Latin American cities. Naturally, the problem may be more acute in some cities than in others, and that will be considered later in this book. Although safety issues appear to affect all socioeconomic groups, there is evidence that the impact of feeling unsafe is stronger for women than for men (although reported victimization is higher for males). In general, problems of safety affect all age groups equally; however, the presence of illegal drug trafficking and levels of confidence in local police seem to affect elderly people much more.

Additional areas that affect the QoL include the existence and quality of sidewalks and pedestrian areas, parks, and public transportation. Somewhat lower in importance, but still significant, are the quality of schools and the availability of housing at affordable prices. The other aspects considered (health services; roads, highways, and freeways; air quality; water quality; and traffic flow) do not have a significant impact on satisfaction with the city. That does not mean that policy makers should disregard these issues, however, because the issues may affect urban QoL (either perceived or "objective") through many other channels.[16]

Many dimensions of the quality of urban life tend to have the same effect on high and low socioeconomic levels, men and women, and individuals of different ages. Exceptions include the state of sidewalks or pedestrian walks (more important for higher-income levels but less important for elderly people) and the availability of good housing at affordable prices

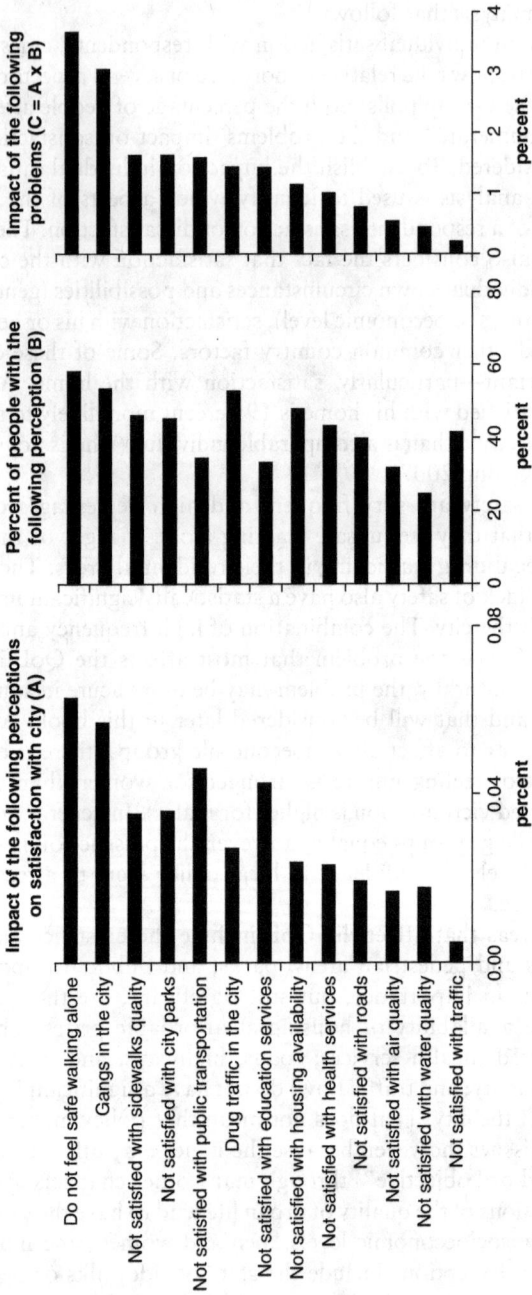

Figure 1.10 Perceived Importance of Selected Urban Problems, 2007

Source: Gallup 2007.

Note: The values in the first panel are the marginal probabilities—that is, how much each factor reduces the probability of being satisfied with one's city. These results come from a logit model for city satisfaction in which the independent variables are those shown in the figure, and gender, age, income quintile, employment status, and housing satisfaction.

(less important for those who are employed). However, this apparently general homogeneity of impacts may result from aggregating a large number of urban centers into a single statistical exercise: within cities, some dimensions of urban life can have differential impacts across groups. Analyzing particular urban areas of greater homogeneity increases the likelihood of identifying which characteristics of homes and neighborhoods are truly important for QoL.

This analysis is the focus of chapters 4 through 8, which consider the QoL in individual cities of five Latin American countries. To provide a foundation for the analytical approach and the findings of each case study, chapter 2 discusses the theoretical underpinnings and the empirical strategies needed to make use of objective and subjective data quantifying the urban QoL and chapter 3 presents a summary of the main empirical results, with a comparative perspective.

Notes

1. For brevity, the term *Latin America* is meant to include the Caribbean, too.
2. According to Cristini and Moya (2008), the Herfindahl-Hirschman Index of Concentration of urban population decreased to half between 1950 and 2005.
3. See the theoretical and empirical analyses of Ades and Glaeser (1995) and Gaviria and Stein (2000).
4. Although the margin of error for the Gallup World Poll is ±3 percent (given sample sizes of 1,000 per country), these figures are subject to larger margins of error because (1) they refer to urban homeowners only, and (2) the individual interviewed in the household is selected at random and may not be well informed about these topics.
5. Figures for telephone coverage come from the Gallup polls, whose margins of error are substantially greater than those of the official household surveys from which the other figures are taken.
6. Assuming that local tax revenues represent 5 percent of the cities' GDPs and assuming a 5 percent annual rate of economic growth, eliminating the deficits would absorb the full revenue increases of almost 11 consecutive years.
7. Fay (2001) calculated the 2000–05 cost of addressing the growing requirements of water and sanitation in Latin America at between 0.05 percent and 0.18 percent of GDP.
8. The questions asked in the poll were these: "Are you satisfied or dissatisfied with your housing or the place you currently live?" and "Are you satisfied or dissatisfied with the city or area where you live?"
9. The option "the same" is included as a possible response, but is not spoken by the interviewer. According to Gallup officials, this is done to prevent many interviewees from choosing that option to avoid taking a position.
10. Notice that not only is the coefficient of having title deeds much higher than that of home ownership, but also the latter is significant only at the 10 percent level.
11. In this case, the reference group comprises all people of the same gender, within the urban areas of the same country, in the same age range, and with a similar level of education.

12. Exploring the causes of perceived safety, or the factors associated with it, is beyond the objective of this chapter. However, it is worth mentioning that perceived safety is associated strongly (with negative sign) with perceived corruption in business and government. When perceived corruption in business and government is used as an explanatory variable of perceived safety, Latin America is not different from the rest of the world.

13. The correlations between the percentage of people who feel safe and the homicide rates (at the country level) are –0.48 for the world (70 countries), but just –0.10 for the 23 Latin American countries (Gallup 2007; PAHO 2007; UN Office of Drugs and Crime 2006).

14. The homicide rates per 100,000 inhabitants in 2007 were 59 in Jamaica and 30 in Trinidad and Tobago (*The Economist* January 31, 2008).

15. Gender has no influence on satisfaction with the city; however, age has a positive influence (although not a statistically significant one) that declines with years. People who have jobs tend to feel better about their city, but this effect also is not significant. Economic levels do not have a discernible positive or negative influence on satisfaction with the city. Country dummies (that capture differences across countries) are important for several countries.

16. For instance, water provision affects satisfaction with housing.

References

Ades, Alberto F., and Edward Glaeser. 1995. "Trade and Circuses: Explaining Urban Giants." *Quarterly Journal of Economics* 110 (1): 195–227.

Ball, Richard, and Kateryna Chernova. 2008. "Absolute Income, Relative Income, and Happiness." *Social Indicators Research* 88 (3): 497–529.

Calderón, Julio. 2001. "Análisis Comparativo de la Población Beneficiada y la No Beneficiada por el Plan Nacional de Formalización." In *¿Ha Mejorado el Bienestar de la Población?* Lima, Peru: Instituto Nacional de Estadística e Informática.

Cristini, Marcela, and Ramiro Moya. 2008. "Ciudades y Calidad de Vida en América Latina y el Caribe: Evolución Histórica y Comparación Internacional." Unpublished manuscript, Inter-American Development Bank, Washington, DC.

Deaton, Angus. 2007. "Income, Aging, Health and Wellbeing around the World: Evidence from the Gallup World Poll." Working Paper 13317, National Bureau of Economic Research, Cambridge, MA.

de Soto, Hernando. 2000. *The Mystery of Capital: Why Capitalism Triumphs in the West and Fails Everywhere Else.* London: Black Swan.

Di Tella, Rafael, Robert MacCulloch, and Hugo Ñopo. 2008. "Happiness and Beliefs in Criminal Environments." RES Working Paper 662, Research Department, Inter-American Development Bank, Washington, DC.

Easterlin, Richard. 1974. "Does Economic Growth Improve the Human Lot? Some Empirical Evidence." In *Nations and Households in Economic Growth: Essays in Honor of Moses Abramovitz*, ed. Paul A. David and Melvin W. Reder, 89–125. New York: Academic Press.

ECLAC (Economic Commission for Latin America and the Caribbean). 1996. "La Situación Latina y el Caribe." Document LC/R.1613, ECLAC, Santiago, Chile.

———. 2006. *Social Panorama of Latin America 2006.* Santiago, Chile: ECLAC.

Fay, Marianne. 2001. "Financing the Future: Infrastructure Needs in Latin America, 2000–05." Policy Research Working Paper 2545, World Bank, Washington, DC.

Fay, Marianne, and Anna Wellenstein. 2005. "Keeping a Roof over One's Head: Improving Access to Safe and Decent Shelter." In *The Urban Poor in Latin America*, ed. Marianne Fay, 91–124. Washington, DC: World Bank.

Galiani, Sebastian, and Ernesto Schargrodsky. 2007. "Property Rights for the Poor: Effects of Land Titling." Business School Working Papers Series, Universidad Torcuato Di Tella, Buenos Aires, Argentina.

Gallup. 2007. Gallup World Poll 2007. http://www.gallup.com/consulting/worldpoll/24046/about.aspx.

Gaviria, Alejandro, and Carmen Pagés. 2002. "Patterns of Crime Victimization in Latin American Cities." *Journal of Development Economics* 67 (1): 181–203.

Gaviria, Alejandro, and Ernesto H. Stein. 2000. "The Evolution of Urban Concentration around the World: A Panel Approach." RES Working Paper 414, Research Department, Inter-American Development Bank, Washington, DC.

Gilbert, Alan. 2001. "La Vivienda en America Latina." Unpublished manuscript, Inter-American Institute for Social Development, Inter-American Development Bank, Washington, DC.

IDB (Inter-American Development Bank). 2005. *The Politics of Policies. Economic and Social Progress in Latin America: 2006 Report*. Washington, DC: IDB.

Lora, Eduardo, and Juan Camilo Chaparro. 2008. "The Conflictive Relationship between Satisfaction and Income." RES Working Paper 642, Research Department, Inter-American Development Bank, Washington, DC.

Luttmer, Erzo F.P. 2005. "Neighbors as Negatives: Relative Earnings and Well-Being." *Quarterly Journal of Economics* 120 (3): 963–1002.

PAHO (Pan American Health Organization), Health Information and Analysis. 2007. *Health Situation in the Americas: Basic Indicators*. Washington, DC: PAHO.

Reid, Michael. 2008. *Forgotten Continent: The Battle for Latin America's Soul*. New Haven, CT: Yale University Press.

Rugiero Pérez, Ana María. 1998. "Experiencia Chilena en Vivienda Social 1980–1995." *Boletín del Instituto de la Vivienda* 13 (35): 3–87.

Szalachman, Raquel. 2000. "Perfil de Déficit y Políticas de Vivienda de Interés Social: Situación de Algunos Países de la Región en los Noventa." Serie financiamiento para el desarrollo 103 (LC/L.1417-P), Economic Commission for Latin America and the Caribbean, Santiago, Chile.

The Economist. 2008. "The Caribbean: Sun, Sea and Murder." January 31, Americas section. http://www.economist.com/research/articlesBySubject/displaystory.cfm?subjectid=348942&story_id=10609414.

UN (United Nations) Department of Economic and Social Affairs, Population Division. 2006. "World Population Prospects: The 2005 Revision." http://www.un.org/esa/population/publications/WUP2005/2005wup.htm.

UN-HABITAT (United Nations Human Settlements Programme). 2003. Global Urban Indicators Database 1998. http://ww2.unhabitat.org/programmes/guo/guo_indicators.asp.

UN Office of Drugs and Crime. 2006. "Ninth United Nations Survey of Crime Trends and Operations of Criminal Justice Systems." http://www.data360.org/pdf/20070531091045.Crime%20Trends.pdf.

van Praag, Bernard M.S., and Ada Ferrer-i-Carbonell. 2004. *Happiness Quantified: A Satisfaction Calculus Approach*. New York: Oxford University Press.

2

Measuring Quality of Life in Latin America's Urban Neighborhoods: A Summary of Results from the City Case Studies

Andrew Powell and Pablo Sanguinetti

Which housing characteristics, neighborhood amenities, and urban public goods are important in determining individuals' levels of well-being or quality of life (QoL)? That is a basic but critically important question for citywide planning authorities, subcity units of government, and neighborhood organizations that regularly must make decisions about the provision of public services as they try to improve living standards for urban populations. Making such decisions is a particularly challenging task, however, because many such services and amenities are not traded in direct markets, and there is little reason for individuals to disclose their true demands or valuations. Without appropriate valuations, how can policy makers decide where to focus their limited resources?

This chapter presents a summary of the results derived from applying two methodologies that may provide such valuations: *hedonic* and *life*

This chapter provides a summary of the results of the individual country chapters and, as such, would have been impossible without the tremendous assistance of the authors of each study: Lorena Alcázar, Raúl Andrade, Guillermo Cruces, Zuleika Ferre, Ada Ferrer-i-Carbonell, Néstor Gandelman, Luis J. Hall, Andrés Ham, Róger Madrigal, Carlos Medina, Leonardo Morales, Jairo Núñez, Giorgina Piani, Juan Robalino, and, Martín Tetaz. We would like to thank the other editors of this book, Eduardo Lora and Bernard M.S. van Praag, for their comments and suggestions, and we thank Mariana Salazni for excellent research assistance.

satisfaction (LS) methodologies. Both approaches first may be used to calculate implicit prices for nonmarket goods; and then, with those prices used as weights, an urban QoL index can be developed. That index would provide a summary of how the salient amenities affect people's well-being. Such an index showing how value varies across neighborhoods and individuals may become a central policy instrument to guide decision making: neighborhoods with particularly low values might become areas for priority actions, or individuals with particular characteristics might become the recipients of targeted polices. Underlying valuations then may be used to make decisions on the value of providing different services, whether involving incentives for improvements in housing quality, urban amenities, and public goods; or involving efforts to reduce the negative impact of urban problems ("bads").

The hedonic approach has a long tradition in the urban economic literature as a method of placing monetary values on the welfare impact of city amenities and public goods.[1] Families' location decisions implicitly reflect preferences regarding a set of characteristics pertaining to the house purchased or rented, the neighborhood where the house is situated, and the amenities offered in that location. In turn, those preferences will affect property prices in the market for land. A better-quality house in a location that offers a wider set of amenities and fewer bads will command a higher price. Given sufficient variation in the house and location combinations present in the market, and assuming that the market functions smoothly, house prices will reflect the value of the full set of relevant housing and neighborhood features and amenities. As examples of this approach, Blomquist, Berger, and Hoehn (1988) and Roback (1982) use hedonic price methods to estimate implicit values of local amenities; the prices then may be used to construct price-weighted QoL indexes.

An alternative and complementary approach is to ask people how satisfied (or happy) they are with their lives, their cities, or their neighborhoods.[2] More recent literature has emphasized this use of subjective satisfaction or happiness indicators for evaluating well-being: for example, Di Tella and MacCulloch (1998); Winkelmann and Winkelmann (1998); Gardner and Oswald (2001); and Frey, Luechinger, and Stutzer (2004).[3] A recent Inter-American Development Bank publication (Lora 2008) that considers many aspects of this approach is devoted to the analysis of general life satisfaction in Latin America and the Caribbean. Because income is included as an explanatory variable in the standard LS regression, the marginal valuations of other significant variables included in the analysis may be computed. Under certain circumstances, including income in the regression allows for calculating an implicit price for various QoL attributes—which again may yield a scheme to weight variables to generate an aggregate QoL index.

There is a small but growing body of literature on estimating QoL indexes for Latin American cities. For example, Amorin and Blanco (2003) use census data for Río de Janeiro (Brazil) to construct a human development index for 126 neighborhoods.[4] Also for Río de Janeiro, Cavallieri and Lopes (2008) present the estimation of a social development index, an equally weighted average of 11 socioeconomic variables normalized between 0 and 1, covering 8,045 subcity areas defined by census radii.[5] For the case of Colombia, using the data provided by the National Survey on Quality of Life, Acosta, Guerra, and Rivera (2005) construct a city-level indicator, based on the methodology proposed by Cortés, Gamboa, and González (1999), that includes sanitary and water services, garbage collection, schooling, overcrowding, and certain housing construction characteristics (quality of floors and walls).

A potential drawback of those analyses is that both the selection of the QoL indicators and the weights used to construct an index tend to be arbitrary.[6] In the analyses in the present report, however, the hedonic and LS approaches both allow the data to determine which indicators should be included and what the weights should be in any QoL index.

Because two methodologies can be used to derive a QoL index, it is natural to ask what the relationship is between is the approaches. Below, it is argued that they are complementary. Indeed, under some circumstances, the most appropriate valuation may be the sum of the prices from each (van Praag and Baarsma 2005). However, comparing the two approaches also may yield interesting information about the functioning of housing and land markets in Latin America.

In general, hedonic regressions result in several significant variables across different cities, with a reasonable degree of consistency in terms of which variables are significant. As discussed below, one interpretation of such results is that housing and land markets function reasonably well in the region, so the wealthy are able to buy better public services by moving to areas that generally have a better QoL. However, one potential indicator that housing markets work is that wealthy buyers will choose better locations and aggravate economic segregation. In turn, economic segregation may feed some bad city characteristics in the region—for example, crime. Across cities and methodologies, crime consistently is found to be one of the most serious bads affecting urban areas in Latin America.

In this chapter, we present a summary of the results of the city-specific analyses. Whereas the country chapters that follow will discuss applications of the two approaches in much greater detail, our focus here is on comparisons across cities and methodologies.

The questions addressed here include the following issues:

- Are housing and neighborhood characteristics important in explaining QoL?
- Are they an important determinant of house prices?
- Using constructed QoL indexes, are there significant disparities in the measured QoL of urban neighborhoods within cities?

- What are the main driving forces pushing QoL up or down in different neighborhoods?
- How might this information be used to monitor QoL and to inform policy actions?

The rest of this chapter is organized in the following way: In the next section, we discuss a set of selected issues regarding QoL monitoring in Latin America. In the subsequent two sections, we summarize first the results obtained using the LS approach to QoL measurement, and then the results gathered with the hedonic pricing approach. Following those discussions, we analyze segregation in Latin America. The final section concludes the chapter.

Monitoring QoL in Latin American Cities: A Discussion of Selected Issues

The cities included in this project are Buenos Aires (Argentina), Bogotá and Medellín (Colombia), San José (Costa Rica), Lima (Peru), and Montevideo (Uruguay).[7] Although the cities cannot be considered a representative sample of all Latin American urban population centers, they certainly are diverse in terms of their history and socioeconomic characteristics. A key aspect that will differentiate this analysis from recent academic and policy work is the level of disaggregation. Here, the objective is to consider a within-city analysis. Thus, many of the QoL indicators that are analyzed are computed at the neighborhood level. In some cases, these subcity areas represent districts or localities within large urban agglomerations; in other cases, they refer to census tracts. This level of disaggregation enables us to gauge how extensively QoL indicators vary across the city space and to consider whether differences in an indicator across households display some spatial pattern.

Definition of the City

In several cases, the urban spaces to be analyzed include the capital of the respective country and its main neighboring districts. For many cities, the formal political boundaries do not reflect the limits of the whole urban area. In such cases, and depending on the availability of information, it is convenient to adopt a metropolitan view in which the urban agglomeration to be studied combines the central city and other surrounding localities that have a close association in terms of the relevant markets for locally produced goods (for example, land, housing, and labor markets). In the case of Buenos Aires, for instance, the urban agglomeration includes the City of Buenos Aires and 24 surrounding municipalities (all of which make up the Buenos Aires Metropolitan Area). For Lima, the analysis covers the 33 districts that form the conurbation of Lima. In the case of San José, the metropolitan area covers 51 localities.[8] This metropolitan approach to the analyses of QoL implies that the urban population covered in the different cases is very significant, representing a large proportion of total urban population in each country. For example, in the case of Argentina, the 13 million people of the Buenos Aires Metropolitan Area represent almost a third of the country's total population.

Choice of Indicators

Another relevant issue is what QoL indicators to monitor. The present project took an open view in that regard, preferring to collect a wide variety of indicators and thus allow the data to reveal which factors are important. Apart from general indicators—such as income, health, and education—indicators pertaining particularly to urban QoL were collected. Those indicators may be divided into ones related to housing characteristics and ones related to neighborhood amenities, the particular indicators being dependent on the city in question. In each city, a survey was conducted for at least three neighborhoods. These surveys permitted a more in-depth analysis of neighborhood amenities, household features, and perceptions and opinions.

Regarding housing characteristics, typical indicators refer to the size of the house (number of bedrooms and bathrooms) and the building's quality of construction (roof, walls, and floor). In relation to neighborhood characteristics, one important focus is the neighborhood's access to the city as a whole and to other areas. Consequently, the distance to a bus stop or a subway entrance, the quality of public transportation services, the quality of roads, and the degree of traffic congestion are neighborhood characteristics that may affect QoL. In addition, neighborhood amenities such as parks, proximity to a riverside promenade (in the case of Montevideo), and even the abundance of trees are relevant characteristics. Two other areas that are highly relevant for QoL are the proximity of educational institutions and such indicators of safety as the crime rate (murders per capita) and victimization rates (robbery).

Although those indicators are largely objective in nature, subjective measures and perceptions also may be used, especially in the LS approach. In particular, the surveys included questions about overall life satisfaction and satisfaction with housing quality and various neighborhood features. Though the overall LS variable is the key dependent variable to be used in the LS approach, other subjective measures of access to and quality of different local public goods and amenities may be incorporated into the analysis.[9] The choice between objective and subjective measures is discussed in greater detail below.

For the hedonic approach, the key dependent variable is housing prices or rents. These data were collected either through the neighborhood surveys (asking how much people are paying if they rent, or how much they would obtain if they were to rent their houses to others) or through such secondary sources as local property tax codes.

Complementarities between the Hedonic and LS Approaches

As discussed above, the hedonic and LS approaches can be viewed as complementary. To understand their relationship, consider an extreme case in which markets function perfectly and the variation in the housing stock is ample enough to include houses with different characteristics and a wide array of neighborhood amenities and disamenities (bads). Under these circumstances, house prices may reflect all the valuations of the relevant neighborhood and housing characteristics, and hence, suitably specified regressions with house prices as the dependent variable may reveal those valuations.

In the extreme case where markets function perfectly, those same characteristics may not be significant in the LS regressions. That may be true because income already is included as one explanatory variable and because the various characteristics are priced correctly, individuals already may buy them through their market-based housing decisions. There is then no extra effect to be found by regressing LS on individual house or neighborhood characteristics. In essence, the importance of, say, a neighborhood amenity already is priced and paid for through the value of the house. Therefore, the interpretation is not that these factors are unimportant, but that markets work well and are in equilibrium.

The fact that income is already taken into account and characteristics are priced correctly implies that using the results of hedonic regressions to calculate prices, and then using those prices as the weights to develop a QoL index, is appropriate. In such a case, the LS approach would not be expected to reveal very much information. Because income is included in the regression and markets are in equilibrium, no additional welfare is obtained from the relevant good (nor is there a reduction in welfare from a bad). These factors are already reflected in prices, and they affect welfare through the income variable.

A more realistic case, however, is one in which housing markets are not perfect. Information problems and transaction costs may be significant, suggesting that disequilibria may persist in housing markets for a considerable period of time.[10] In this case, it is possible that both the LS and hedonic regression approaches will find significant effects for a particular characteristic. Moreover, some characteristics change quite quickly over time; for example, bus routes change, patterns of crime may shift, and some neighborhoods may be "gentrified." Other characteristics, however, are much more permanent. A river or coastal area, for instance, is a fixture; the slope of the land cannot be changed easily; and parks rarely move (although they may be improved). These more structural features (again assuming there is enough variation in the housing stock) may be priced in the cross-section of house prices at a given time, whereas characteristics that shift over time may not be priced appropriately in the snapshot of house prices typically available. Hedonic regressions may reveal some valuations, but not others, depending on the nature of the characteristic in question. And where hedonic regressions do reveal values, they may reveal those valuations only imperfectly because the market may be moving slowly toward equilibrium.

Furthermore, there may be insufficient variation in a particular characteristic across the housing stock for that characteristic to be priced. For example, if all houses have exactly the same type of roof, then the quality of roofing will not be reflected in house prices. Likewise, if the crime level is constant across neighborhoods, that disamenity will not be priced. In those cases, prices will not reflect the full marginal effect of the characteristics on welfare. In that situation, hedonic regressions may not find the characteristic significant, whereas those factors may be picked up by the LS approach.

Those issues are discussed further in van Praag and Baarsma (2005), where the authors suggest that the hedonic and LS approaches are complements. Indeed, they show that, if certain conditions are met, the correct valuation actually is the sum of the coefficients from the two approaches. However, that is feasible only if the same sample and the same variable are included in both analyses—and that generally is not the case. Moreover, it is also of interest to compare the two approaches and to understand what the combination of results implies for how housing markets operate in the region. A summary of the results from both approaches is presented below, and the results are then compared and discussed in the light of this discussion.

The LS Approach to Measuring QoL

As explained in detail in chapter 3 (see also Frey, Luechinger, and Stutzer 2004), LS is a relatively new approach to placing a value on public goods. This method corresponds more closely to a stated-preference approach. As reported, subjective well-being can serve as an empirically adequate and valid approximation for individual utility. It is an obvious and straightforward strategy for directly evaluating public goods in utility terms. By measuring the marginal utility of a public good, as well as the marginal utility of income, we are able to calculate the trade-off between income and public goods (the implicit price).[11]

LS has certain advantages over hedonic methods (and they will be analyzed in the next section). First, because the LS approach is not based on observed behavior, the underlying assumptions are less restrictive and nonuse values can be measured to some extent. Furthermore, individuals are not asked to value the public good directly, but to evaluate their general subjective satisfaction. Arguably, this task is less cognitively demanding and does not allow for strategic behavior—two issues that have been critical problems affecting contingent valuation methods.

The LS approach has been applied successfully to value different public goods and policies, such as environmental externalities. For example, van Praag and Baarsma (2005) analyze the noise nuisance in the area of the Amsterdam Airport (Schiphol). For the case of housing and neighborhood amenities, Cattaneo et al. (2007) provide evidence that certain basic housing characteristics generate significant improvement in health and self-reported levels of QoL satisfaction, even though they are poorly correlated with family income.

In the basic empirical analysis of the LS approach, a microeconometric happiness function is estimated in which an individual's utility is approximated by self-reported subjective well-being. Explanatory variables are his or her income and a vector of socioeconomic variables. In addition, exposure to different neighborhood and city amenities (or disamenities) could be included. The typical regression has the following form:

$$LS_{ij} = a + b\,y_{ij} + c\,age_{ij} + d\,age_{ij}^2 + e\,fs_{ij} + g\,H_{ij} + h\,Z_j + v_{ij}, \qquad (2.1)$$

where y, *age*, and *fs*, respectively, represent income, age, and family size of individual i living in neighborhood j. H and Z, respectively, are two vectors of housing and neighborhood characteristics. The error term $v_{ij} = n_i + z_j$ is a composite error term that combines a neighborhood-specific error component, z_j, and a house-specific error component, n_i. Equation (2.1) is the typical LS regression, with the addition of housing and neighborhood features. In this regard, it is important to mention that empirical applications of this approach consistently have found that income has a positive effect on life satisfaction (b positive) and that age has a negative but decreasing impact (c negative and d positive).

The estimation of equation (2.1) is subject to potential omitted variables bias. In cross-section applications of these regressions (which will be summarized in a later section), estimation can be seriously biased if unobserved factors are covariate with LS and the measured public good. A key issue is to control for potentially collinear variables, although the lack of the relevant indicators generally limits this procedure. Alternatively, instruments for the public good variables could be used.

Table 2.1 presents an overview of the results of LS regressions for the six cities studied. A set of housing and neighborhood characteristics is found to be important for each city, with reasonable homogeneity across different urban areas. The table indicates statistically significant coefficients in a regression of LS on a set of standard variables (income, age,

Table 2.1 Overall LS Regressions for the Six Case Cities: Summary of Results and Significant Factors

Argentina (Buenos Aires)	Colombia (Bogotá)	Colombia (Medellín)	Costa Rica (San José)	Peru (Lima)	Uruguay (Montevideo)
Housing characteristics					
Not included (because a two-stage technique was used)	Number of rooms	Number of rooms	Quality of floors	Condition of walls	Quality of walls
		Satellite TV services			
	Quality of floors	Quality of floors			
Neighborhood characteristics					
Security during the day	Safety in the neighborhood	Presence of prisons	Safety (presence of gangs)	Safety (robbery)	Safety (vandalism in neighborhood)
Sidewalk condition in rain	Robbery				
	Drug dealing			Condition of street	Running water
Cultural and sports activities	Recreation/sports centers	Distance to places of cultural value		Trust in neighbors	Street lights
Amount and quality of green areas	Quality of energy services				

(continued)

Table 2.1 Overall LS Regressions for the Six Case Cities: Summary of Results and Significant Factors *(continued)*

	Argentina (Buenos Aires)	Colombia (Bogotá)	Colombia (Medellín)	Costa Rica (San José)	Peru (Lima)	Uruguay (Montevideo)
Traffic		Quality of garbage collection	Distance to main or connector street			
		Quality of telephone services				
Evaluation of neighbors		Average education in the neighborhood				
Other controls						
Income	Income	Income	Income	Income	Income	Income
Age	Age	Age	Age	Age	Age	Age
Marital status	Marital status	Marital status	Marital status	Marital status	Marital status	Marital status
Household size	Family size	Family size	Family size	Family size	Family size	Family size
Education		Health variables				

Source: Authors' compilation.
Note: LS = life satisfaction.

sex, marital status, and so forth) and a set of house and neighborhood characteristics.[12]

At least one indicator of the quality of house construction appears to be significant in all cases.[13] The particular proxy varies between the quality of floors and the quality of walls, but at least one appears in each case. In the case of the two Colombian cities (Bogotá and Medellín), the number of rooms also appears to be significant, although that is not true for the other cities.

With respect to neighborhood characteristics, security may be *the* most important and consistent issue in Latin American cities—a finding that is consistent with the cross-country findings on city satisfaction discussed in chapter 1. For example, in San José, the presence of gangs negatively affects life satisfaction. In Bogotá, Lima, and Montevideo, safety is seen as an important neighborhood attribute. Access to such basic services as electricity, water and sewerage, garbage collection, and telephone service also appears to be important. For Bogotá, inefficiencies in the provision of certain infrastructure services—energy, garbage collection, and telephone service—have a negative and significant impact on subjective well-being.

Note that some neighborhood characteristics are objective, in that they can be verified by an external observer: for example, the presence of garbage in the streets or the availability of pay phones. (In general, information on the objective variables was reported by interviewers in this project.) But several subjective neighborhood characteristics based on residents' own opinions also were included. Among the subjective variables, good neighbors are found to be particularly valuable in Argentina and Peru, as is the perceived condition of sidewalks in Peru.

Several neighborhood characteristics that might be considered important a priori do not seem to influence individuals' satisfaction. Perhaps it is surprising that traffic (or congestion) was significant only in Buenos Aires. That finding is consistent with the cross-country results reported in chapter 1, where traffic problems did not affect city satisfaction. However, one view is that traffic congestion is a disamenity that people grow used to and of which they eventually become unaware. As a result, they do not cite it as one of the most important disadvantages when they are asked.

Apart from judging which housing and neighborhood characteristics are particularly important, the LS approach can be used also to place a value on living in a neighborhood or on a particular house or neighborhood characteristic.[14] Because income influences life satisfaction along with certain characteristics (say, the condition of sidewalks), the trade-off between greater income and better sidewalks can be used to estimate the value of improving sidewalks. At no point do interviewed people actually express how much they are willing to pay for these characteristics. The LS approach is particularly helpful, therefore, because it can be used to value amenities that do not yet exist or for which no market price is available.

To illustrate how the LS approach can be used to price or value neighborhood amenities, table 2.2 shows the values for those neighborhood characteristics that turned out to be significant for three neighborhoods in Buenos Aires.[15] The table not only presents the valuation of individual neighborhood characteristics and amenities, but also shows how they are combined into a QoL index. Thus, the approach may be used to place

Table 2.2 Values of Neighborhood Characteristics, Selected Buenos Aires Neighborhoods

Neighborhood dummies	Monthly income compensation (%)	(US$)
Avellaneda	0.00	0.00
Caballito	−1.47	−11.66
Palermo	−1.28	−10.15
Neighborhood characteristics		
Annoying noise during the day	0.38	3.01
Good sidewalk conditions when raining	−0.38	−2.99
Good conditions of pavement/ streets	−0.40	−3.13
Cultural and sports activities	−0.22	−1.75
Amount and quality of green areas	−0.32	−2.51
Low traffic in neighborhood	−0.23	−1.86
Security during the day	−0.45	−3.59
Evaluation of neighbors	−0.64	−5.10
Pay phones	−0.35	−2.78

Neighborhood	Change from average to own neighborhood (income variations)	
	Neighborhood QoL index (US$)	Average monthly income (US$)
Avellaneda	−319	763
Caballito	463	807
Palermo	455	866
San Cristóbal	−558	704

Source: Chapter 4 of this volume.

a value on a neighborhood as such, as well as on specific neighborhood characteristics. For instance, good condition of pavement on streets has an estimated value of a monthly payment of $3.13. In the same way, living near green areas and parks commands a monthly income of around $2.51. The significant value for the neighborhood dummies suggests that differences in value go beyond the differences in the set of characteristics considered. In other words, this value is in addition to the measured differences in neighborhood characteristics, as reflected in the regression results. Overall, the combinations of all these characteristics (those that are observable and those that are captured by the dummies) imply that people living in Caballito and Palermo enjoy a QoL that is equivalent to a monthly payment of approximately $450, compared with that of people living in a neighborhood with the average supply of local public services and amenities.

The LS approach then provides one possible route to determining which amenities actually are considered valuable, to placing values on those characteristics, and to monitoring the valuations over time to see if they change as socioeconomic developments occur and as the characteristics of cities change.

The Hedonic Approach to Valuing Neighborhood Characteristics and Their QoL Impact

As mentioned above, a second way to estimate monetary values for local public goods and neighborhood amenities is hedonic pricing. This approach considers valuations based on actual behaviors and extracts preferences from market prices. Valuations are inferred, considering house prices or equivalent rents of properties with different characteristics. So long as enough variation in the relevant attributes is present in the sample of houses, values for each characteristic may be inferred from the information revealed by transaction prices.

The valuations may be derived from microeconomic fundamentals, considering the households' and firms' location decisions as a function of the characteristics of neighborhoods and houses. (A more in-depth theoretical account is provided in chapter 3.) Intuitively, implicit prices for various QoL attributes are obtained from a "spatial equilibrium," where a worker-resident receives an equilibrium wage and pays an equilibrium price for housing services. At this equilibrium, the worker-resident is just as happy living in that location as he or she would be moving to a different one. For the equilibrium to be sustainable, differences in urban amenities between alternative locations must be compensated by differences in prices of the local traded goods: housing prices and wages.[16]

The urban economics literature usually has assumed that city amenities affecting the QoL are reflected not only in land or housing prices, but also in wages. The key assumption is that city borders also place limits on labor markets in that choice of residence affects access to job opportunities. In contrast, the analysis presented in this book focuses on within-city variations in QoL. Because it is reasonable to assume that job opportunities do not differ greatly among workers within neighborhoods, valuations of amenities will be captured in house prices, not in wage differentials. Within-city location is not expected to limit labor opportunities if worker mobility is relatively high. To implement this methodology empirically, complementary data on real estate prices are needed. Ideally, for each subcity area j, information on housing prices and characteristics needs to be collected for a representative sample of housing units. Thus, the hedonic regression to be estimated would have the following form (Gyourko, Linneman, and Wachter 1999):

$$\ln p_{ij} = \text{constant} + \gamma_1 H_i + \gamma_2 Z_j + v_{ij}, \; v_{ij} = \delta_j + \eta_i, \qquad (2.2)$$

where p_{ij} is the rental price of house i located in neighborhood j, H_i is a vector of individual house features (number of rooms, quality of construction, square meters, and so forth), Z_j is a vector of neighborhood j amenities (crime rate, green space, and the like), and v_{ij} is the composite error term that is a combination of neighborhood-specific error component δ_j and house-specific error component η_i. The city-specific error component is common to all houses in the neighborhood, and it represents systematic uncontrolled differences in amenity characteristics across subcity areas; however, it also may capture systematic uncontrolled differences in *house quality* across neighborhoods. Either of those two factors would imply that the composite error term across houses within the same subcity area will be correlated, violating the ordinary least squares (OLS) independence assumption.[17]

The brief discussion of the hedonic approach provided above suggests the rather restrictive assumptions made by this theory. As mentioned earlier, the presumption that the real estate market is in equilibrium implies that households have a great deal of information on buying-selling opportunities in the real estate market, that prices of houses and land adjust rapidly, that transaction and moving costs are low, and that there are no other market restrictions (for example, price controls). Only if those assumptions are met can we expect the impact of public goods or bads to be reflected fully in housing rents and prices.

Beyond the theoretical concerns about whether the application of hedonic pricing is justified, from the empirical point of view, there is the problem of unobserved house and neighborhood characteristics and the consequent bias produced by omitted variables. In the literature, this problem is manifested in results that vary across different regression specifications or, occasionally, in variables that even appear to have the wrong sign. (The practical relevance of this problem will be discussed in the context of the estimation results presented later in the chapter.)

Table 2.3 offers a summary of the results of the hedonic regressions. There is considerable variation across the selected urban areas in terms of features that affect house prices. For example, in the San José metropolitan area, the slope of the land in a neighborhood and vulnerability to volcanic eruptions negatively affect property values. In Montevideo, proximity to the coastal promenade is an important feature of a neighborhood that contributes to the values of the houses. In some cities, proximity to a main avenue or thoroughfare may be considered an asset, whereas it may indicate congestion or pollution in another context. Thus, whereas closeness to a subway station contributes to higher house prices in Buenos Aires or Medellín, distance to the TransMilenio transportation system does not affect house prices in Bogotá. In those cities where basic domiciliary services coverage is still deficient in some areas, its influence on house prices can be gauged. The results indicate that access to running water, access to sewerage, and access to piped gas are associated with higher house prices.

Other neighborhood variables that proved to be important in several of the cities considered include proximity to schools, proximity to a park or a green space, and security. It is interesting to note that, in some cities, variables that relate to segregation by socioeconomic characteristics impact property prices. In Bogotá and Medellín, the proportions of people who belong to the highest socioeconomic stratum and of those who have attained the average level of education by census tract have a significant positive impact on property values (even after controlling for housing and other neighborhood characteristics). In fact, these two variables explain approximately 20 percent of the variance of prices in Bogotá and 30 percent in Medellín.

These quantitative estimates should be considered with caution because identification problems may produce biases in the results. Segregation is an endogenous response of location decisions to market prices, so that causality could go from prices to the chosen indicator of segregation. At the same time, these neighborhood-level variables may be capturing other unobservable characteristics of houses and neighborhoods. At least qualitatively, nonetheless, these results suggest that spatial segregation could result in a negative externality for poor/low-educated families living in those city areas. (We will come back to this issue when we discuss policy implications.)

House prices also depend strongly on the characteristics of the particular home in question. Location definitely is not all that matters when it comes to the cost of housing or equivalent rents. Here there is more homogeneity regarding the variables found to be significant. In particular, the number of rooms (total rooms or bedrooms); the number of bathrooms; and the conditions of walls, roof, and floors typically were found to be

Table 2.3 House and Neighborhood Characteristics Revealed in House Prices, Case Cities

Argentina (Buenos Aires)	Colombia (Bogotá)	Colombia (Medellín)	Costa Rica (San José)	Peru (Lima)	Uruguay (Montevideo)
Housing characteristics					
Age	Number of rooms	Number of rooms	Number of rooms	Number of rooms	Number of rooms
Garage	Garden	Number of bathrooms	Number of bathrooms		Number of bathrooms
Condition of walls	Garage	Fixed phone line	Condition of walls	Condition of walls	Condition of walls
	Condition of floor	Internet or satellite TV	Condition of floor		Condition of floor
	Size of house	Garage	Condition of roof	Condition of roof	Condition of roof
Number of bathrooms	Size of plot	Condition of floors	Exclusive bathroom		Exclusive kitchen
		Condition of walls			
Neighborhood characteristics					
Drug dealing	Homicide rate	Environmental risks	Safety	Sidewalks in good condition	Access to running water
Public transportation stops	No bus/train terminal	Distance to subway	Slope		Access to sewerage

Distance to subway	Distance to restaurant	Distance to bus terminal	Eruption vulnerability	Access to gas
	Running water	Distance to main or connector street	Distance to fire department	Condition of street
Distance to green space	Average education	Running water	Neighborhood roads	Condition of sidewalk
	Education inequality	Gas main	Length of primary road	Street lights
	Schools per capita	Average education	Length of secondary road	Access to La Rambla (Ocean Promenade)
	Distance to universities	Distance to university	Distance to parks	
	Lower unemployment	Distance to places of cultural value		

Source: Authors' compilation, based on the Inter-American Development Bank's Latin American Research Network Project on Quality of Life in Urban Neighborhoods in Latin America and the Caribbean, http://www.iadb.org/research/projects_detail.cfm?id_sec=8&id=91.

significant. In Buenos Aires, the age of the house was important (with a negative coefficient); and, in some cities, the presence of a garage and an exclusive kitchen were important.

Policy makers frequently need to know the relative importance of the different variables because they must decide where to invest scarce resources. Should investments be made in the quality of housing construction or in providing neighborhood amenities? In the case of Bogotá, approximately 30 percent of the variance in housing prices is explained by identified neighborhood amenities, whereas 51 percent of price variation is explained by housing attributes. For Medellín, the numbers are 37 percent and 25 percent, respectively. In the metropolitan area of San José, neighborhood amenities explain 39 percent of the variation in rents. Neighborhood features, although not everything, definitely are significant. That fact is quite important from the perspective of urban planers and local authorities because it suggests that QoL, as reflected in property values, can be improved by supplying better local public goods and neighborhood amenities.

The hedonic approach provides a direct means of evaluating these types of interventions in monetary terms. Using the coefficients from the regressions, an implicit price can be estimated (expressed in monthly terms) for different housing and neighborhood attributes. Table 2.4 presents an exercise considering San José. The implicit prices in the right-hand column indicate how much the monthly rental of an average house would change with an additional unit of the specified characteristic. For example, each degree of slope of land implies a lower monthly housing cost of about 60 cents, whereas an extra unit of safety (measured as neighborhood crimes reported per week) would imply a $25 increase in the cost of housing per month.[18]

Using the implicit prices in table 2.4, an index of the overall value of neighborhood characteristics can be generated. When that value is combined with the average value of housing characteristics, an overall neighborhood QoL index, expressed in monetary terms, can be calculated. Using this technique, it is possible to obtain the average QoL index, measured in terms of monthly house rental value by district (including both housing and neighborhood characteristics across 51 neighborhoods). In San José, this value ranges from $143 to $370 per month. Table 2.5 lists the top 10 and bottom 10 neighborhoods in San José, based on that measure. The contribution of the neighborhood amenities and other characteristics to this rental value ranges from –$67 to $27. It may take negative values because some neighborhood characteristics—such as the probability of a volcanic eruption—are bads. The contribution of housing characteristics ranges from $183 to $343, reflecting the diverse quality of housing construction across neighborhoods in San José.

As expected, wealthier neighborhoods, such as Sánchez, San Rafael, and San Isidro, have relatively high rental values attributable to neighborhood

Table 2.4 Hedonic Estimation of Implicit Prices for Housing and Neighborhood Characteristics, Metropolitan Area of San José, Costa Rica

Amenities/Disamenities	Estimated coefficient	Implicit price (2000 US$)
Housing characteristics		
Number of bedrooms	0.55***	30.84
Number of rooms (not bedrooms)	0.33***	18.80
Floor in good condition	0.24***	13.63
Walls in good condition	0.44***	24.82
Walls of cinder blocks	0.82***	45.72
Roof in good condition	0.32***	18.23
Ceiling in good condition	0.43***	24.46
Water source: communal organization	−0.36***	−20.24
Water source: rain	−0.82**	−46.07
Water source: well	0.13	7.44
Water source: river	−0.89***	−49.63
Sewer: septic tank	−0.10***	−6.03
Sewer: latrine	−0.21*	−11.72
Sewer: other	−0.33***	−18.60
No sewer	0.09	5.05
Exclusive bathroom for the household	0.48***	27.07
Electricity not supplied by Instituto Costarricense de Electricidad	−0.24***	−13.66
No electricity supplied	−0.70**	−39.15
Total contribution of housing characteristics (%)	60.84	
Neighborhood characteristics		
Safety index	0.46***	25.82
Degree of slope	−0.01***	−0.57
Precipitation (mm^3)	−0.12**	−6.99
Risk of eruption	−0.13**	−7.52
Log distance to national parks (km)	−1.25***	−70.09
Log distance to clinics (km)	0.01	0.57
Log distance to secondary schools (km)	0.02	1.18

(continued)

Table 2.4 Hedonic Estimation of Implicit Prices for Housing and Neighborhood Characteristics, Metropolitan Area of San José, Costa Rica *(continued)*

Amenities/Disamenities	Estimated coefficient[a]	Implicit price (2000 US$)
Log distance to primary schools (km)	0.00	0.19
Log distance to rivers (km)	0.06***	3.42
Log distance to fire departments (km)	0.05**	3.14
Log closeness to Sabana Park (km)	−0.54***	−30.58
Log distance to Peace Park (km)	1.35***	75.56
Length of primary roads (km)	−0.46***	−25.89
Length of secondary roads (km)	0.23***	13.31
Length of urban neighborhood roads (km)	0.57***	31.77
Neighborhood classified as poor	−0.35***	−19.91
Total contribution of neighborhood characteristics (%)	39.15	

Source: Chapter 6 of this volume.

Note: km = kilometers; mm^3 = cubic millimeters. The price of amenities is measured at mean prices in 2000 dollars (308 colones = 1 dollar). Where no asterisk appears, the coefficient does not differ from zero with statistical significance.

a. Specified to two decimal places.

*p < .10 **p < .05 ***p < .01.

variables; poorer areas, such as Aserri, Patarrá, and Concepción, have lower values. Although these findings are not surprising, they illustrate how neighborhood characteristics may exacerbate income differentials in terms of the distribution of QoL. These valuations also provide a guide to where scarce resources might be concentrated most effectively to improve that distribution. However, there also are some unexpected results. For example, Mata Redonda ranks very high (3rd) in housing/neighborhood characteristics, but rather low (10th) in neighborhood amenities; and Escazú ranks low (26th) in housing characteristics, but very high (4th) in neighborhood amenities. Those disparities illustrate that there is considerable space for action in both areas. Public policy has contributed to these results, and it may be used further to enhance the welfare of people living in areas where neighborhood valuations are at the lower end.

A similar exercise using the hedonic approach to calculate monetary values for neighborhood amenities in Buenos Aires is presented in table 2.6. The table lists the top 10 and bottom 10 neighborhoods, ranked by their characteristics and the housing price per square meter. Characteristics include the distance to different types of urban infrastructure, such as avenues, schools, parks, freeways, train stations, and subways. The

Table 2.5 Ranking of Districts by Housing and Neighborhood Characteristics, Using Hedonic Prices to Construct a QoL Index, Metropolitan San José, Costa Rica

Neighborhood	Neighborhood plus housing characteristics		Neighborhood characteristics		Housing characteristics	
	Rank	Value (US$)	Rank	Value (US$)	Rank	Value (US$)
Top 10						
Sánchez	1	370	1	27	1	343
San Rafael	2	285	2	9	8	275
Mata Redonda	3	275	10	−23	2	299
Carmen	4	264	11	−24	3	287
San Vicente	5	258	8	−20	6	277
Anselmo Llorente	6	254	13	−28	4	281
San Isidro	7	245	3	−5	23	250
San Pedro	8	238	20	−32	10	271
San Juán	9	237	16	−30	11	267
Sabanilla	10	237	35	−39	7	276
Bottom 10						
Alajuelita	42	172	48	−59	34	230
Hospital	43	169	40	−42	42	211
San Jocesito	44	166	46	−54	38	220
San Felipe	45	165	36	−40	46	205
Cinco Esquinas	46	164	28	−37	48	200
Patarrá	47	154	15	−29	51	183
San Juán de Dios	48	148	50	−62	45	210
Tirrases	49	144	51	−67	43	211
Concepción	50	143	49	−61	47	204
Aserri	51	143	47	−57	49	199

Source: Hall, Madrigal, and Robalino 2008.
Note: QoL: = quality of life. Rounding errors may mean sums are not exact.

"Amenities Index Implicit Price Difference" column in table 2.6 presents the estimated 2006 U.S. dollar values of the neighborhood characteristics for the average house in the indicated city area. The "Average Amenities Index" column indicates the percentage difference in price given by the considered amenities (0.05 means that property values rise 5 percent in

Table 2.6 Using Hedonic Prices to Construct a QoL Index,
by Neighborhood, City of Buenos Aires, Argentina

Neighborhood	Amenities index implicit price difference (value, US$)	Average amenities index (scale –1 to 1)	Rank by amenities index (47 neighborhoods)	Average price per square meter (US$)	Rank by price per square meter (47 neighborhoods)
Top 10					
Chacarita	218.7	0.186	1	1,021	14
Colegiales	214.0	0.166	2	1,174	7
Puerto Madero	209.2	0.064	18	2,810	1
San Nicolás	204.2	0.159	3	1,159	8
Palermo	202.9	0.129	7	1,507	3
Belgrano	184.7	0.136	5	1,269	5
Villa Ortuzar	178.0	0.148	4	1,118	9
Recoleta	158.2	0.105	10	1,453	4
Retiro	154.3	0.091	14	1,721	2
Villa Crespo	138.8	0.128	8	1,016	16
Bottom 10					
Monte Castro	–42.8	–0.051	36	862	30
Villa Devoto	–44.5	–0.056	38	960	22
Villa Soldati	–44.9	–0.070	40	680	45
Villa Lugano	–46.4	–0.081	43	605	47
Mataderos	–60.4	–0.082	44	754	42
Villa Luro	–63.1	–0.079	42	836	36
Liniers	–63.6	–0.076	41	852	34
Versalles	–89.0	–0.108	45	873	28
Villa Riachuelo	–90.0	–0.124	46	760	41
Villa Real	–126.6	–0.164	47	850	35

Source: Cruces, Ham, and Tetaz 2008.

the presence of amenities). As seen for some neighborhoods, even the rather small number of amenities considered implies a significant increase in property values (19 percent for Chacarita, 17 percent for Colegiales). At the other extreme, lack of these amenities in some other areas implies a significant reduction in property prices (for example, –16 percent for Villa Real and –12 percent for Villa Riachuelo). Overall, we see that wealthier neighborhoods (as judged by the average price of property per square meter), such as Recoleta and Palermo, are included in the top 10; whereas poorer ones, such as Villa Lugano and Mataderos, are in the bottom 10. It is interesting that some relatively expensive neighborhoods are at the bottom of the table (for example, Villa Devoto), and neighborhoods in the middle of the income distribution (such as Villa Crespo) are among the top 10. With respect to the city's 2006 average price per square meter of real estate, (approximately $1,041), the implicit price differences given by this index range from $219 to –$127, with an average of $72.50 or just less than 7 percent of the average property value.

The correlation between the price per square meter and the index is positive, but far from 1.00—thus reflecting a significant but imperfect relationship between property prices and the index (the price/index correlation is 0.43, and the price/rank correlation is 0.71). That imperfect correlation again suggests that factors other than basic housing features and neighborhood characteristics determine real estate prices. In the case of Buenos Aires, the ordering developed also may be used as a guide for public investment to improve the distribution of QoL.

Interpretation of the LS and Hedonic Results, and Comments on the Issue of Segregation

As discussed above, this project holds that LS and hedonic approaches should be considered complementary. The hedonic regressions find a set of housing and neighborhood characteristics to be significant, and that finding implies that housing markets in the region do function reasonably well in that they reveal considerable information about what individuals consider to be important. However, the LS regressions also reveal a set of variables to be significant. Although housing markets function, it is clear that they do not function perfectly. This finding implies that not all characteristics are priced appropriately at all times. Both sets of results should be considered relevant and be taken into account by policy makers.

The results may also suggest some answers to the relevant policy-making question of how to finance the provision of public goods. Amenities that are reflected in housing prices may be financed through property taxes, and those reflected in life satisfaction may be financed through general taxation.

Because of different sources of data, different definitions of variables, and different samples, it is not possible here to make very fine comparisons between the two sets of results for each city; nor is it feasible to add the monetary valuations from each approach, as suggested by van Praag and Baarsma (2005). Rather than conducting more narrow experiments to compare or harness together the two approaches, this project takes a broad view of what factors may be important for individuals' QoL. However, it is interesting to note that security issues, for example, come through as highly important in both approaches. Although house prices reflect part of the value of living in a safer neighborhood, they do not appear to reveal the full value of safer streets. The monetary valuations from the hedonic regression in this instance are likely to underestimate the value of heightened safety. On the other hand, hedonic regressions find that access to public transportation is important. LS regressions generally do not find that to be true. Hence, the market may reflect the value of this characteristic more fully, and the valuations in the hedonic regressions then may be fully revealing. If they compare the results in this way, policy makers may use both sets of results to consider likely true valuations.

An implication of the finding that housing markets reveal a wide set of neighborhood characteristics also suggests that Latin American cities are likely to be characterized by deep economic segregation. Segregation has received attention in the literature on urban economics, from both a theoretical and an applied perspective. Tiebout (1956) advances a theoretical model where inhabitants organize themselves into different areas, depending on their preferences for public goods. Different preferences imply an economic rationale for segregation. As homogeneous subcity areas develop, they exacerbate segregation at the city level. This economic segregation contrasts with ethnic or other motives for segregation.

A prediction of the Tiebout model, borne out by evidence from the United States, is that the more segregated an urban area is, the more local governments may develop to serve the needs of each homogeneous subcity zone. Vandell (1995), in an extension of the same argument, holds that the greater the income inequality, the greater the level of segregation, because higher-income families will outbid lower-income families for property with desirable characteristics.[19] The result is that richer areas will cluster closer to desirable amenities. More generally, according to that view, market forces are likely to generate areas where residents have similar attributes, perhaps including neighborhood characteristics such as natural features or parks and the provision of higher-quality public services.

Therefore, it should come as no surprise that Latin American cities are highly segregated, given the region's high income inequality and the finding here that housing markets do reflect a wide set of public goods and bads.[20] Moreover, the urban economics literature also concludes that rapid development of cities allows the demand for segregation to be both quicker and deeper (Watson 2005). As discussed in chapter 1, the region's large cities have developed very rapidly over the past 50 years, producing precisely the conditions in which segregation can flourish.

In the case of Montevideo, the high-income strata are concentrated spatially in very few neighborhoods. In two of these neighborhoods, Carrasco and Pocitos, more than 90 percent of the population belongs to the highest socioeconomic level. It is no coincidence that these areas are clustered closest to Montevideo's most famous natural feature, La Rambla or the promenade along its beaches. In metropolitan Lima, districts on the periphery of the city are poorer, and higher-income districts are located closer to the center of the metropolitan area.

Given that house prices reflect neighborhood characteristics and that neighborhoods tend to be segmented by income (socioeconomic strata), there is an implication that QoL also will be highly segmented. In Bogotá, the spatial distribution of the Índice de Calidad de Vida (a QoL index) and the Necesidades Básicas Insatisfechas (Unsatisfied Basic Needs) indicators demonstrate that the poorest families with the lowest QoL indicators consistently are located in the southern and western census sectors of the city; and those who are better off are located in the northern and eastern sectors that match the highest socioeconomic strata.

Segregation also is apparent when other characteristics, such as educational attainment, are considered. Within a limited geographic space in Greater Buenos Aires, areas where 25–50 percent of the population holds a university degree are located adjacent to areas with significantly lower educational levels. Highly educated residents tend to concentrate in the northern half of the City of Buenos Aires and in the three municipalities north of that—an area that constitutes the *corredor norte* (the northern suburban corridor that follows the shore of the Río de la Plata). The same pattern is apparent when the proportion of the population with at least one category of deficit in basic needs—a widely used measure of structural poverty captured with census data—is analyzed. In 2001, the outer area of Greater Buenos Aires had, by far, the highest concentration of population living under these conditions.

Greater Buenos Aires (on average, a wealthy city by Latin American standards) displays high levels of segregation of urban services.[21] Moreover, although access to the public network for water is relatively high for all residents (84–100 percent), there are several pockets where more than 10 percent of households are not connected to this network[22]—specifically in the urban outskirts. Moreover, some areas within the City of Buenos Aires are poorly covered, corresponding to some of the city's poorer areas (or *villas miseria*). To underline the segregation patterns in the city, the neighborhoods with higher socioeconomic status (such as Caballito and Palermo) have a significantly higher number of leisure-related and educational facilities, more trees, and more garbage bins per block than do areas with a greater number of inhabitants with lower socioeconomic status (such as Avellaneda and San Cristóbal).

In Montevideo, there also is significant variation of services across city areas. Dwellings in a neighborhood corresponding to a high-medium socioeconomic status have access, on average, to 8.0–8.4 public services; dwellings in a low-medium socioeconomic neighborhood have access to only 5.6–7.1 public services. In general, there is a positive correlation between the socioeconomic status of the inhabitants of a neighborhood and the number of basic services that are offered in Montevideo: the higher the socioeconomic status, the more services offered. In metropolitan Lima, the findings are slightly more mixed. Neighborhoods such as La Victoria, which has a medium-low income status, may be considered to be in the geographic center of the urban area and to have better access to public services (including transportation, police officers and security, and hospitals and other health facilities), whereas neighborhoods such as Los Olivos (with a medium socioeconomic status) and Villa El Salvador (a low-income neighborhood) are located on the city's periphery where access to public services is more restricted. For the cases of Bogotá and Medellín, the data show that the strong pattern of spatial segregation by socioeconomic level found is observed also when the allocation of basic services is considered. For example, the distribution of piped gas is concentrated in a few neighborhoods within the city, and these areas coincide with high-income neighborhoods.

In summary, the evidence suggests that there are important disparities in access to local public services and urban amenities across neighborhoods in Latin American cities. Therefore, the following questions arise: Is this segregation bad? If so, what should be done about it?

Returning to the Tiebout model, there is a theoretical argument that some types of segregation may be good. If segregation does reflect different preferences, then the variation across areas enables inhabitants to choose the area that corresponds most with their desires. This view implies that subcity areas will be relatively homogeneous in their demands for public services; and it suggests that voting mechanisms in an area would ensure less disappointment regarding taxation and service provision because people would tend to vote for the same options, given homogeneity. Therefore, if segregation produces a larger set of local governments offering different bundles of services according to inhabitants' tastes, then segregation also may be desirable—just as variety is important for consumers when shopping.

This positive side to segregation may be easily outweighed by a set of negatives; there are several reasons to be quite concerned about the strong pattern of socioeconomic spatial segregation outlined above. First, because the distribution of socioeconomic indicators also is reflected in the allocation of basic urban public services and neighborhood amenities, cities do not appear to be working as a compensating mechanism to moderate QoL differences across the urban population. Indeed, segregation in services and amenities implies that inequality may be even deeper in QoL than in income. Evidence also reveals that segregation extends racial divisions. For example, research in the United States suggests that Blacks living in more highly segregated cities have significantly lower educational and future-earnings outcomes than do Blacks living in less-segregated areas, when current socioeconomic variables are controlled for (Cutler and Glaeser 1997). Moreover, a highly segregated city population generally is less likely to demand high-quality public services (Alesina, Baqir, and Easterly 1999). The theory here is that a more-segregated population across a metropolitan area is one in which collective action is made more problematic; therefore, inhabitants are less likely to be able to communicate their demands effectively.

There also are additional costs to creating separate areas of high and low income—particularly, the potential flourishing of crime and violence in the low-income areas and the resulting spillover to all areas. Indeed, the efficiency of Tiebout-style sorting may turn negative if such spillovers (not contemplated in the original model) are significant. Given the major concerns with crime found by both the hedonic and LS approaches and across all cities, one view is that the high perceptions of serious crime in the region are a result of highly segregated cities. This view, by itself, constitutes an important reason to be concerned about the high levels of economic segregation in the region. Although there may be some theoretically positive aspects to segregation, many people find practical disparities in income and in access to basic services intolerable on moral grounds; and, although it is difficult to find conclusive evidence, they have serious concerns that segregation fosters crime and the perception of a lack of security.[23]

A number of policies could be followed to reduce segregation. But, first, it should be realized that if house prices reveal services and amenities being offered (as generally is shown in this volume), then whatever policies have been pursued in that regard have not been particularly successful to date. If policies to diminish segregation had been pursued strongly and had been effective, then researchers should find that house prices are not very revealing of neighborhood characteristics, because those interventions in the market presumably would have upset the price signals. It is beyond the scope of this book to present an evaluation of policies to date, but logic suggests that new policies must be advanced or current ones made more effective. The types of interventions that might be considered include subsidizing basic services in poorer areas and taxing richer areas more heavily. Another approach would be to use zoning to encourage the movement and mixing of people with different socioeconomic characteristics to diminish segregation. However, that is not easy to accomplish. Redevelopment or rejuvenation of urban areas may provide the best opportunity to ensure diminished segregation, and city planners certainly should consider the importance of ensuring the mixing of socioeconomic groups in areas that are redeveloped.

Conclusion

This chapter tries to summarize a very large set of results that readers will find in the subsequent chapters of this publication. Using LS and hedonic approaches, quantitative measures are obtained regarding the values that people and markets implicitly assign to specific characteristics of housing quality, access to different goods and services, and neighborhood amenities (such as parks) and disamenities (such as crime).

Apart from housing quality and access to public services, safety stands out as the aspect that most significantly affects urban areas' QoL. It is interesting that objective measures of crime do not always correlate with perceptions of safety. Creative policy thinking is required not only to reduce the actual incidence of crime, but also to ensure that urban populations feel safe. All the cities and countries analyzed here appear not to have been able to provide the perception of a safe environment for their urban populations.

At a more local level, municipal governments should establish information systems for monitoring the variables affecting QoL in urban neighborhoods. There are interesting and useful experiences in setting up these monitoring systems, including those of the City of London (London Sustainable Development Commission 2005), of Canadian cities (Treasury Board of Canada Secretariat 2000), and of the Urban Audit Program of the European Union (European Communities 2000). In Latin America and the Caribbean, Bogotá and its Bogotá Cómo Vamos scheme is another well-known example.

What variables and what questions should be included in these initiatives? The lessons learned from the analysis presented in this chapter suggest that research should cover both quantitative and qualitative indicators. In particular, investigators should use secondary sources (censuses and household surveys) to gather quantitative information at a highly disaggregated, census-tract level of basic socioeconomic and housing indicators. These secondary sources of information should be complemented by surveys (with subcity representation). In addition to covering some quantitative socioeconomic and housing variables, those surveys should include subjective questions about satisfaction with several dwelling and neighborhood characteristics (beyond overall life satisfaction).

One key objective of such subjective questions is to gauge the consistency between objective QoL indicators and people's perceptions of those variables. A second purpose of subjective survey questions is to extract an implicit value for certain public goods (or bads). And it is very important to develop and monitor a data set comprising house prices and rents. These data may be gathered through secondary sources (real estate quotations) and by rent and home value questions within the survey.

National statistical offices in some countries collect valuable information on many relevant variables. Typically, however, the focus is at the national level, with no regional or city-level disaggregation. Moreover, not all relevant variables are collected, and rarely are subjective opinions sought. (An exception is Bogotá's QoL survey, the Encuesta de Calidad de Vida.) Efforts are needed to link the valuable information already available at the national level with other information sources (including subjective surveys) and to provide results that are useful at different levels of government (including regions, cities, and subcity jurisdictions).

Nonetheless, the purpose of these local QoL monitoring systems is not merely to gather information in an integrated and consistent way. If these data are to inform the policy process, they must become part of the public debate and must influence the policy agenda. Those ends could be better achieved if there were public access to the information, and if the main results were presented to the public in a framework that ensures a certain level of independence with respect to the authorities.

The monitoring of QoL indicators at the city level can reveal existing overall disparities in QoL across neighborhoods and can identify the main causes of those disparities. This question then arises: How should this diagnosis be used to guide policy interventions? In other words, which disparities should be given priority in terms of public investment and compensation schemes? The clearest case is when the survey reveals that certain areas of the city lack basic services (say, running water) or are subject to a particular disamenity (say, pollution), and people's perceptions are consistent with those facts. Such evidence surely could support a public program to address the problems.

But beyond such obvious and clear-cut use of the information to drive public policy, the analysis undertaken in this chapter also suggests other, less direct ways to interpret the data and derive policy prescriptions. In particular, both the LS and hedonic approaches may be used to determine actual monetary valuations of improvements in services or provision of better amenities. Moreover, comparing the LS and hedonic approaches provides further insights. For example, where both approaches suggest that a particular issue is important, it is likely that both approaches underestimate true valuations. If a characteristic is found to be significant in the LS approach, it implies that markets are not fully reflecting individuals' true valuations. On the other hand, finding that a characteristic is not significant in the LS approach does not necessarily imply that there is no public policy concern. Furthermore, the results found using both approaches could be used to answer the very important policy question of how to finance provision of public goods. Amenities that are reflected in housing prices are amenable to financing through property taxes, and those reflected by the LS approach may be financed through general taxation.

In addition, in the extreme case where markets fully reflect all valuations, economic segregation is likely to be very deep and cities are likely to be characterized by severe inequality in QoL. In turn, spillovers between neighborhoods well may reduce the QoL of all inhabitants. In particular, one view is that deep economic segregation feeds crime. Because the lack of a sense of security may be the most serious issue found to affect QoL in the cities analyzed here, the link between segregation and crime surely is an important issue for further analysis.

Notes

1. Pioneering work using the hedonic approach to evaluate, for example, the impact of air pollution may be found in Ridker (1967) and Ridker and Henning (1967). Chay and Greenstone (2005) provide an updated treatment of the same issue, taking identification problems into account. Hedonic methods also have been used widely in estimating the value of school quality. Early work focusing on the United States is presented in Kain and Quigley (1975) and Li and Brown (1980). For more recent estimations, see Black (1999); Clapp and Ross (2002); and Bayer, McMillan, and Ferreira (2003).

2. This question also may be applied to a specific dimension of life satisfaction—such as how satisfied a person is with his or her house.

3. For application to other economic issues—such as the costs of unemployment, the inflation-unemployment trade-off, macroeconomic volatility, and inequality—see, respectively, Clark and Oswald (1994); Di Tella, MacCulloch, and Oswald (2001); Wolfers (2003); and Alesina, Glaeser, and Sacerdote (2001).

4. The human development index is a welfare measurement that combines three indicators: (1) longevity, measured by life expectancy at birth; (2) educational attainment, measured as a weighted average rate of adult literacy (two-thirds weight) and the combined primary and secondary gross enrollment rates (one-third weight); and (3) standard of living, measured by income per capita.

5. The 11 indicators are (1) access to a water network within the house, (2) access to sewerage services, (3) proper waste disposal collection, (4) average size of household, (5) number of bathrooms per house, (6) percentage of illiteracy among household members older than 15 years, (7) percentage of heads of household with less than 4 years of schooling, (8) percentage of heads of household with 15 or more years of schooling, (9) average income of heads of household (in terms of minimum wages), (10) percentage of heads of household with income up to two minimum wages, and (11) percentage of heads of household with income of 10 or more minimum wages.

6. An exception is Acosta, Guerra, and Rivera (2005). Although the authors arbitrarily select the indicators, they determine the weights across nine regions of Colombia, using a principal component analysis.

7. The project also included La Paz and Santa Cruz in Bolivia, but the results are not considered here because of substantial methodological differences.

8. Unlike the other areas studied, the analyses of Bogotá and Medellín refer only to the formal political borders of the two cities.

9. As described in chapter 3 and used in practice in chapter 7, additional LS dimensions or domains may be included in the analysis.

10. That situation may occur, for example, because of imperfect information about certain features of a neighborhood—features such as crime, which cannot be associated easily with a specific location as a result of its mobile nature.

11. As indicated in Frey, Luechinger, and Stutzer (2004), measures of self-reported subject well-being passed a series of validation exercises in the sense that they reflect objective circumstances affecting individuals' well-being. Another critical assumption made by this approach, which makes it possible to identify the impact of public goods on welfare, is that utility is cardinal and interpersonally comparable. This assumption, though problematic on theoretical grounds, proved to be less problematic empirically. For example, Frey and Stutzer (2002) report very similar quantitative results in microeconometric estimations of happiness function, using ordinal and cardinal measures of satisfaction.

12. The distinction here between what is a house characteristic and what is considered a neighborhood characteristic is somewhat artificial because the data

are at the level of each household. In practice, we may draw a distinction based on the relative variation across individual houses in a subneighborhood. For example, most houses in a (small) subneighborhood will have or will not have access to water; therefore, access to water is considered a neighborhood characteristic here.

13. The Argentina study adopted a slightly different methodology where housing satisfaction was included in the regression and so individual housing characteristics were not included. However, a second-stage regression was performed to explain housing satisfaction and here, too, the quality of house construction was found to be a significant variable.

14. Chapter 3 provides a description of the theory and applications of these techniques in practice. See also Frey, Luechinger, and Stutzer (2004) and Ferrer-i-Carbonell and van Praag (2004).

15. These valuations stem from a two-stage technique (developed by van Praag, Frijters, and Ferrer-i-Carbonell 2003) wherein a first-step overall LS is regressed on income and a set of domains (including satisfaction with the neighborhood), and a second-step neighborhood satisfaction is regressed on a set of more objective neighborhood characteristics. The coefficient on income in the first regression and the coefficients on neighborhood satisfaction in the second step are then combined to find the trade-off between income and, say, improving security during the day. That trade-off implies how much someone would be willing to pay to obtain a little more security, so it may be interpreted as the price of additional security.

16. For a description of the microeconomic fundamentals behind hedonic pricing of QoL indicators, see Gyourko, Linneman, and Wachter (1999).

17. In particular, it will imply a downward bias to OLS-based standard errors (Moulton 1986). Thus, the potential problem of the presence of group effects needs to be addressed by correcting the standard error by clustering or running a random effect estimation (assuming city fixed effects are not correlated with any of the Z variables). Of course, this problem will be minimized by better data on individual housing characteristics and by more data for neighborhood-level QoL attributes.

18. Housing cost refers to "equivalent rent," which is either the rent itself or a calculation of the opportunity cost of inhabiting the self-owned house (as estimated by the owner, albeit somehow subjectively). Any differences between renters and owners in relation to their preferences are ignored in this analysis.

19. Vandell (1995) divides characteristics into four categories: (1) housing and lot characteristics; (2) neighborhood amenities; (3) accessibility characteristics; and (4) resident attributes, such as race, income, wealth, education, family composition, and occupation.

20. Here we focus on economic rationales for segregation; but there also may be other rationales, such as religious or racial divisions.

21. As discussed in the penultimate section of this chapter, segregation may have other detrimental effects.

22. Because 10 percent is very different from the average, this finding implies a high degree of segregation.

23. For an interesting discussion, see Wassmer (2002).

References

Acosta, Olga, José Alberto Guerra, and David Rivera. 2005. "Acceso de los hogares a los principales servicios públicos y sociales y percepciones de calidad sobre estos servicios." Serie Documentos 76, Economía, Universidad del Rosario, Bogotá, Colombia.

Alesina, Alberto, Reza Baqir, and William Easterly. 1999. "Public Goods and Ethnic Divisions." *Quarterly Journal of Economics* 114 (4): 1243–84.

Alesina, Alberto, Edward Glaeser, and Bruce Sacerdote. 2001. "Why Doesn't the United States Have a European-Style Welfare State?" *Brookings Papers on Economic Activity* 2: 187–277.

Amorin, Érica, and Mauricio Blanco. 2003. "O Indice do Desenvolvimento Humano (IDH) na Cidade do Río de Janeiro." Colecao Estudos Da Cidade, Prefeitura Da Cidade do Río de Janeiro.

Bayer, Patrick, Robert McMillan, and Fernando Ferreira. 2003. "A Unified Framework for Measuring Preferences for Schools and Neighborhoods." Economic Growth Center Discussion Paper 872, Yale University, New Haven, CT.

Black, Sandra E. 1999. "Do Better Schools Matter? Parental Valuation of Elementary Education." *Quarterly Journal of Economics* 114 (2): 577–99.

Blomquist, Glenn, Mark Berger, and John Hoehn. 1988. "New Estimates of Quality of Life in Urban Areas." *American Economic Review* 78 (1): 89–107.

Cattaneo, Matías D., Sebastián Galiani, Paul J. Gertler, Sebastián Martinez, and Rocío Titiunik. 2007. "Housing, Health and Happiness." Policy Research Working Paper 4214, World Bank, Washington, DC.

Cavallieri, Fernando, and Gustavo Peres Lopes. 2008. "Índice de Desenvolvimento Social—IDS: comparando as realidades microurbanas da cidade do Río de Janeiro." Coleção Estudos Cariocas 20080401, Río de Janeiro, Brazil.

Chay, Kenneth Y., and Michael Greenstone. 2005. "Does Air Quality Matter? Evidence from the Housing Market." *Journal of Political Economy* 113 (2): 376–424.

Clapp, John, and Stephan Ross. 2002. "Schools and Housing Markets: An Examination of School Segregation and Performance in Connecticut." Working Paper 2002-08, Department of Economics, University of Connecticut, Storrs.

Clark, Andrew E., and Andrew J. Oswald. 1994. "Unhappiness and Unemployment." *Economic Journal* 104 (424): 648–59.

Cortés, Darwin C., Luis Fernando Gamboa, and Jorge I. González. 1999. "ICV: Hacia una medida de estándar de vida." *Coyuntura Social* 21 (November): 159–80.

Cruces, Guillermo, Andrés Ham, and Martín Tetaz. 2008. "Quality of Life in Buenos Aires Neighborhoods: Hedonic Price Regressions and the Life Satisfaction Approach." Latin American Research Network Working Paper R-559, Research Department, Inter-American Development Bank, Washington, DC.

Cutler, David, and Edward Glaeser. 1997. "Are Ghettos Good or Bad?" *Quarterly Journal of Economics* 112 (3): 827–72.

Di Tella, Rafael, and Robert MacCulloch. 1998. "Partisan Social Happiness." Unpublished manuscript, Harvard Business School, Cambridge, MA.

Di Tella, Rafael, Robert MacCulloch, and Andrew J. Oswald. 2001. "Preferences over Inflation and Unemployment: Evidence from Surveys of Happiness." *American Economic Review* 91 (1): 335–41.

European Communities. 2000. *The Urban Audit: Towards the Benchmarking of Quality of Life in 58 European Cities.* Luxembourg: Office for Official Publications of the European Communities. http://ec.europa.eu/regional_policy/urban2/urban/audit/ftp/vol3.pdf.

Ferrer-i-Carbonell, Ada, and Bernard M.S. van Praag. 2004. *Happiness Quantified: A Satisfaction Calculus Approach.* Oxford, U.K.: Oxford University Press.

Frey, Bruno, Simon Luechinger, and Alois Stutzer. 2004. "Valuing Public Goods: The Life Satisfaction Approach." Working Paper 1158, CESifo Group, Munich, Germany.

Frey, Bruno, and Alois Stutzer. 2002. *Happiness and Economics: How the Economy and Institutions Affect Human Well-Being*. Princeton, NJ: Princeton University Press.

Gardner, Jonathan, and Andrew J. Oswald. 2001. "Does Money Buy Happiness? A Longitudinal Study Using Data on Wind Falls." Unpublished manuscript, University of Warwick, Coventry, U.K.

Gyourko, Joseph, Peter Linneman, and Susan Wachter. 1999. "Analyzing the Relationships among Race, Wealth, and Home Ownership in America." *Journal of Housing Economics* 8 (2): 63–89.

Hall, Luis J., Róger Madrigal, and Juan Robalino. 2008. "Quality of Life in Urban Neighborhoods in Costa Rica." Research Network Working Paper R-563, Research Department, Inter-American Development Bank, Washington, DC.

Kain, John F., and John M. Quigley. 1975. *Housing Markets and Racial Discrimination: A Microeconomic Analysis*. Cambridge, MA: National Bureau of Economic Research.

Li, Mingche, and James Brown. 1980. "Micro-Neighborhood Externalities and Hedonic Prices." *Land Economics* 56 (2): 125–41.

London Sustainable Development Commission. 2005. *2005 Report on London's Quality of Life Indicators*. London: Greater London Authority.

Lora, Eduardo, ed. 2008. *Beyond Facts: Understanding Quality of Life*. Washington, DC: Inter-American Development Bank.

Moulton, Brent. 1986. "Random Groups Effects and the Precision of Regression Estimates." *Journal of Econometrics* 32 (3): 385–97.

Ridker, Ronald. 1967. *Economic Costs of Air Pollution, Studies in Measurement*. New York: Frederick A. Praeger.

Ridker, Ronald, and John Henning. 1967. "The Determinants of Residential Property Values with Special Reference to Air Pollution." *Review of Economics and Statistics* 49 (2): 246–57.

Roback, Jennifer. 1982. "Wages, Rent and the Quality of Life." *Journal of Political Economy* 90 (6): 1257–78.

Tiebout, Charles. 1956. "The Pure Theory of Public Expenditures." *Journal of Public Economy* 64 (5): 416–24.

Treasury Board of Canada Secretariat. 2000. "Quality of Life—A Concept Paper: Defining, Measuring and Reporting Quality of Life for Canadians." Ontario. http://www.tbs-sct.gc.ca/pubs_pol/dcgpubs/pubsdisc/qol1-eng.asp.

Vandell, Kerry. 1995. "Market Factors Affecting the Spatial Heterogeneity among Urban Neighborhoods." *Housing Policy Debate* 6 (1): 103–39.

van Praag, Bernard M.S., and Barbara Baarsma. 2005. "Using Happiness Surveys to Value Intangibles: The Case of Airport Noise." *Economic Journal* 115 (500): 224–46.

van Praag, Bernard M.S., Paul Frijters, and Ada Ferrer-i-Carbonell. 2003. "The Anatomy of Subjective Well-Being." *Journal of Economic Behavior & Organization* 51 (1): 29–49.

Wassmer, Robert W. 2002. "An Economic View of Some Causes of Urban Spatial Segregation and Its Costs and Benefits." Unpublished manuscript, California

State University, Sacramento. http://www.csus.edu/indiv/w/wassmerr/segrega
tionincity.pdf.

Watson, Tara. 2005. "Metropolitan Growth and Neighborhood Segregation
by Income." Unpublished manuscript, Williams College, Williamstown, MA.
http://www.williams.edu/Economics/seminars/watson_brook_1105.pdf.

Winkelmann, Liliana, and Rainer Winkelmann. 1998. "Why Are the Unemployed
So Unhappy? Evidence from Panel Data." *Economica* 65 (257): 1–15.

Wolfers, Justin. 2003. "Is Business Cycle Volatility Costly? Evidence from Surveys
of Subjective Well-Being." *International Finance* 6 (1): 1–26.

3

Toward an Urban Quality of Life Index: Basic Theory and Econometric Methods

*Bernard M.S. van Praag and
Ada Ferrer-i-Carbonell*

It readily is apparent that some cities are more pleasant to live in than others. That assessment is based on considerations such as safety, the presence of green spaces, access to educational and health facilities, and adequate street lighting. This volume calls attention to how those aspects of urban life affect overall quality of life (QoL), with the ultimate goal of developing operational indexes to measure the effects of urban life. In turn, those indexes can be used to compare the amenities offered by different neighborhoods within a city and their contributions to citizens' QoL. Then one may try to differentiate urban amenities with respect to their contributory impacts to get a better understanding of the type of urban policy that will be most favorable for citizen's QoL.

But what is QoL? Numerous definitions have been proposed by philosophers, psychologists, and other scholars (see, for example, Nussbaum and Sen 1993), many of whom make distinctions among terms such as *quality of life, happiness,* and *satisfaction.* Economists, for their part, refer to individual utility or well-being. Until recently, however, differences between those two concepts largely have been ignored in empirical practice.

Following Pareto (1909) and Robbins (1932), neoclassical economists traditionally have held that individual satisfaction cannot be observed

The authors wish to thank Eduardo Lora for support at different stages of the chapter and two anonymous referees for useful comments.

directly. However, assuming that individuals maximize their utility or satisfaction, observing purchase behavior allows conclusions to be drawn regarding the shape of indifference curves. In this view, survey information on satisfaction or happiness is rejected as unnecessary and even misleading.

Observing only purchases, however, does not provide a way to determine the contribution to individuals' utility or well-being of those goods (or bads) that are not bought directly in the market, but presumably are important for well-being. Such amenities and disamenities include aspects of the urban environment, ranging from air quality to the level of personal security. Under certain assumptions, those and other urban features should be reflected in housing prices; and thereby the standard approach may be extended to assess those features' contributions to QoL.

A second problematic assumption in the neoclassical approach is that individuals have reached the most optimal situations available to them. As will be discussed later in this chapter, there are many reasons to believe that people do not see their present conditions as optimal, even if they originally viewed their decisions in that light. That fact is particularly pertinent regarding choices in housing, education, or work.

Finally, the neoclassical approach denies the possibility of measuring differences in satisfaction derived from different situations, yielding only preference orderings but no cardinal measurement of differences in satisfaction. A growing body of studies by psychologists and economists over the last four decades, however, has led to an emerging consensus on the cardinal measurability of subjective well-being through the use of surveys that investigate how people evaluate diverse aspects of life and life satisfaction in general.

Measured in that way, life satisfaction depends on a number of factors—not only those that lend themselves to the standard approach of revealed preferences. Satisfaction depends not only on income; it also depends, for instance, on health, family situation, and working conditions. Life satisfaction also is influenced by the quality of the urban environment, reflected in factors such as personal safety, crime, traffic, street and sanitary conditions, and access to education. Until recently, economists focused mainly on private variables, such as the life satisfaction impact of one's own income or work situation (Clark and Oswald 1994; van Praag 1971), health (Ferrer-i-Carbonell and van Praag 2002; Oswald and Powdthavee 2007), and relative income (Easterlin 1995; Ferrer-i-Carbonell 2005; Luttmer 2005). However, economists often have excluded other highly relevant factors that are difficult to measure and frequently are not included in the data sets at hand. These factors, which cannot be bought on the market, have been ignored on the grounds that traditionally they are within the research field of other behavioral sciences. Nonetheless, such factors have an undeniable effect on QoL.

Because this volume focuses on the quality of the living environment, level and availability of public services are of primary importance. The financing of those services through tax revenues or direct payments (such as road tolls), however, means that public authorities' decisions will affect the level of private consumption. A choice may exist, for example, between better and cheaper public transportation and private automobile ownership. Similarly, within the public budget, officials must choose among alternatives such as policing, street lights, and education.

Decisions on taxes and spending theoretically are made by a legislature or by other authorities who take citizens' preferences into account. Because preferences hardly are homogeneous, and because some citizens are more successful than others in making their opinions known, decision makers may not possess sufficient information about what makes people happy.

This volume makes a first attempt to construct data sets on the urban quality dimension of human happiness and to present some analysis of those data. This is a very new field of study, particularly in Latin America, so the Inter-American Development Bank commissioned the studies in this volume from several national research groups. The Bank described the main research objectives and suggested some tools of analysis, but it avoided overly stringent requirements for the content of the national studies. Given the data constraints faced by various research groups, each study has its own level of detail.

This chapter provides a methodological framework for interpreting the studies in this volume. The two methodologies proposed to researchers were the hedonic price and the life satisfaction (LS) approaches. Other alternatives exist—most notably, stated-preference approaches such as contingent valuation. In the context of urban amenities, Dolan and Metcalfe (2007) compare the value of urban renewal, using the three methods, and they conclude that those methods give rise to different values.

The structure of this chapter is as follows. The next two sections present the theoretical foundations of the hedonic price and the LS approaches,[1] respectively, followed by a discussion of the relationship between the two. Three subsequent sections address the empirical strategies that may be used to make the two approaches operational. Particular attention is paid to the LS approach, given the nature of the data and the difficulties involved in their econometric use. The final section summarizes the methodologies proposed and their potential to help address relevant policy questions.

The Hedonic Price Approach

This volume includes applications of both the hedonic price and the LS approaches. The former approach (Rosen 1979; Roback 1982; Blomquist, Berger, and Hoehn 1988; and Gyourko 1991) was developed to obtain monetary valuations of public goods, such as green areas, security, congestion, and other urban features. The rationale for this approach is quite simple: if two otherwise identical houses are located in safe and unsafe parts of a city, and if the monthly rent for the safe-area house is $1,000 while the monthly rent for the unsafe-area house is $500, it then seems plausible to assign the difference in value to the difference in safety. The value of safety per month may thus be evaluated by the rent difference of $500.

This idea may be generalized to a great extent. Assume that the rent per month of a specific house n located at a specific location within neighborhood $j(n)$ is p_n. The rent will vary with the characteristics of the house, such as the number of rooms, whether it is an apartment or an independent house, how far it is from key amenities or services, and the physical infrastructure and other attributes of the neighborhood. In short, the rent of a house depends on a vector of characteristics of the house and its specific location, H_n, and a vector of neighborhood characteristics, $Z_{j(n)}$ (characteristics that are common to all the houses in the neighborhood). It therefore follows that relationships of the type $p_n = p(H_n, Z_{j(n)})$ may be posited. For instance, let Z_{1j} be for the neighborhood $j(n)$ the number of minutes it takes the police to arrive after an emergency, and let Z_{2j} be the walking distance (in minutes) to the nearest subway station. After suitable transformations of the variables, a linear relationship for the logarithm of the rent could be estimated as

$$\ln(p_n) = \alpha_0 + \alpha_1 Z_{1j(n)} + \alpha_2 Z_{2j(n)} + \alpha_3 H_n + \alpha_4 \ddot{Z}_{j(n)}, \tag{3.1}$$

where $\ddot{Z}_{j(n)}$ stands for the vector Z without the two first components; α_0, α_1, and α_2 are scalars; and α_3 and α_4 are vectors. Let us assume that we estimate $\hat{\alpha}_1 = -0.02$ and $\hat{\alpha}_2 = -0.01$. These estimates imply that for every extra minute it takes the police to arrive, rents would drop by 2 percent. Similarly, every minute less of walking time to the nearest subway station would increase rent by 1 percent.[2] It therefore seems attractive to interpret these coefficients as *shadow prices*.

Notice that $Z_{1j(n)}$ and $Z_{2j(n)}$ are *hedonic* dimensions that cannot be bought separately in a different market. Also, problems in one dimension could be compensated for by advantages in another. For example, two extra minutes of walking time to the subway could be compensated by one minute less in police arrival time. In this way, it is possible to use a common denominator (that is, the amount of rent to be paid) to compare different factors. This ratio, the market substitution between two characteristics, is equal to α_1 / α_2.

Equation (3.1) now may be seen as a budget curve in the sense that it describes all houses as bundles of characteristics that can be leased at a specific rent level p. Assume that individuals have direct utility functions of the type $U(H_n, Z_{j(n)})$; and that, in equilibrium, indifference curves (in the characteristics space) will be tangent to the budget curve. Formally, this means that

$$\frac{\partial U}{\partial Z_{1j(n)}} \Bigg/ \frac{\partial U}{\partial Z_{2j(n)}} = \frac{\partial p}{\partial Z_{1j(n)}} \Bigg/ \frac{\partial p}{\partial Z_{2j(n)}} = \frac{\alpha_1}{\alpha_2}. \tag{3.2}$$

It follows that the ratios α_1/α_2 also describe the slope of the indifference curve, if the individual consumer is assumed to be in his or her optimum. Under that assumption, there is equality between the market substitution ratio and the subjective trade-off between characteristics. It follows also that the rent equation (3.1) may be interpreted as a local approximation of the indifference curve (up to a positive factor of multiplication). Relative utility changes thus can be assessed by

$$\Delta U \approx \alpha_1 \Delta Z_{1j(n)} + \alpha_2 \Delta Z_{2j(n)} + \alpha_3 \Delta H_n + \alpha_4 \Delta \ddot{Z}_{j(n)} \tag{3.3}$$

for a specific individual if the bundle $(H_n, Z_{j(n)})$ is changed into $(H_n, Z_{j(n)}) + (\Delta H_n, \Delta Z_{j(n)})$. However, this is only a local approximation. In this way, the relative impact of changes in different variables on subjective well-being may be compared.

The hedonic price approach, used by all research groups in this volume, offers interesting and even surprising results. All the groups were able to find a wealth of information in public records, including data on factors such as domiciliary services, distance to schools, and vulnerability to natural disasters. These data were complemented by information drawn from individual questionnaires filled out by the inhabitants of the houses considered.

One problem, however, renders this method less attractive than it might appear at first: the underlying assumption of neoclassical economics that each person not only looks for the best position he or she can reach, but also is able to reach it. In other words, the housing market is a free-access competitive market and is always in equilibrium. That assumption, which implies that every observed respondent is in the best position he or she can attain, is unlikely to hold in practice. This is especially true for the housing market, where regulations and lack of information on many relevant variables may prevent full competition, where individuals' choices—in most cases, made many years ago—are very costly to reconsider, and where the monetary and psychic transaction costs of moving to a new home are considerable. Moreover, housing markets frequently are rationed—for example, by public housing programs or zoning restrictions. If the equilibrium assumption does not hold, then market substitution rates will not equal subjectively perceived substitution rates.

Indeed, it is not reasonable to assume that individuals observed in a dynamic reality live in an optimal situation. Most serious decisions—such as those involving education, job choice, housing, the number of children, and the choice of a partner in life—are long-term decisions with long-lasting consequences. It is by no means certain that individuals at any arbitrary later moment still feel that they have reached the greatest possible well-being or level of satisfaction, even if all those decisions were made in a fully rational manner. It is much more probable that, at present, individuals would choose other situations, if they were not hampered by rather enormous transition costs (see Bruni and Sugden 2007). Hence, individuals in reality are rarely in an optimum situation.

A second problem with this method in relation to housing is its implicit assumption that the choice of a house is the only consumer choice affected by external factors such as safety, commuting distance, and sanitation. In fact, the choice of a car and the decision whether to buy a car are determined partly by such external factors as well. For instance, the decision to buy a car depends on such considerations as road congestion, road conditions, and auto accessibility to schools and hospitals. Likewise, external variables may affect many other choices. It is not obvious that the trade-off ratios between urban variables when buying a car would be the same as when renting a house; and if the trade-off ratios between urban variables are unequal, depending on the specific commodity considered, it is unclear which trade-off ratio should be analyzed. Although having well-defined estimates of the rent equation $p_n = p(H_n, Z_{j(n)})$ remains interesting, because it describes the possibilities on the housing market, it does not necessarily give a complete evaluation of the individually perceived trade ratios between, for example, safety and distance to the subway.

A feature of the hedonic approach is that it only assumes an ordinal utility function. Using the ordinal assumption only does not allow for translating an income gain into a utility gain; nor does it allow for interpersonal comparison of levels of well-being (QoL).

Here is where the LS approach comes into play. That approach does not assume that the individual is at any time observed in his optimum in a perfect market. Moreover, the LS approach allows for both ordinal *and* cardinal satisfaction measurements.

The LS Approach

Happiness economics—the term apparently coined by Clark and Oswald (1994), with predecessors in van Praag (1971), Easterlin (1974), and the so-called Leyden School—is diametrically opposed to mainstream neoclassical economics in that it does not assume beforehand that individuals optimize their utility by situating themselves in a point of tangency between an indifference curve and the budget curve.[3] Instead, the happiness or LS approach starts empirically by *asking* individuals how *satisfied* they are with their life or how *happy* they are.[4] The rationale for this approach is empirical evidence that individuals are able to evaluate their satisfaction with life as a whole. Such evaluation may take the form of verbal categories, such as "bad," "adequate," and "good"; or it may use a numerical scale on which, for instance, 0 stands for the worst conceivable situation and 10 stands for the best conceivable situation. It has been demonstrated that these measurements are well correlated with various aspects of behavior associated with happiness, such as frequency of laughter in moments of social interaction. People who are happy according to such measurements also are considered happy by their friends and families; such individuals express positive emotions more frequently and are more optimistic, sociable, and extrovert.

No uniformity so far exists on how to phrase satisfaction questions. Respondents may be asked, generally speaking, How *happy* are you with your life? or How *satisfied* are you with your life? Possible responses include selections from a list of four verbal levels (for example, "bad," "insufficient," "sufficient," or "good") or from a numerical scale of 0 to 10, depending on the questionnaire design. Respondents also may be asked to evaluate other aspects of their lives (called *life domains*), such as their health, financial situation, and housing. In spite of the fact that there are different wordings of satisfaction questions, in practice the results are fairly well comparable.

Given the LS question as described above, it may be assumed that life evaluation depends on a set of variables describing the individual situation, such as income, age, marital status, number of working hours, health situation, family size, travel distance to work, and type of work—in short, a vector x of k different variables $x_1,\ldots,x_k$. These can be called *aspects* or *dimensions* of one's life situation. Some of these aspects or dimensions, like the number of working hours or travel time to work, can be influenced by the respondents themselves; others, like age, cannot be changed by the individual. These dimensions also may include urban and environmental features, like safety, cleanliness, or climate variables.

Figure 3.1 presents three curves, representing three satisfaction levels (W). In this example, life satisfaction depends on only two aspects or dimensions, x_1 and x_2. The higher the curve, the higher the satisfaction level. By construction, these are *satisfaction indifference curves*. In practice, the number of response categories is finite—say, 0, 1, 2, \ldots, up to 10. It follows that a dense and continuous map of indifference curves cannot be observed; but it is possible to observe 11 of them, corresponding to the response categories $0,1,\ldots,10$. It is surprising that simply questioning individuals enables the construction of indifference curves, without assuming optimizing behavior or functional specifications. In fact, the identifying power of neoclassical marginal conditions is not needed.

A question of terminology should be clarified before this discussion continues. The term *indifference curve* traditionally is derived from the analysis of consumer behavior, where the individual ranks *commodity* bundles according to preferences. In the present context, the term has a

Figure 3.1 Satisfaction Indifference Curves

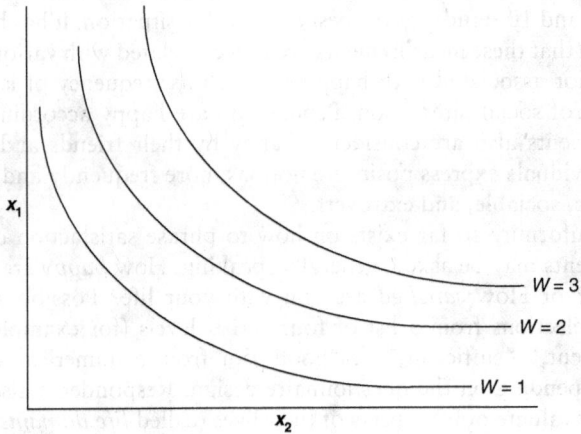

Source: Authors' illustration.

wider meaning in which the space of alternatives consists of different *life situations*. A life situation is described by a vector x of relevant characteristics, such as age, income, housing situation, and street safety. Some of those characteristics involve market goods that can be purchased, and others do not.

It can be assumed that each indifference curve is described by the equation $f(x_1, x_2, \ldots, x_k) = W$ (constant), where the value of W indicates the *level* of the indifference curve. If two situations— $\left(x_1^1, x_2^1, \ldots, x_k^1\right) = x^{(1)}$ and $\left(x_1^2, x_2^2, \ldots, x_k^2\right) = x^{(2)}$ where $W^{(1)} < W^{(2)}$—are compared, then $x^{(2)}$ is preferred over $x^{(1)}$. In that case, the individual's perceived trade-off ratio may be defined as the subjective trade-off ratio between any two dimensions. The ratio is defined as the required compensation in dimension x_2 when the quantity of dimension x_1 is reduced by one unit, such that there is no change in the indifference curve level. This trade-off ratio is called "subjective" because it is defined by the subjective satisfaction measure. However, here the trade-off ratios between urban aspects are not derived by observation of purchase behavior (for example, purchase of houses), but by direct observation of how urban features affect satisfaction with life as a whole or with urban dimensions in particular.

The trade-off ratio is found by solving for Δx_2 in the equation

$$f(x_1 + \Delta x_1, x_2 + \Delta x_2, x_3 \ldots, x_k) = f(x_1, x_2, \ldots, x_k), \qquad (3.4)$$

taking Δx_1 as given. If the function $f(.)$ is differentiable, this yields as a limiting value the slope coefficient of the indifference curve at x, which is $\lim_{\Delta x_1 \to 0} (\Delta x_2 / \Delta x_1) = -f_1 / f_2$, also known as the substitution rate or trade-off ratio, where f_i stands for the partial derivative with respect to x_i.

If the satisfaction indifference curve is linear in x for a specific level C, then the equation of the curve will be

$$\alpha_1 x_1 + \alpha_2 x_2 + \ldots + \alpha_k x_k = C; \qquad (3.5)$$

and then the trade-off ratio between x_1 and x_2 is constant all along the indifference curve and equal to $-\alpha_1/\alpha_2$. If all indifference curves are parallel lines, there is *one* common trade-off ratio equal to $-\alpha_1/\alpha_2$.

The Relationship between the Hedonic and LS Approaches

The relationship between the hedonic and LS approaches now may be discussed, following the analysis of van Praag and Baarsma (2005)—the first authors to suggest the complementarity between the two methods.

For convenience, consider two individuals who are identical in all respects (including their incomes and their houses). These individuals live in neighborhoods that are very similar in all respects, except that one has green areas and one does not. If the assumptions of competitive housing markets and market mobility in the hedonic approach hold, housing rents in the neighborhood with green spaces should be higher by exactly the amount that compensates for the additional utility produced by having green areas. Consequently, the first individual (with green spaces in the neighborhood) should report the same level of satisfaction as the second individual because both have the same means and are free to move to the other neighborhood if they wish to do so. This finding implies that both would be placed on the same satisfaction indifference curve, but that their locations on that curve would differ: the first would be "consuming" more green areas (implicitly paying for them through higher rents) but spending less on other goods than the second. The level of satisfaction W thus can be represented as a function of income y and housing rents p, which depends on the existence of green areas in the neighborhood (denoted by z):

$$W(y, p(z); z). \qquad (3.6)$$

When the hedonic price assumptions hold, the satisfaction levels of the two representative individuals are necessarily equal:

$$W(y, p(z_1); z_1) = W(y, p(z_2); z_2). \qquad (3.7)$$

Notice that, because rents differ between the two neighborhoods only as a result of access to green areas, equation (3.7) in reduced form is

$$W(y,z_1) = W(y,z_2), \tag{3.8}$$

which implies that the same level of satisfaction will be perceived by the two individuals, *irrespective* of whether they have access to green areas! Therefore, when hedonic price assumptions hold, neighborhood features do not have any *additional* influence on satisfaction when income is controlled for. The intuitive reason is that the satisfaction derived from access to the green areas is captured already in the satisfaction derived from income, because access to the green areas implicitly is paid for in housing rents.

More often than not, however, neighborhood features such as green spaces, recreational areas, or safety conditions do have an influence on life satisfaction after controlling for income; that is,

$$W(y,z_1) \neq W(y,z_2). \tag{3.9}$$

Or, in other words, two individuals in identical circumstances and with equal income, but living in houses with different rents, may be at different levels of satisfaction. This inequality implies that the standard hedonic price assumptions do not always hold. In some cases, neighborhood features do not have any influence on housing rents. Access to cultural centers is such a case, according to some of the studies presented in this volume. In other cases, however, there may be some difference between rents in neighborhoods that have some feature—such as better security—and those that do not. This suggests that the housing market is frequently unable to achieve equilibrium: other things being constant, those people who live in safer neighborhoods manifest more life satisfaction, even though they may be paying rents that are higher because of that factor.

In that case, we cannot equalize the slope of the price curve with the subjective trade-off ratio. However, the trade-off ratio, derived from the estimated indifference curve discussed at the end of the previous section, can be used to calculate the compensation that would be required to equalize the satisfaction levels of the two groups of individuals. If one dimension in the satisfaction indifference map is income and the other is security, the subjective trade-off ratio $-\alpha_1/\alpha_2$ would be the ratio between the marginal utility (or satisfaction) of income and the (additional) marginal utility of security (where the word *additional* refers to the fact that part of the utility already may be captured in the income coefficient, as explained above). The value of that ratio is the monetary compensation needed to equalize the satisfaction between individuals in more-secure (z_1) and less-secure (z_2) neighborhoods.

Notice that this monetary compensation is additional to what individuals in the more-secure neighborhood pay as extra rents, which is measured by the coefficient of the security variable in the hedonic price. Therefore, the total value of security or, in more technical terms, the *total shadow cost* of any neighborhood feature z is

$$(p(z_1) - p(z_2)) + \Delta y, \tag{3.10}$$

where housing rent p depends on whether the neighborhood has the feature z, and Δy is the monetary compensation obtained from the subjective trade-off ratio of the LS approach.

As the previous discussion shows, the hedonic and LS approaches are complements. Taken separately and using only rather stringent assumptions, neither approach provides an adequate measure of the value of neighborhood features. The hedonic approach requires that housing markets function perfectly for the feature in question. The LS approach estimates the residual shadow cost, if prices are not equilibrium prices; and, consequently, rent differences do not completely compensate for the differences between houses. The hedonic approach may be sufficient to value most of the characteristics of the dwellings—such as the number and sizes of rooms, the quality of floors, and the availability of some domiciliary services—because these are mostly private, excludable goods with competitive markets. By itself, the LS approach may be adequate to find the "value,"—that is, the equivalent income that would provide the same satisfaction—of things that money does not buy, such as trust in others or friendships (see Lora 2008, ch. 4). But most neighborhood features and amenities do not fall clearly into either the market or the nonmarket category. The reason is simply that housing markets may operate *only to some extent* as intermediate markets for access to such features as transportation, green areas or recreation places, safety, and quiet, among others. Therefore, it is left to empirical analysis to establish the market and nonmarket components of the values of neighborhood characteristics and amenities.

The hedonic and LS approaches may be considered further complementary from a different angle that, although noteworthy, is not pursued empirically in this volume. It may be argued that discrepancies in the trade-offs obtained with the hedonic and happiness methods reflect the differences between ex ante and ex post evaluations, as related to different concepts of utility introduced by Kahneman, Wakker, and Sarin (1997). Whereas the happiness approach reflects individuals' evaluations after they have made a decision (ex post), the hedonic method reflects the decisions made at the time of the market transaction (ex ante). Because individuals mispredict (as a result of unexpected adaptation or cognitive dissonance, among other reasons), ex ante and ex post evaluations do not necessarily coincide. For example, individuals may underestimate their capacity to adapt to local amenities. That underestimation, in turn, raises the fundamental and unsolved question, Which evaluations should policy makers take into account? To this point, no convincing answer has been given.

Econometric Methods

In light of the previous discussion, a combination of hedonic price regressions and LS regressions would be required to determine the full value of neighborhood amenities and features. Ideally, both types of estimations should be done jointly; but that would require information for all variables to be available for the observation sample. Thus, for each individual n in the sample, it would be necessary to have data on the two main dependent variables—housing rents or prices p_{nj}, and subjective well-being or life satisfaction W_n—and on the four main sets of explanatory variables: (1) an individual's personal and family characteristics F_n, (2) income y_n, (3) housing features H_n, and (4) neighborhood amenities and characteristics $Z_{j(n)}$. As explained, the basic hedonic and LS regressions, respectively, are

$$p_n = p(H_n, Z_{j(n)}) \tag{3.11}$$

$$W_n = W(F_n, y_{nj}, H_n, Z_{j(n)}). \tag{3.12}$$

Notice that if all the explanatory variables of subjective well-being are combined, this refers to the vector of life satisfaction *aspects* x defined above. That is, the vector $x_n = (F_n, y_n, H_n, Z_{j(n)})$.

In practice, simultaneous estimation of both regressions with a fully consistent data set lies beyond the scope of this book because the national data sets to be merged worked with different definitions and universes. For this reason, the two basic regressions are estimated independently in the country cases in this volume (which limits interpretation of the results).

As mentioned in chapter 2, the hedonic regression usually estimated is of the following form:

$$\ln(p_n) = \text{constant} + \gamma_1 H_n + \gamma_2 Z_{j(n)} + v_n \qquad v_n = \delta_{j(n)} + \eta_n. \tag{3.13}$$

In addition to the explanatory variables, the equation includes the composite error term v_n, which is a combination of a neighborhood-specific error component $\delta_{j(n)}$ in which $j(n)$ stands for n's neighborhood, and a house-specific error component η_n. The neighborhood-specific error component is common to all houses in the same neighborhood j, and it represents all those amenity characteristics that do not vary within a neighborhood.

Because estimating the hedonic price regression at the neighborhood or city level does not present any further major conceptual difficulties, the rest of this section is devoted to the estimation of the LS regression, considering a few novel methods that have been suggested and applied in the literature. Several of the studies in this volume use these novel methods—known as cardinal ordinary least squares (COLS) and probit-adapted ordinary least squares (POLS)—that were introduced by van Praag and Ferrer-i-Carbonell (2008b). The outcome of this section is that all methods fortunately yield about the same results with respect to the estimation of the subjective trade-off ratios $-\alpha_1/\alpha_2$.

In practical econometrics, the estimation problem can be summarized as follows: There are both a variable W to be explained (in this case, life satisfaction self-reported on a scale of 0 to 10 or a monotonous transformation w of W) and a set of explanatory variables $(F_n, y_n, H_n, Z_{j(n)})$. Recall that F stands for individual and family characteristics, y is income, H stands for house characteristics, and Z stands for neighborhood characteristics. Then one may stipulate an approximate relationship:

$$w_n = \alpha_1 F_n + \alpha_2 y_n + \alpha_3 H_n + \alpha_4 Z_{j(n)} + \eta_n, \tag{3.14}$$

where η_n stands for the residual error—that is, the difference between w_n and the structural estimate $(\alpha_1 F_n + \alpha_2 y_n + \alpha_3 H_n + \alpha_4 Z_{j(n)})$. The best estimates of the unknown parameters α are then those values that minimize the sum of squared residuals.[5]

$$\sum_{i=1}^{N} \left[w_n = \alpha_1 F_n + \alpha_2 y_n + \alpha_3 H_n + \alpha_4 Z_{j(n)} \right]^2, \tag{3.15}$$

where N stands for the total number of households. The problem is which transformation w of W—that is, which *cardinalization*—should be taken. In a growing number of papers, researchers take simply the response values from 0 to 10.

In the older versions of satisfaction questions, numerical response categories sometimes were avoided; instead, the answers were cast in verbal ratings, such as "not satisfactory," "somewhat unsatisfactory," "satisfactory," and "very satisfactory." In that case, the dependent variable is a *verbal* rating. Although verbal ratings can be converted into positions on a numerical scale, that step clearly introduces some arbitrariness. Whereas some authors employ such conversions, others use probit or logit specifications, maintaining that the ordinary least squares (OLS) specification would create an arbitrary cardinalization of life satisfaction.[6]

The probit and logit specifications, however, imply *arbitrary cardinalizations* as well. Recall that the probit model assumes a latent model:

$$w_n = \alpha_1 F_n + \alpha_2 y_n + \alpha_3 H_n + \alpha_4 Z_{j(n)} + \eta_n, \tag{3.16}$$

where it is assumed that the response categories correspond with a partition of the real axis into T intervals $(-\infty, \mu_1], (\mu_1, \mu_2], \ldots, (\mu_{t-1}, \mu_t], \ldots, (\mu_{T-1}, \infty)$, such that w_n belongs to the t_n^{th} interval, where t_n stands for n's response category, and η is assumed to be distributed as a normal standardized random variable with mean equal to 0 and variance equal to 1. By definition, the chance of observing a response in interval t by respondent n is then

$$P_n(t) = N[\mu_t - (\alpha_1 F_n + \alpha_2 y_n + \alpha_3 H_n + \alpha_4 Z_{j(n)})]$$
$$- N[\mu_{t-1} - (\alpha_1 F_n + \alpha_2 y_n + \alpha_3 H_n + \alpha_4 Z_{j(n)})]. \qquad (3.17)$$

The probit estimates are found by maximizing with respect to α and μ the sample probability—that is, the product of the chances $\prod_{n=1}^{N} P_n(t_n)$. The latent cardinalization is caused by the choice of the distribution of ε. A similar story holds for the logit, where the assumption that the error follows a normal distribution function is replaced by the logistic distribution function. Again, here w may be interpreted as a (an ordinal) utility level, and equation (3.18) may be interpreted as describing an indifference surface corresponding to a specific satisfaction level w_n:

$$w_n = \alpha_1 F_n + \alpha_2 y_n + \alpha_3 H_n + \alpha_4 Z_{j(n)}. \qquad (3.18)$$

At first glance, there seems to be a serious problem because it is not clear which specification should be chosen for the estimation method. In practice, however, the problem is minimal because these two methods yield about the same gradient vectors α, except for a multiplication factor. Indeed, Amemiya (1981) has found that probit and logit specifications yield the same estimates, apart from a multiplicative factor (see also Ferrer-i-Carbonell and Frijters 2004).

Although the numerical estimates look rather different when using different cardinalizations, the trade-off ratios look very similar when the estimators are "normalized." Let $\hat{\alpha}^{(1)}$, $\hat{\alpha}^{(2)}$ be two estimators of the gradient vector corresponding to two cardinalizations. Then their ratios may be easily compared by "normalizing"[7] both vectors—that is, by dividing them by their respective norms $|\hat{\alpha}| = \sqrt{\sum \hat{\alpha}_i^2}$. Likewise, van Praag and Ferrer-i-Carbonell (2008b) present estimation results for a satisfaction question, using four different cardinalizations—namely ordered probit, OLS, COLS, and POLS—showing that the four estimates yield about the same trade-off ratios.

In sum, regardless of the cardinalization method used, approximately the same estimate of the gradient of the satisfaction indifference curve will be found (apart from a method-specific proportionality factor) and, as a consequence, approximately the same subjective trade-off ratios. The reliability of those estimates, in terms of their standard errors, will be about the same as well. In plain language, there are many methods that yield similar results.

All of these techniques also may be used to assess the effect of urban amenities. Instead of considering life satisfaction as the dependent variable, such an analysis would focus on *satisfaction with the urban environment*. Variables typically considered in this domain of satisfaction include such features as "public street lighting" and "vandalism in the neighborhood." The problem with this type of estimated equation is that researchers frequently include too many correlated explanatory variables (mostly dummy variables), which leads to statistically nonsignificant estimates for many effects. The chapters that follow, however, also provide many meaningful estimates and, thus, offer one of the first large-scale and consequential studies on urban environment in the literature.

A final point regarding econometric methods is the possible cardinalization of LS variables. An individual who is very satisfied with his or her life would report 8 or 9 (on a 10-point scale), and an unsatisfied individual in all likelihood would report low-number answers; but the relative magnitude of the answers is not significant if an ordinal interpretation is followed. A problem is that ordinal scales do not allow for interpersonal or intertemporal comparisons. Normative statements comparing individuals' levels of happiness are possible only if some strong assumptions are made. First, it must be assumed that the wording of questions is emotionally translated by respondents in the same way and that they evaluate parallel situations similarly. This assumption has been examined, with roughly positive results (see van Praag 1991). A second point is that one cardinalization and, henceforth, one cardinal utility function must be agreed on for all individuals.

A cardinal measure is required to compare or analyze life satisfaction between individuals. For example, a simple statistic, such as national average life satisfaction (that is, the average of individual life satisfactions), is based on the implicit assumption of cardinality. Therefore, a careful approach to cardinalization is relevant. One way to cardinalize is to transform the responses on the LS scale, using a probability distribution function that has a range between 0 and 1. This choice has nothing to do with a probabilistic content of the phenomenon under consideration; rather, it concerns only the analytical suitability of this procedure. A normal distribution function of the type $N\,[\alpha_1 F_n + \alpha_2 y_n + \alpha_3 H_n + \alpha_4 Z_{j(n)};\ 0,\sigma]$, which can vary between 0 and 1, seems a reasonable choice. This formulation gives rise to the cardinal median transformation[8]:

$$\frac{\alpha_1 F_n + \alpha_2 y_n + \alpha_3 H_n + \alpha_4 Z_{j(n)}}{\sigma} = \bar{w}_n, \tag{3.19}$$

where $\bar{w}_n$ is the average between the upper and the lower bounds for each LS interval. After applying this transformation to the discretely measured satisfaction questions, one can run a simple linear regression model on satisfaction data. Different alternatives likewise can be obtained to estimate the same model. In van Praag and Ferrer-i-Carbonell (2008b), the COLS and POLS methods are described in detail. These methods are merely two of many different possible cardinalizations of the satisfaction answers. When a specific cardinalization is accepted, it makes sense to consider *average* happiness in a society (see, for example, Easterlin 1974 and van Praag and Ferrer-i-Carbonell 2008a) or the inequality of the distribution of happiness in a population.

Life as a Whole and Its Partition into Domains: Two-Layer and Multilayer Models

As discussed above, satisfaction with life as a whole can be examined; it is possible to use the same tools to observe and analyze satisfaction with respect to specific aspects or domains of life, such as health, employment, and housing. This section considers how the satisfaction with different domains may be linked to satisfaction with life as a whole. Although subjective well-being can be understood through either a top-down or bottom-up approach (Diener 1984; Headey, Holmstrom, and Wearing 1985; Lance et al. 1989), this section combines both approaches. In the bottom-up approach, domain satisfactions determine (and are components of) satisfaction with life as a whole. This yields the so-called two-layer satisfaction model.[9] The top-down approach, in contrast, may be visualized by thinking of an individual who is optimistic or pessimistic. That trait not only affects the individual's outlook on life as a whole (that is, yielding a higher or lower evaluation of life than that of the average individual), but also affects the individual's evaluation of different domains. The top-down approach aspect may be represented by a variable Z, which is a common determinant of satisfaction with life as a whole and of the domain satisfactions. In essence, that variable captures the psychological traits of the individual.

The two-layer model can be operationalized by asking about respondents' satisfaction with many different domains of life. Examples include satisfaction with job, health, and financial situations; social relationships; marriage; the government; the housing situation; one's neighborhood; and the supply of urban amenities—the focus of the present volume.

The answers to these questions are domain satisfactions. It is clear that individuals may not be equally satisfied with all domains of life. For instance, a person may be at once highly satisfied with his or her financial situation and highly dissatisfied with his or her health. Satisfaction with life as a whole—say, *LS*—may be seen as an aggregate measure or as a weighted average of domain satisfactions (*DS*), where the most important domains are given the most weight. Satisfaction with life thus depends on degree of satisfaction with the various (k) aspects of life, that is, $DS_1, \ldots, DS_k$. An example of such a two-layer model is shown in figure 3.2. The underlying idea is that domain satisfactions are formed first, and then their weighted aggregate is satisfaction with life as a whole. In other words, domain satisfactions are components of "satisfaction with life as a whole."

This analysis can be operationalized by the following model equation:

$$LS = LS(DS_1, \ldots, DS_k). \tag{3.20}$$

For instance, one might think of a linear aggregate:

$$LS = \alpha_1 DS_1 + \ldots \alpha_k DS_k + \varepsilon_{LS}, \tag{3.21}$$

where the DSs are operationalized by the cardinal median or COLS method.

An advantage of this intuitively plausible decomposition is that many variables that have no significant direct impact on LS (called x in figure 3.2) do have a significant impact on one or more domains. For instance, income has a rather limited impact on satisfaction with life as a whole; but it has a rather considerable impact on some of its components— notably, satisfaction with financial situation, health, and job. On the other hand, income may have a positive effect on financial satisfaction while it has a negative effect on health or job satisfaction, because higher income frequently entails a greater workload. The total effect of income on life as a whole is then a weighted addition of the three effects via the three domain satisfactions. It may be that the total effect on life satisfaction (LS) is then rather small or nonsignificant because positive and

Figure 3.2 Two-Layer Model of Domain and Life Satisfaction

Job satisfaction

Financial satisfaction

House satisfaction

x

Health satisfaction → Satisfaction with life as a whole

Leisure satisfaction

Environment satisfaction

Source: Authors' illustration.

negative effects on the domain satisfactions cancel out in the aggregate. In other words, the estimated *direct* effect of income on *LS* may be too small to matter. Similarly, the presence of electric lights on the streets is not a significant explanatory variable of life satisfaction, but it may be important as an explanatory variable for satisfaction with urban amenities—which, in turn, is a sizable component of satisfaction with life as a whole.

It is obvious that, as a rule, objective variables already used to explain one or more domain satisfactions should not be included a second time as explanatory variables in equation (3.21) for *LS* as a whole, because doing so would lead to identification problems. It also is evident that more domains and layers may be used than the two that are suggested here. For instance, using a British data set, van Praag and Ferrer-i-Carbonell (2008b) further decompose job satisfaction according to four types of job satisfaction—that is, with pay, security, the work itself, and hours worked. The only requirement for such multilayer decompositions clearly is whether such further differentiations make intuitive and empirical sense. For example, van Praag and Ferrer-i-Carbonell (2008b) use the British Household Panel Survey to decompose life satisfaction into five different domain satisfactions—namely, satisfaction with job, financial situation, health, house, and leisure. They find that, in descending order, the domains health, financial situation, and job situation score the highest. The model was later extended to three layers by distinguishing subdomains of the job situation, such as job security and pay.

The cardinalizations of the domain satisfactions and life satisfaction discussed above significantly simplify computation, permitting the use of OLS and related techniques instead of multiequation probit-type models involving series of highly complex integrations. Van Praag and Ferrer-i-Carbonell (2008b, ch. 4) provide an example in which the same model is estimated by means of ordered probit and by the corresponding COLS-variant for a large panel data set. Whereas ordered probit required a computation time of about 1.5 hours with panel data techniques, the OLS-variant took about 1 minute. The results were virtually the same, except for a proportionality factor. Although the time needed for computation clearly is not very important in itself, the fact that one method was about 90 times faster than the other method cannot be ignored.

Toward an Index of the Quality of Urban Life

Various institutions calculate indexes for monitoring the QoL and attractiveness of cities. The preface to this volume mentions such instruments as the Quality of Living survey produced by Mercer, which studies 215 cities around the world, and the Global Cities Index produced by *Foreign Policy* magazine, which classifies 60 cities. These indexes are considered "objective" because they are constructed on the basis of objective statistics available for all the cities covered. However, they are not truly objective in that the combination of those indicators into a single index requires subjective judgments by experts who assign a weighting system to the variables and dimensions. Another limitation of these city rankings is that they do not reflect the needs and interests of the inhabitants of the cities studied; rather, they reflect the criteria of the experts themselves.

Those limitations are avoided in the monitoring systems that cities, countries, and regions have set up in recent decades—systems such as the Eurostat Urban Audit system, which covers 357 cities; the Quality of Life Project that covers a dozen New Zealand cities; and the isolated experiences of various cities in Brazil, Colombia, and other countries. These systems use subjective information with the explicit purpose of reflecting the interests, needs, and opinions of cities' inhabitants, instead of the judgments of experts. However, these monitoring systems do not have indexes, which synthesize information. Consequently, there is no way to compare QoL between cities or track it in a single city over time.

The two approaches presented in this chapter offer the possibility of constructing QoL indexes that overcome some of the limitations of those two monitoring methods. As discussed above, the hedonic price and LS methods produce valuations of the facilities and features of neighborhoods that may be used directly as weightings to construct QoL indexes, without resorting to using arbitrary judgments. These valuations can reflect the needs, interests, and opinions of local people better than other methods can reflect them.

When the hedonic price and LS approaches are used separately, two different QoL indexes can be constructed to reflect the QoL contributions made by neighborhood facilities and features through the housing market as well as through nonmarket channels. Ideally, both indexes can be combined to obtain a single index encompassing the total QoL contributions of each of the facilities and features considered. However, as mentioned in the previous section, this ideal is difficult to achieve because of the limitations of the information. The chapters that follow present examples of one or the other type of index, but in no case is a joint index calculated.

It could be argued that life satisfaction directly reported by individuals is tantamount to the sought-after total index because direct reporting incorporates all aspects of people's well-being, according to their own assessments. The main problem with that argument is that such assessments do not specifically measure the QoL in neighborhoods or cities because life satisfaction involves many other individual factors. To be useful in discussing cities' problems and in local government decision making, an index of the quality of urban life must be limited to aspects that are truly urban.

Calculation of QoL indexes by the hedonic price or LS approach is operationally very simple. Consider the hedonic price approach:

1. The (statistically significant) coefficients in the hedonic price regression for each feature of homes or neighborhoods are the contributions of a unit of the corresponding feature to the rental price of the home. For example, the coefficient of the variable "distance in minutes from the nearest bus station" (which is expected to be negative) is the value that every minute (less) of distance adds to the rent of a home. If the value of the rent has been converted to logarithms, then this coefficient will be the percentage value added to the rent.

2. Therefore, for each home, the contribution of each feature can be obtained as the product of the respective coefficient and the value of that feature (less a reference value) for that home. Note that it is necessary to use a reference value to be able to interpret the results. In the example of distance to the bus station, if the unit is minutes (not the logarithm), the reference value can be 0 (that is, the home located right at the bus stop).

3. Adding all the contributions attributable to all the urban features for each home gives the total contribution of urban conditions to the price of each home. Naturally, it is possible to distinguish different groups of features (physical infrastructure, security, and so forth). According to the reference values chosen, contributions may be negative. For example, if the reference values are the averages of each variable, there will be negative contributions for some homes and positive ones for others.

4. Averaging the values of the contributions by neighborhood gives a value that, among other things, can be used to make a ranking of the neighborhood QoL that is attributable to urban features, according to the criteria revealed in the housing market. This value also is the average implicit transfer that the homeowners in each neighborhood receive from the urban features.

5. When hedonic price regressions consider various neighborhoods, dummy variables for each neighborhood may be included to capture the influence of unobserved features that are common to each one.

6. These calculations are the baseline for evaluating over time the QoL in the city or its neighborhoods, or across socioeconomic levels. Because the valuations are available and the significant features of the neighborhoods are known, all that is required to update indexes on a regular basis is obtaining information on how these features have changed.

7. Obviously, the baseline of the indexes will tend to lose relevance as the housing market changes or the needs and interests of the population change. This fact means that the regression equations have

to be revised every few years (as occurs with other indexes, such as price indexes).

Consider now the procedure for obtaining QoL indexes using the LS approach:

1. The starting point is either satisfaction with life as a whole or satisfaction with one's house or living environment. At this point, money trade-offs can be found by including household income. If the income variable has been converted to logarithms (as is desirable), then the trade-off ratio will be the relative change in income that is equivalent to the satisfaction produced by the urban feature. The calculations are made by dwelling unit.
2. For each household, each feature's equivalent in income now can be calculated as the product of the respective trade-off ratio and the value of that feature (less a reference value) for that household. The same precautions as for hedonic prices apply.
3. Adding for each individual all the contributions attributable to all the urban features yields the total contribution (measured in equivalent income) that urban conditions make to life satisfaction, beyond what has been paid for those conditions through the market price of the home (or other prices). As in the hedonic price approach, it is possible to separate different groups of urban features (physical infrastructure, security, and the like). The same approach can be used to find other factors' contributions to life satisfaction. It should be remembered that these contributions may be negative, depending on the reference values.
4. Averages can be obtained from the contributions of the urban features (totals or by group) for the individuals in each neighborhood. The value will be the quality of urban life index (in equivalent income), according to individual satisfaction. Neighborhoods can be ranked as well. The observations made in points 5–7 of the hedonic price approach also apply to the LS approach.

The calculations based on the LS approach answer a crucial question for public decision makers: Which urban problems have the greatest impact on life satisfaction, and on which groups of individuals? If satisfaction with the city is used as a dependent variable, instead of life satisfaction, it is also possible to identify the problems that weigh most heavily in people's opinions of the management of the city.

Because some urban features influence both home prices and life satisfaction, it also is possible to know which of the city's problems should be given priority by government authorities, considering their impact on the well-being of different groups of individuals. This approach also helps identify the cases in which it is possible or desirable to finance the provision of certain services (or the solution of certain urban problems) through property taxes, and the cases in which it is not desirable to do so.

For management of cities, the most attractive feature of the proposed indexes is that they form a permanent monitoring system. Changes in the indexes for the city as a whole, or for a given neighborhood or socio-economic level, show whether there is an improvement in the aspects of the city that are important to its people. They also indicate if activities undertaken by builders, on the one hand, and by local authorities, on the other hand, are concentrating more on some neighborhoods or on certain socioeconomic groups than on others. If subjective information is collected about people's satisfaction with specific aspects of cities, it becomes possible to evaluate whether perceptions of the problems correspond with their seriousness, based on objective indicators; and whether the gaps between perception and reality differ between one area of a city and another, especially between high-income and low-income areas.

Obviously, there are caveats to be expressed as well. In particular, it does permit an unambiguous comparison of QoL across different cities only if the inhabitants of the different cities have the same tastes for urban quality. The reason is very simple: if what the people of Buenos Aires (Argentina) love most about their city is excitement and diversity, and the people of Montevideo (Uruguay) consider order and uniformity to be the most valuable aspects of the city, then the two groups have different preferences. However, for now it has not been settled that inhabitants in different cities or quarters of cities have such widely divergent preferences. Frequently, such differences can be attributed to reference effects, whereby one quarter is much richer than another and hence has much higher material standards. Another cause of seeming difference may be differences in climate, such as temperature, altitude, or windiness.

The proposed method may allow for comparison between cities, provided that the citizens of the cities to be compared may be assumed to have the same preference functions. This preference alignment has to be established. The LS (or urban satisfaction) method does compare problems across cities, and it ranks problems according to their importance from the point of view of the subjective well-being of individuals (and of social groups). As discussed above, this method also can assign values to the provision of public goods, which is essential for making informed decisions about public expenditures.

The method also can be used to compare neighborhoods in a single city or district (provided the tastes and needs of the people are relatively homogeneous). Because the method offers valuations of public goods to which all *neighborhoods* have access, neighborhoods' QoL can be broken down into the components attributable to the quality of homes and the components attributable to the main public goods. Moreover, because public goods can be valued, this approach facilitates comparisons between alternative public investments or spending projects, without introducing the conceptual and practical complications of other methods of valuing public goods (such as contingent prices).

The precision with which these questions can be answered naturally depends on the quality and level of detail of the objective and subjective information available. The monitoring systems of the population's general QoL, which already exist in some cities, offer most of the information needed; paradoxically, however, some of them do not collect information on the two key variables—the prices of home sales or rents and satisfaction with life (or, at least, satisfaction with the city).

Conclusion

In this chapter, we have summarized two rather new and important methods to get more insight into the question: What are the weaknesses and the strong points that a city presents to its inhabitants? These are positive and negative external effects for the inhabitants. For urban policy, one needs to have an idea of the magnitude of those effects because they co-determine inhabitants' QoL. Both methods give a clue to translate these effects in terms of money, even when the external effects are not sold and purchased separately on a market and, consequently, there are no market prices for those effects. The methods presented above are empirical methods by which it becomes possible to price external effects from the standpoint of the urban policy maker, and to evaluate specific urban quality dimensions in terms of a numerical index.

The chapters that follow present the practical application of these methodologies in a series of country studies. As such, they differ in relation to the issues they address and in relation to aspects of their methodology. At the moment, we are certainly in the experimental stage. The various studies hereafter do not use the same streamlined instrument of analysis; they use all their own specifications and various estimation methods. Nevertheless, these pilot studies have determined that it is feasible to implement a system for monitoring the quality of urban life that is easy to operate at a reasonable cost and is based on sound concepts. Such a system—the ideal of many academics and observers of urban problems—may not be far from becoming a reality. A successful monitoring system will enable local governments, analysts of urban problems, and the communities themselves to debate the problems of cities and their possible solutions in a more informed manner.

Notes

1. The section on the LS approach borrows and elaborates on themes initiated in chapters 2–4 of van Praag and Ferrer-i-Carbonell (2004).
2. Percentages are obtained because the *logarithm* of the rent is considered.

3. Recent surveys of the newly developing field of happiness economics are found in Frey and Stutzer (2002a, b), Graham (2008), and van Praag and Ferrer-i-Carbonell (2008b).

4. The validity of such questions and their capacity to measure a concept that is shared among all individuals are thoroughly discussed by Clark, Frijters, and Shields (2008).

5. More sophisticated optimum criteria are not examined in this section.

6. For examples of different applications and methods, see Blanchflower and Oswald (2004); Di Tella, Haisken-De New, and MacCulloch (2007); Di Tella, MacCulloch, and Oswald (2001); Easterlin (1995); Easterlin and Zimmermann (2006); Helliwell (2007); Oswald and Powdthavee (2007); and van Praag and Ferrer-i-Carbonell (2008b).

7. This normalization device may be replaced by many others.

8. For a more detailed description of the cardinalization procedure, see van Praag and Ferrer-i-Carbonell (2008b, ch. 2).

9. That model was proposed, estimated, and applied first in Ferrer-i-Carbonell and van Praag (2002); van Praag, Frijters, and Ferrer-i-Carbonell (2003); and van Praag and Baarsma (2005). It subsequently was elaborated in van Praag and Ferrer-i-Carbonell (2008a,b). A similar layered model is estimated by Kapteyn, Smith, and van Soest (2008).

References

Amemiya, Takeshi. 1981. "Qualitative Response Models: A Survey." *Journal of Economic Literature* 19 (4): 1483–536.

Blanchflower, David G., and Andrew J. Oswald. 2004. "Well-Being Over Time in Britain and the USA." *Journal of Public Economics* 88 (7-8): 1359–86.

Blomquist, Glenn C., Mark C. Berger, and John P. Hoehn. 1988. "New Estimates of Quality of Life in Urban Areas." *American Economic Review* 78 (1): 89–107.

Bruni, Luigino, and Robert Sugden. 2007. "The Road Not Taken: How Psychology Was Removed from Economics, and How It Might Be Brought Back." *Economic Journal* 117 (516): 146–73.

Clark, Andrew E., Paul Frijters, and Michael Shields. 2008. "Relative Income, Happiness, and Utility: An Explanation for the Easterlin Paradox and Other Puzzles." *Journal of Economic Literature* 46 (1): 95–144.

Clark, Andrew E., and Andrew J. Oswald. 1994. "Unhappiness and Unemployment." *Economic Journal* 104 (424): 648–59.

Diener, Ed. 1984. "Subjective Well-Being." *Psychological Bulletin* 95 (3): 542–75.

Di Tella, Rafael, John Haisken-De New, and Robert MacCulloch. 2007. "Happiness Adaptation to Income and to Status in an Individual Panel." Working Paper 13159, National Bureau of Economic Research, Cambridge, MA.

Di Tella, Rafael, Robert MacCulloch, and Andrew J. Oswald. 2001. "Preferences over Inflation and Unemployment: Evidence from Surveys of Happiness." *American Economic Review* 91 (1): 335–41.

Dolan, Paul, and Robert Metcalfe. 2007. "Valuing Non-Market Goods: A Comparison of Preference-Based and Experience-Based Approaches." Unpublished manuscript, Tanaka Business School, Imperial College, London.

Easterlin, Richard A. 1974. "Does Economic Growth Improve the Human Lot? Some Empirical Evidence." In *Nations and Households in Economic Growth: Essays in Honor of Moses Abramowitz*, ed. Paul A. David and Melvin W. Reder, 89–124. New York: Academic Press.

———. 1995. "Will Raising the Incomes of All Increase the Happiness of All?" *Journal of Economic Behavior & Organization* 27 (1): 35–47.

Easterlin, Richard A., and Anke Zimmermann. 2006. "Life Satisfaction and Economic Outcomes in Germany Pre- and Post-Unification." Discussion Paper 2494, Institute for the Study of Labor, Bonn, Germany.

Ferrer-i-Carbonell, Ada. 2005. "Income and Well-Being: An Empirical Analysis of the Comparison Income Effect." *Journal of Public Economics* 89 (5-6): 997–1019.

Ferrer-i-Carbonell, Ada, and Paul Frijters. 2004. "How Important Is Methodology for the Estimates of the Determinants of Happiness?" *Economic Journal* 114 (497): 641–59.

Ferrer-i-Carbonell, Ada, and Bernard M.S. van Praag. 2002. "The Subjective Costs of Health Losses Due to Chronic Diseases: An Alternative Model for Monetary Appraisal." *Health Economics* 11 (8): 709–22.

Frey, Bruno S., and Alois Stutzer. 2002a. *Happiness and Economics: How the Economy and Institutions Affect Well-Being*. Princeton, NJ: Princeton University Press.

———. 2002b. "What Can Economists Learn from Happiness Research?" *Journal of Economic Literature* 40 (2): 402–35.

Graham, Carol. 2008. "The Economics of Happiness: New Lenses for Old Policy Puzzles." In *The New Palgrave Dictionary of Economics*, 2nd ed., ed. Steven N. Durlauf and Lawrence E. Blume. New York: Palgrave Macmillan.

Gyourko, Joseph. 1991. "How Accurate Are Quality-of-Life Rankings across Cities?" *Business Review (Federal Reserve Bank of Philadelphia)* Mar/Apr: 3–14.

Headey, Bruce, Elsie Holmstrom, and Alexander Wearing. 1985. "Models of Well-Being and Ill-Being." *Social Indicators Research* 17 (3): 211–34.

Helliwell, John. 2007. "Life Satisfaction and Quality of Development." Plenary lecture for the International Conference on Comparative Development in Honor of the Platinum Jubilee of the Indian Statistical Institute, Delhi, India, December 19.

Kahneman, Daniel, Peter Wakker, and Rakesh Sarin. 1997. "Back to Bentham? Explorations of Experienced Utility." *Quarterly Journal of Economics* 112 (2): 375–405.

Kapteyn, Arie, James Smith, and Arthur van Soest. 2008. "Comparing Life Satisfaction." Working Paper WR-623, RAND Corp., Santa Monica, CA.

Lance, Charles E., Gary J. Lautenschlager, Christopher Sloan, and Philip E. Varca. 1989. "A Comparison between Bottom-Up, Top-Down, and Bidirectional Models of Relationships between Global and Life Facet Satisfactions." *Journal of Personality* 57 (3): 601–24.

Lora, Eduardo, ed. 2008. *Beyond Facts: Understanding Quality of Life. Development in the Americas*. Washington, DC: Inter-American Development Bank/David Rockefeller Center for Latin American Studies, Harvard University.

Luttmer, Erzo F.P. 2005. "Neighbors as Negatives: Relative Earnings and Well-Being." *The Quarterly Journal of Economics* 120 (3): 963–1002.

Nussbaum, Martha, and Amartya Sen, eds. 1993. *The Quality of Life*. Oxford, U.K.: Oxford University Press.

Oswald, Andrew J., and Nattavudh Powdthavee. 2007. "Obesity, Unhappiness, and the Challenge of Affluence: Theory and Evidence." *Economic Journal* 117 (521): F441–54.

Pareto, Vilfredo. 1909. *Manuel d'économie politique*. Paris: Girard & Brière.

Roback, Jennifer. 1982. "Wages, Rents, and Quality of Life." *Journal of Political Economy* 90 (6): 1257–78.

Robbins, Lionel. 1932. *An Essay on the Nature and Significance of Economic Science*. London: Macmillan.

Rosen, Sherwin. 1979. "Wage-Based Indexes of Urban Quality of Life." In *Current Issues in Urban Economics*, ed. Peter Mieszkowski and Mahlon Straszheim, 74–104. Baltimore, MD: Johns Hopkins Press.

van Praag, Bernard M.S. 1971. "The Welfare Function of Income in Belgium: An Empirical Investigation." *European Economic Review* 2 (3): 337–69.

———. 1991. "Ordinal and Cardinal Utility: An Integration of the Two Dimensions of the Welfare Concept." *Journal of Econometrics* 50 (1–2): 69–89.

van Praag, Bernard M.S., and Barbara E. Baarsma. 2005. "Using Happiness Surveys to Value Intangibles: The Case of Airport Noise." *Economic Journal* 115 (500): 224–46.

van Praag, Bernard M.S., and Ada Ferrer-i-Carbonell. 2004. *Happiness Quantified: A Satisfaction Calculus Approach*. New York: Oxford University Press.

———. 2008a. "A Multi-Dimensional Approach to Subjective Poverty." In *Quantitative Approaches to Multidimensional Poverty Measurement*, ed. Nanak Kakwani and Jacques Silber, 135–54. New York: Palgrave Macmillan.

———. 2008b. *Happiness Quantified: A Satisfaction Calculus Approach*. Oxford, U.K.: Oxford University Press.

van Praag, Bernard M.S., Paul Frijters, and Ada Ferrer-i-Carbonell. 2003. "The Anatomy of Subjective Well-Being." *Journal of Economic Behavior & Organization* 51 (1): 29–49.

4

Well-Being at the Subcity Level: The Buenos Aires Neighborhood Quality of Life Survey

Guillermo Cruces,
Andrés Ham, and Martín Tetaz

The purpose of this chapter is to provide indicators of the quality of life (QoL) in urban neighborhoods and the factors that determine it in the Buenos Aires Metropolitan Area (AMBA). Although disparities in other Latin American cities may be attributed to geographic characteristics such as slope, rivers, and hills, the AMBA spatial configuration stems mostly from historic, political, and economic factors. The urban area is characterized by overlapping government jurisdictions and policy responsibilities. The limited presence of "metropolitan" authorities generates severe coordination problems in policy making at the urban level, and the overlapping of revenue sources creates important cooperation problems. These characteristics make AMBA an interesting case study for the interaction between urban public policy and QoL.

The analysis presented is thus related to aspects of QoL that can be influenced through policy—urban infrastructure, service delivery and

The team responsible for this project was directed by Guillermo Cruces. Team members include Gonzalo Fernández, Leonardo Gasparini, Andrés Ham, and Martín Tetaz, from Centro de Estudios Distributivos, Laborales y Sociales, Universidad Nacional de La Plata; and Fernando Alvarez de Celis, from Geographic Information Systems, Autonomous City of Buenos Aires Government. The team gratefully acknowledges comments and support from the coeditors of this book; and from Ada Ferrer-i-Carbonell, Hugo Ñopo, and colleagues from other cities' teams participating in seminars in Washington, DC, in September 2007 and January 2008, as well as discussions with Gary Fields.

availability, and crime, among others. Identifying disparities in these indicators at the subcity level is the main motivation for this study.

By definition, QoL is a multidimensional concept. The challenge of providing subcity-specific indicators thus resides in informational sources, and in the aggregation of measures of living standards and amenities availability. The first contribution of the chapter is the presentation of the Neighborhood Quality of Life Survey (NQLS), which encompasses information on the respondent's neighborhood, satisfaction with life, and the characteristics of household and dwelling. The second contribution is analysis and comparison of QoL indexes derived from two alternative methodologies. On the one hand, the analysis follows the urban economics literature by deriving the implicit market valuation of neighborhood amenities through augmented hedonic regressions of property prices. On the other hand, an original extension of the life satisfaction (LS) approach is developed, and it derives the implicit valuation of public goods and externalities from subjective questions. In this case, the LS approach is applied to the valuation of neighborhood amenities and characteristics.

Description of AMBA

In colonial times, the Spanish founded Buenos Aires on mainly flat land at the shore of the Río de la Plata. It evolved as Argentina's main trading port, its financial and economic center, and its political capital. The city quickly expanded and absorbed neighboring localities, making it presently the largest urban agglomeration in the country. According to the 2001 census, the total population of the City of Buenos Aires was 2,770,000.

As in many large cities, however, the boundary of the municipal authority does not reflect the whole area of influence that is part of the same urban area. In fact, the National Institute of Statistics and Census presents periodic data on both the City of Buenos Aires and its 24 surrounding municipalities as the "Buenos Aires Agglomerate" or Gran Buenos Aires." Together, these areas contain a population of 13 million, making AMBA[1] the third-largest urban area in Latin America, after Mexico City (Mexico) and São Paulo (Brazil).

The urban area is divided into multiple municipal authorities, and it lacks a centralized administration or major entity coordinating public policy among the different levels involved. Consequently, four levels of authority coexist within the area: the subnational (Gobierno de la Ciudad), national, provincial, and municipal governments. The federal government retains control of overall aspects of AMBA's urban policy, including transportation, policing, and the port authority. Responsibility for other areas of urban policy, however, is delegated to each municipality. This fragmentation of responsibilities means that there is no single level of government responsible for the city, and there is relatively little comparable geographic and socioeconomic information available for the whole metropolitan area.[2]

The available socioeconomic indicators for AMBA originate in the 2001 census. AMBA presents important disparities in living standards and socioeconomic outcomes by neighborhood and other subcity areas—a relatively common occurrence in large cities in developing countries, where it is not unusual for affluent areas to grow side by side with slums that have low-quality housing and limited or no access to public services.

Different aspects of this heterogeneity can be illustrated by means of the available data sources. Cruces, Ham, and Tetaz (2008) show that areas of great affluence in AMBA are adjacent to areas with significantly lower levels of socioeconomic indicators. Using educational levels as a proxy, they find that better-off areas are concentrated in the northern half of the City of Buenos Aires and in the three municipalities north of it (constituting the so-called north corridor). Separating AMBA into the City of Buenos Aires and Gran Buenos Aires highlights within-city disparities even more intensely: almost one third of the population of the City of Buenos Aires has tertiary education and only 5.0 percent has completed less than primary education; in the municipalities of the greater metropolitan area, correlative figures are 14.4 and 19.6 percent, respectively. The contrast is even more stark between the City and Gran Buenos Aires' outskirts.[3]

Real estate prices of vacant land vary significantly across AMBA. In broad terms, the same spatial pattern as with other indicators is observed, with higher property prices concentrated along the north corridor and some main bands along railway lines. However, higher prices are found near the center. For instance, land south of the City of Buenos Aires (considered a lower-level socioeconomic area) is still relatively expensive. This effect may be explained by the land's proximity to downtown Buenos Aires and to the north corridor. The outer areas of Greater Buenos Aires have significantly lower property prices, except for a few pockets situated mostly along the rings.

These marked within-city disparities carry over to other indicators, such as literacy, child mortality, access to public services, and unsatisfied basic needs. (See Cruces, Ham, and Tetaz 2008 for a more detailed description.) These strong geographic patterns also carry over into other characteristics, such as urban infrastructure and the levels of subjective satisfaction of the population, as discussed below for a subsample of the metropolitan area drawn from the NQLS.

Description of the NQLS

The objective of any study concerning QoL should focus both on the interaction of subjective evaluations of living conditions and on objective

indicators of amenities and service availability. With that in mind, the
NQLS was designed as a two-step data collection process, comprising a
household survey and a geographic module with objective indicators collected at the street level.

The sample size necessary for attaining a degree of representativeness
for relevant subcity levels in all of AMBA (with 13 million inhabitants),
or even within the City of Buenos Aires (almost 3 million), was beyond
the resources available to this project. The data collection effort thus was
conceived as a pilot program to be conducted in portions of four selected
neighborhoods.[4] The limited range of the pilot program offered the advantages of being able to use a longer household questionnaire and to collect
more infrastructure data than would have been the case in a larger study.
This rich data set is the main data source of the ensuing analysis.

The selected areas are relatively small (roughly 1 square kilometer)[5]
and they all lie within well-defined neighborhoods, so that all interviewees within an area have the same reference point when asked about their
neighborhood.[6] Three of the selected areas (Caballito, Palermo, and San
Cristóbal) are in the City of Buenos Aires. The fourth area, Avellaneda,
belongs to a bordering municipality in Greater Buenos Aires. Its inclusion
permits the incorporation of residents from Greater Buenos Aires while
maintaining a representative sample of the City's population.

For the household component of the survey, about 250 interviews were
carried out in each of the four neighborhoods in November 2007. The survey was directed at decision makers in the household—those more likely
to make location choices and to pay the rent and the property taxes. A
separate team of geographers collected objective indicators for each block
in the selected areas. These indicators included, among other things, the
number of trees, lampposts, and traffic lights; and the availability of shops
and public transportation. These data were geo-referenced and matched to
each surveyed household by block of residence.

The upper half of table 4.1 summarizes the main demographic
indicators of the NQLS sample.[7] The average age of survey respondents
is 44.2 years, higher than the average in Caballito and Palermo and lower
than the average in Avellaneda and San Cristóbal. Slightly less than half of
the respondents are male, and about 57 percent are heads of households.
Avellaneda has the highest proportion of respondents with only some
primary education (9 percent), followed by San Cristóbal (8 percent),
Caballito (6 percent), and Palermo (5 percent); Palermo has, by far, the
highest level of respondents with some tertiary education (71 percent),
followed by Caballito (60 percent), Avellaneda (55 percent), and San
Cristóbal (45 percent). Household income behaves in a similar fashion,
with Caballito and Palermo having a higher total household income and
per capita income than Avellaneda and San Cristóbal. Because Avellaneda
has a larger average household size, this neighborhood has the lowest per
capita income. The differences are large, with Palermo's household per
capita income more than 60 percent higher than that of Avellaneda.

Table 4.1 Summary Statistics: Household, Respondent, and Dwelling Characteristics

Variable	Avellaneda	Caballito	Palermo	San Cristóbal	Total
Household and respondent characteristics					
Age (years)	45.8	43.0	41.9	45.9	44.2
Male respondent (%)	49.2	46.3	46.9	49.2	47.9
Respondent is head of household (%)	55.3	55.3	57.3	60.5	57.1
Some primary education (%)	9.0	5.8	5.0	8.2	7.0
Some secondary education (%)	33.8	30.0	23.1	43.4	32.5
Some tertiary education (%)	54.9	59.5	71.2	44.9	57.7
Total household income (pesos)	2,416	2,621	2,912	2,197	2,539
Per capita income (pesos)	781	1,145	1,257	892	1,012
Household size (number of members)	3.6	2.9	2.8	3.0	3.1
Number of children	1.8	1.2	1.1	1.5	1.4
Dwelling characteristics					
Owns home (%)	64.7	55.6	55.8	57.4	58.4
Own estimate of rent for owners (pesos)	1,120	1,220	1,348	966	1,164
Rent for non-owners (pesos)	833	1,010	1,064	749	924
Home with garden (%)	52.6	23.3	31.2	21.9	32.4
Parking space/garage (%)	47.4	28.8	27.7	9.8	28.6
Home is a house (%)	78.2	16.7	35.8	29.3	40.3
Number of bathrooms/ toilets	1.69	1.50	1.54	1.32	1.52
Number of bedrooms	3.02	2.59	2.61	2.63	2.72
Years in neighborhood	20.7	14.2	13.3	15.7	16.0
Thinks about moving (%) (alternative: satisfied with neighborhood)	20.3	13.2	14.2	19.9	16.9

Source: Authors' calculations, based on the Neighborhood Quality of Life Survey (NQLS).

Note: Household and respondent characteristics correspond to the X variable in the regressions. Housing and dwelling characteristics correspond to the HC variable in the regressions.

The lower half of table 4.1 presents a series of housing and dwelling characteristics.[8] Avellaneda respondents are much more likely to live in houses (instead of apartments) than are residents of the three neighborhoods within the City of Buenos Aires (78 percent versus 27 percent, respectively). Properties are larger in the suburbs, with a higher number of bathrooms, bedrooms, garages, and gardens. Rental prices are highest in Palermo, followed by Caballito, Avellaneda, and San Cristóbal; and the same order (although with consistently higher values) holds true when comparing the estimated rent that owners believe they would get for their property. Respondents in Avellaneda have been living in the same neighborhood for 20.7 years, significantly longer than those in the other areas. Finally, respondents in the two poorer areas report a significantly greater desire to change neighborhoods than do respondents in the other two neighborhoods (approximately 20 percent versus 14 percent, respectively) when "satisfied with the neighborhood" is the alternative.

The NQLS also collected extensive information on general life satisfaction and subjective satisfaction with a series of life domains. The results from these questions also point to specific patterns among the four selected neighborhoods, as shown in table 4.2. The neighborhood levels of satisfaction revealed by answers to these questions are expressed on a 1-to-10 scale, with 10 being the highest possible valuation for the domain.[9] The results are in line with the happiness literature (see chapter 3), where residents in the two more affluent neighborhoods report significantly higher levels of general life satisfaction than do those in the two worse-off areas. In this case, Caballito fares slightly better than Palermo, and Avellaneda fares slightly worse than San Cristóbal. When considering the level of satisfaction with QoL in the neighborhood, Caballito again scores higher than the average level of responses, followed closely by Palermo (although the difference is not significant), and then by Avellaneda and San Cristóbal (the last with a significantly lower level than the other three). In general, the lower levels of satisfaction are in one of the two poorer neighborhoods, and the higher levels are in one of the two richest neighborhoods.

Table 4.3 presents a set of in-depth subjective evaluations of neighborhood characteristics that are relevant for urban QoL.[10] As in table 4.2, the answers are on a 1–10 scale, covering such areas as sidewalk and street conditions, cleanliness, presence of trees, security, green areas, and cultural activities, among others. The same clear pattern of two distinct groups of neighborhoods emerges in table 4.3 as in previous tables. Considering the average evaluation of these aspects, San Cristóbal and Avellaneda have similarly lower levels than do Palermo and Caballito (although Caballito has a significantly higher level than does Palermo). Neighbors in the better-off areas of the City of Buenos Aires thus have a higher evaluation of these important aspects of public goods and services than do those in worse-off areas.

Table 4.2 General Life Satisfaction and Satisfaction
with Life Domains
On a scale of 1–10

Type of satisfaction	Avellaneda	Caballito	Palermo	San Cristóbal	Total
General life satisfaction	7.59	8.00	7.88	7.68	7.79
Satisfaction with neighborhood QoL	7.08	7.82	7.71	6.75	7.34
Satisfaction with own economic situation	6.99	7.23	7.26	6.68	7.04
Job satisfaction	7.88	7.93	8.27	8.04	8.03
Satisfaction with friends	8.76	9.02	9.05	9.03	8.96
Satisfaction with emotional life	7.94	8.07	8.10	7.85	7.99
Satisfaction with physical health	7.75	8.18	8.11	7.85	7.97
Satisfaction with mental health	7.99	8.16	8.20	7.90	8.06
Satisfaction with home	8.11	8.34	8.12	8.18	8.19
Simple average	7.79	8.08	8.08	7.77	7.93

Source: Authors' calculations, based on the Neighborhood Quality of Life Survey (NQLS).

Note: QoL = quality of life. On the scale, 10 = the highest possible valuation for the domain. In the regressions, general life satisfaction corresponds to the *GS* variable, neighborhood QoL satisfaction corresponds to the *NS* variable, and other life domains satisfaction corresponds to the *DS* variable.

The evaluations in table 4.3, however, reflect both subjective satisfaction and objective availability of public goods and services. For instance, Palermo has some of the best and largest green areas in AMBA, so it is not surprising that its residents report a higher level of satisfaction with this characteristic; and of the four neighborhoods, Avellaneda is the most suburban and quiet, which is reflected in its residents' average evaluation of traffic (the highest of the four areas).

Table 4.4 presents the proportion of respondents in each neighborhood who report some problem or characteristic in their area.[11] Reports of annoying levels of noise vary greatly in the city. Although Avellaneda seems to

Table 4.3 Subjective Evaluation of Neighborhood Characteristics
On a scale of 1–10

Characteristic	Avellaneda	Caballito	Palermo	San Cristóbal	Total
Sidewalk conditions when raining	5.27	5.85	5.37	5.11	5.40
Conditions of pavement/streets	5.74	6.22	5.32	5.65	5.73
Street and sidewalk cleanliness	5.01	6.42	5.83	5.39	5.66
Sidewalk forestation	5.56	6.92	6.58	6.02	6.26
Garbage collection in neighborhood	6.42	7.47	6.95	7.06	6.97
Access to public transportation	7.83	7.78	7.47	7.55	7.66
Cultural and sports activities in neighborhood	5.57	6.84	6.13	5.79	6.07
Amount and quality of green areas	5.12	7.07	7.28	5.96	6.36
Police performance in neighborhood	4.61	5.70	5.88	5.25	5.35
Street and sidewalk lighting at night	6.62	6.81	6.70	6.14	6.57
Traffic in neighborhood	6.13	5.63	5.97	5.03	5.70
Security during the day	5.30	6.49	6.42	5.73	5.98
Security during the night	4.49	5.59	5.33	4.33	4.93
Evaluation of neighbors	7.59	7.77	7.38	7.22	7.49
Simple average	5.80	6.61	6.33	5.87	6.15

Source: Authors' calculations, based on the Neighborhood Quality of Life Survey (NQLS).

Note: On the scale, 10 = the highest possible valuation for the characteristic. Neighborhood evaluation corresponds to the *NE* variable in the regressions.

Table 4.4 Neighborhood Characteristics Indicators
Proportion of respondents stating that a characteristic is present

Characteristic	Avellaneda	Caballito	Palermo	San Cristóbal	Total
Annoying noise during the day	0.23	0.49	0.32	0.48	0.38
Annoying noise during the night	0.17	0.28	0.23	0.30	0.24
Annoying noise on weekends	0.17	0.23	0.25	0.23	0.22
Pollution	0.55	0.61	0.53	0.58	0.57
Visual contamination	0.24	0.42	0.37	0.36	0.35
Stray dogs	0.56	0.21	0.32	0.31	0.35
Beggars	0.54	0.61	0.50	0.59	0.56
Street prostitution	0.04	0.08	0.10	0.23	0.11
Drug dealing	0.42	0.21	0.24	0.39	0.32
Abundant shops	0.40	0.79	0.68	0.63	0.63

Source: Authors' calculations, based on the Neighborhood Quality of Life Survey (NQLS).
Note: Neighborhood characteristics correspond to the SC variable in the regressions.

be the quietest, by far—at least according to its residents' evaluation— Caballito and San Cristóbal, the two densest areas, have significantly higher levels of reported annoying noise during the day and the night. Drug dealing is significantly higher in the two poorest neighborhoods, with approximately 40 percent of respondents reporting it in Avellaneda and San Cristóbal, compared with 21 percent in Caballito and 24 percent in Palermo. Street prostitution is highest in San Cristóbal, by far, and lowest in suburban Avellaneda.

Whereas these subjective evaluations of neighborhood characteristics seem to be clear-cut, with two low-evaluation and two high-evaluation neighborhoods, the objective characteristics show a mixed pattern. Table 4.5 presents 21 indicators from the geographic module of the NQLS.[12] These indicators correspond to the average availability of different types of urban infrastructure per block.

The heterogeneity among neighborhoods in the indicators in table 4.5 is greater than in the previous tables. For instance, there are significantly more trees and plants per block and significantly fewer broken pieces of sidewalk per block in Caballito and Palermo than in Avellaneda and San Cristóbal.

Table 4.5 Neighborhood Characteristics per Block, Household
Survey, NQLS Geographic Module
Number per block

Characteristic	Avellaneda	Caballito	Palermo	San Cristóbal	Total
Trees and large plants	15.90	19.10	18.50	15.70	17.40
Wooden posts	12.10	0.20	0.90	1.20	3.44
Steel posts	0.76	5.53	7.36	4.47	4.60
Street lighs	3.69	4.43	3.72	2.99	3.73
Public transportation stop	0.06	0.17	0.41	0.15	0.20
Garbage bins and containers	0.05	2.60	3.06	2.00	1.97
Policemen	0.00	0.06	0.13	0.13	0.08
Rubbish bags during the day	5.68	2.32	4.70	2.48	3.75
Broken sidewalk	7.06	1.60	2.71	5.99	4.23
Leisure-related venues	0.36	0.80	1.71	0.60	0.88
Residential units (houses, appartment blocks)	11.10	11.60	10.90	8.97	10.70
Tall buildings	0.53	6.95	6.23	6.21	5.07
Health facilities	0.01	0.09	0.18	0.02	0.07
Educational facilities	0.06	0.09	0.11	0.00	0.07
Commercial facilities	0.76	2.55	3.41	4.46	2.80
Parking lots	6.58	6.26	3.79	0.11	4.23
Visual contamination	6.15	2.66	4.89	2.63	4.04
Red lights	0.51	1.09	2.07	1.79	1.37
Pay phones	0.13	0.32	0.39	0.29	0.28
Street name posts	2.02	1.35	1.71	1.70	1.68
Estate agent signs	0.34	0.60	0.56	0.61	0.53

Source: Authors' calculations, based on the Neighborhood Quality of Life Survey (NQLS).

Note: These neighborhood characteristics correspond to the *OC* variable in the regressions.

Some of the differences in patterns reflect the fact that Avellaneda belongs to a different jurisdiction (outside the City of Buenos Aires): particularly, fewer tall buildings, less visual contamination, wooden posts for street signs (not common within the City borders), fewer pay phones, fewer real estate agent signs, and fewer garbage bins and containers. The relatively higher level of income of Palermo residents and the neighborhood's status as an entertainment area are reflected in some indicators—for instance, in the significantly higher number of leisure-related venues, signs of visual contamination, and educational facilities per block.

The results by neighborhood, so far, indicate the presence of two distinct sets of areas: one set has two neighborhoods where the rent is higher and residents have higher incomes, education levels, and degrees of satisfaction with their lives and their neighborhoods; and one set has two areas with lower levels of all those indicators.

The rest of the chapters in this volume will use the indicators presented in this section in a multivariate regression context to study urban QoL through the relationship of neighborhood characteristics with property prices and with life satisfaction.

Inferring QoL at the Neighborhood Level, Using Hedonic Price Regressions

In a summary of findings and methodologies, Blomquist (2006) postulates the derivation of a QoL index at the city level from the "full implicit prices" of city amenities. In Blomquist's model, these full prices are derived from the joint location and work decisions of the households. For a model within a city, differences in wages are not relevant. The data in table 4.1 indicate that there are significant differences in the rents paid (or estimated, in the case of owners) by respondents in the four neighborhoods included in the NQLS.[13] A QoL index can be derived using the neighborhood variables included in the survey, exploiting the greater availability of neighborhood characteristics in the data set.

The results presented in table 4.6 correspond to an ordinary least squares (OLS) regression of the logarithm of monthly rent as a function of property characteristics (HC variables, from table 4.1) and both objective (OC variables, table 4.5) and subjective evaluations (NS, NE, SC variables, tables 4.2–4.4) in the regression. Following the methodology described in chapter 3, the regression is of the following form:

$$\log(\text{rent}) = \alpha + \sum_h \eta_h HC_h + \sum_c \theta_c OC_c + \gamma NS + \sum_n \lambda_n NE_n$$
$$+ \sum_s \phi_s SC_s + u. \tag{4.1}$$

Table 4.6 Augmented Hedonic Price Regressions for
Monthly Rent

Dependent variable: Log of monthly rent	OLS
Property characteristics (HC variables)	
Medium-quality construction	0.1388
	[1.45]
High-quality construction	0.2578
	[2.60]***
Garden	−0.0311
	[0.84]
Garage	0.1383
	[3.56]***
House	−0.0057
	[0.13]
Number of bathrooms/toilets	0.1378
	[4.60]***
Number of bedrooms	0.0219
	[1.45]
Rents the property	−0.1663
	[4.60]***
Objective characteristics (OC variables)	
Steel posts	0.029
	[3.41]***
Public transportation stops	0.1227
	[3.03]***
Leisure-related venues	−0.0355
	[2.01]**
Health facilities	0.1193
	[2.05]**
Subjective evaluations and characteristics (NE and SC variables)	
Neighborhood satisfaction	−0.0076
	[0.50]
Annoying noise on weekends	0.1032
	[1.96]**
Pollution	0.0943
	[2.58]**
Drug dealing	−0.0978
	[2.42]**

(continued)

Table 4.6 Augmented Hedonic Price Regressions for
Monthly Rent *(continued)*

Dependent variable: Log of monthly rent	OLS
Abundant shops	−0.0821
	[2.43]**
Sidewalk conditions when raining	0.0238
	[2.37]**
Conditions of pavement/streets	−0.0272
	[2.64]***
Constant	6.3121
	[33.21]***
Observations (n)	616
R^2	0.37

Source: Authors' calculations, based on the Neighborhood Quality of Life Survey (NQLS).

Note: HC = housing and dwelling characteristics; NE = neighborhood evaluation; OC = objective neighborhood characteristics; OLS = ordinary least squares. Robust *t*-statistics appear in brackets. In line with project guidelines, only variables with coefficients significant at the 10 percent level are included in the table.

*p < .10 **p < .05 ***p < .01.

Because the objective of the exercise is to compute neighborhood QoL indexes, the regression does not include neighborhood controls.[14] The results for housing characteristics in table 4.6 are fairly standard. Better-built properties (as assessed by the interviewers) and those with more bathrooms command a higher rental price, and owners tend to report a higher estimated price than do renters.

Only four of the objective characteristics (collected by a team of geographers, independent of the household survey) are significant. The number of steel posts for lighting and electricity cables (as opposed to wooden posts) and the number of public transportation stops per block have both a positive and strongly significant effect on rental prices, pointing toward the importance of infrastructure quality and public transportation availability. The number of health facilities also has a positive and significant impact, highlighting the importance for rental prices of service availability in the neighborhood. Finally, there is a negative and significant coefficient for the number of leisure-related venues per block, possibly reflecting the penalty imposed by the relatively lower levels of peace and quiet.

Some of the subjective variables (reported by the interviewees) also have a significant effect on rental prices in these regressions. The presence of drug trafficking in the neighborhood's streets implies a strong and significant penalty on rental prices (about 10 percent), which highlights the importance of security-related characteristics of the neighborhoods; and the evaluation (on a 1-to-10 scale) of sidewalk conditions when raining has a positive and significant effect on rents, reflecting the importance of neighborhood infrastructure maintenance. The presence of abundant shops is negatively correlated with rental prices, a result similar to the one reported for leisure-related venues. The neighborhood QoL satisfaction measure, denoted by the variable *NS*, does not seem to be significantly correlated with rental prices.

There are also some counterintuitive results. The presence of pollution and annoying noises during the weekends has a positive and significant effect on rental prices, whereas the evaluation of pavement and street conditions has a negative and significant coefficient. These variables could be expected, a priori, to have the opposite effect on rental prices; and the results for pollution and noise are that both factors are probably associated with more fashionable or affluent areas.[15]

These results (summarized in table 4.7) can be used to compute the implicit value of neighborhood characteristics, according to the methodology developed in chapter 3. The sample average rental price was $337 (in 2007 dollars); and the implied rental differences (for the index based only on objective characteristics) were a penalty of $8 for Avellaneda; and premiums of about $8, $35, and $52 for San Cristóbal, Caballito, and Palermo, respectively. Inclusion of the subjective variables in the index implied larger differences and a reordering at the bottom, with Avellaneda slightly better off than San Cristóbal.

The derivation of policy recommendations from these results is marred by the fact that some coefficients appear to be of the "wrong" sign, reflecting market equilibrium rather than demand or supply forces. The following section derives another set of measures of neighborhood QoL from an alternative methodological perspective.

Table 4.7 QoL Index and Implicit Price Differences for NQLS Neighborhoods

Neighborhood	Monthly rent (US$)	Index based on objective characteristics	Implicit price difference	Index based on all characteristics	Implicit price difference
Avellaneda	339	−0.032	−8.3	0.090	38.8
Caballito	361	0.084	35.4	0.199	88.6
Palermo	368	0.113	51.7	0.249	118.3
San Cristóbal	275	0.018	7.9	0.086	34.0
Average	337	0.047	22.2	0.158	70.9

Source: Authors' calculations, based on the Neighborhood Quality of Life Survey (NQLS).

QoL in Urban Neighborhoods: The LS Approach

This section presents a further analysis of QoL at the subcity level, focusing on the interaction of subjective evaluations and objective indicators. As discussed in the previous section, the urban economics literature explains differences in QoL by city or subcity area, assuming that city or neighborhood amenities are capitalized in property prices and wages (Gyourko, Kahn, and Tracy 1999). An alternative strand of research, related to the happiness literature surveyed in chapter 3, attempts to derive valuations for intangibles and externalities by studying the impact of the relevant factors on life satisfaction.

This section presents an extension of that alternative strand. The main difference consists of the joint modeling in this chapter of the relationships between income and general life satisfaction, on the one hand, and between life satisfaction and neighborhood QoL, on the other hand. This methodology computes the impact of the variables related to urban QoL in monetary terms. In addition to the availability of detailed data on objective and subjective evaluations of well-being at the neighborhood level, the distinguishing features of this study are the distinction in the analysis between endogenous and exogenous variables, and the resulting estimation of a system of equations that accounts for the potential endogeneity in the variables incorporated into the analysis.

Estimation: Methodological Issues

QoL can be approximated through the general life satisfaction (*GS*) variable included in the NQLS data, whereas the *NS* variable provides information on neighborhood satisfaction. A series of conditions needs to be met to apply the two-equation valuation method to the neighborhood QoL setting. First, a relationship must exist between general life satisfaction and neighborhood satisfaction. Second, an unbiased estimator of the effect of *NS* on *GS* must be available. Third, the neighborhood characteristics must be correlated with neighborhood satisfaction. Finally, these characteristics must affect *GS* only through their effect on *NS* (that is, they are exogenous to the determination of *GS*). If these conditions are met, it is possible to estimate the following system of equations:

$$GS = \alpha + \sum_c \beta_c X_c + \rho Y + \gamma NS + u \tag{4.2}$$

$$NS = \alpha_2 + \sum_n \lambda_n NE_n + \sum_s \phi_s SC_s + \sum_c \theta_c OC_c + v, \tag{4.3}$$

where the *X* variables represent individual characteristics; *Y* is the level of income; *NS* is neighborhood satisfaction; *GS* is general life satisfaction;

and the other groups of variables represent objective and subjective neighborhood characteristics: OC_c are c objective geographic characteristics, SC_s are s neighborhood characteristics, and the nNE_c variables are subjective evaluations of neighborhood characteristics.

Under the conditions mentioned, equations (4.2) and (4.3) can be estimated as a system, instead of sequentially, correcting for the probable endogeneity of the NS variable in the GS regression. This endogeneity bias is corrected by instrumenting NS with the neighborhood characteristic variables, resulting in an unbiased γ coefficient. A monetary valuation of neighborhood amenities and characteristics then can be derived from their indirect impact on general life satisfaction through their effect on neighborhood satisfaction.

Estimation: Regression Results

As a first approximation, the two equations in the system can be estimated independently. Because the dependent variables are both ordered on a 1-to-10 scale, the model is estimated by cardinal OLS (COLS), which first transforms all ordered variables (dependent and independent) to a form similar to the normal distribution, and then applies OLS to estimate the model (see chapter 3 for methodological details).[16]

The results from these simple regressions are presented in the "COLS" columns of table 4.8 (NS regressions) and table 4.9 (GS regressions). Starting with the latter table, the results match well-established results in the happiness literature (see Oswald 1997, among others): life satisfaction increases with income, is lower for men than for women, and decreases with age. Marital status, education, and household and family size variables do not have a significant effect. Last, and most interesting for the purpose of this study, the level of satisfaction with neighborhood QoL (the NS variable) has a positive and strongly significant effect on GS.[17]

Regarding the determinants of neighborhood satisfaction, the COLS column of table 4.8 presents the estimation results of NS as a function of the OC, SC, and NE variables by COLS. Of the objective indicators and neighborhood characteristics, only the presence of pay phones and parking lots seems to have a positive and significant effect on neighborhood satisfaction. The subjective variables with a negative and significant effect on neighborhood satisfaction are related to externalities (noise and beggars), whereas those with a positive effect are related to social interactions (evaluation of the neighbors), safety (evaluation of neighborhood security during the day), neighborhood amenities and infrastructure (evaluation of traffic conditions; green areas; and the state and cleanliness of pavement, streets, and sidewalks), and the evaluation of local cultural and social activities.

From this preliminary analysis, it appears that there is indeed a relationship between life satisfaction and neighborhood satisfaction (GS and NS), and that the NE, SC, and OC variables are relevant determinants of

Table 4.8 Neighborhood Satisfaction Regressions, OLS and 3SLS

Dependent variable: Neighborhood satisfaction	COLS	3SLS (COLS)
Objective characteristics (OC variables)		
Parking lots	0.0128	0.0131
	[1.89]*	[1.82]*
Pay phones	0.0707	0.0761
	[2.05]**	[2.26]**
Subjective characteristics (SC variables)		
Annoying noise during the day	–0.0754	–0.0651
	[1.95]*	[1.65]*
Beggars	–0.0501	–0.0416
	[1.52]	[1.27]
Subjective evaluations (NE variables)		
Sidewalk conditions when raining	0.0793	0.0865
	[2.43]**	[2.99]***
Conditions of pavement/streets	0.0668	0.0557
	[1.90]*	[1.76]*
Street and sidewalk cleanliness	0.0482	0.0499
	[1.46]	[1.75]*
Cultural and sports activities	0.0414	0.0402
	[2.31]**	[2.37]**
Amount and quality of green areas	0.0733	0.0829
	[2.60]***	[3.44]***
Traffic in neighborhood	0.0533	0.0616
	[1.98]**	[2.40]**
Security during the day	0.0895	0.0927
	[2.39]**	[2.81]***
Evaluation of neighbors	0.1190	0.1208
	[5.35]***	[6.62]***
Some subjective evaluation missing	0.2111	0.2239
	[4.57]***	[4.87]***
Constant	0.4919	0.4898
	[6.14]***	[6.76]***
Observations (n)	938	847
R^2	0.33	

Source: Authors' calculations, based on the Neighborhood Quality of Life Survey (NQLS); complete regression output is available in Cruces, Ham, and Tetaz (2008).

Note: 3SLS = three-stage least squares; COLS = cardinal ordinary least squares; OLS = ordinary least squares. COLS transformation is included. Robust *t*-statistics appear in brackets. In line with project guidelines, only variables with coefficients significant at the 10% level are reported for neighborhood variables.

*$p < .10$ **$p < .05$ ***$p < .01$.

Table 4.9 General LS and Neighborhood Satisfaction
Regressions, OLS and 3SLS

Dependent variable: General life satisfaction	COLS	3SLS (COLS)
Satisfaction with neighborhood QoL	0.3343 [8.25]***	0.4748 [7.87]***
Log total household income	0.0794 [2.09]**	0.0882 [2.33]**
Household size	−0.0003 [0.02]	−0.0013 [0.09]
Male	−0.0903 [2.31]**	−0.077 [1.92]*
Married	0.0801 [1.61]	0.0728 [1.53]
Age (log)	−3.9599 [3.85]***	−3.4052 [3.53]***
Age (log), squared	0.5459 [3.87]***	0.4668 [3.56]***
Number of children	−0.0015 [0.06]	−0.0065 [0.35]
Some secondary education	−0.0549 [0.53]	−0.0528 [0.66]
Some tertiary education	−0.0259 [0.25]	−0.0512 [0.63]
Imputed income	−0.0086 [0.16]	0.0081 [0.16]
Constant	7.1764 [3.85]***	6.0576 [3.46]***
Observations (n)	932	847
R^2	0.12	

Source: Authors' calculations, based on the Neighborhood Quality of Life Survey (NQLS); complete regression output is available in Cruces, Ham, and Tetaz (2008).

Note: 3SLS = three-stage least squares; COLS = cardinal ordinary least squares; LS = life satisfaction; QoL = quality of life. COLS transformation is included. Robust t statistics appear in brackets. In line with project guidelines, only variables with coefficients significant at the 10 percent level are reported for neighborhood variables.

*p < .10 **p < .05 ***p < .01.

neighborhood satisfaction. The latter result implies that the *NE, SC,* and *OC* variables might be appropriate instruments to correct for the potential endogeneity of *NS* in the *GS* regression. The neighborhood characteristics have an impact on general life satisfaction only through their effect on neighborhood satisfaction.[18]

The estimation of the two-equation system is carried out by three-stage least squares (3SLS) estimation on the COLS-transformed variables, and the results validate the intuition that *NS* is endogenous in the *GS* regression. The main difference from the joint estimation is the coefficient of the *NS* variable (0.4748), which is significantly higher than the OLS coefficient of the "COLS" column (0.3343) in table 4.9. The endogeneity of the *NS* variable in the *GS* regression thus implies a downward bias for *NS* in an OLS regression, implying that equations (4.2) and (4.3) in the system cannot be estimated independently—and that the QoL estimates from such estimation would be biased through the *NS* coefficient. The 3SLS coefficient for income on *GS* is slightly higher than the OLS estimate, and the coefficients of the other *X* variables on *GS* are qualitatively similar to those reported in the "COLS" column of table 4.9.

The first regression in the system is reported in the "3SLS" column of table 4.8, and the results are similar to those in the "COLS" column (OLS estimation): the same objective and subjective variables have a significant impact on neighborhood satisfaction.

Estimation: QoL Indexes

The estimation results in the "3SLS" columns of tables 4.8 and 4.9 can be used to compute QoL indicators for the NQLS neighborhoods in the fashion discussed in detail in chapter 2. Table 4.10 reports the average valuations of neighborhood characteristics for the four quarters in the NQLS data sets, using only the objective characteristics *OC* (first results column) and using the objective and subjective characteristics (*OC, NE,* and *SC* variables, second results column).

The first column indicates that objective characteristics are valued relatively little, on average, for the whole sample—$17 compared with an average income of $793. This average, however, masks a large variability between neighborhoods: moving from Caballito or Palermo to the synthetic "average" neighborhood would require average compensations of $125 and $97, respectively, whereas San Cristóbal residents would give up $165 to move to the average neighborhood. Avellaneda residents seem to be close to the average neighborhood in terms of objective characteristics. Although Caballito appears to have a higher QoL than Palermo, according to this methodology, the difference is small and the two neighborhoods are still clearly in the upper group.

The second results column of table 4.10 computes the compensation based on all neighborhood characteristics, yielding similar qualitative

Table 4.10 Monetized Value of LS-Based Neighborhood
QoL Index

Neighborhood	Income value of LS index, based on objective characteristics (US$)	Income value of LS index, based on all neighborhood characteristics (US$)	Average monthly income (US$)
Avellaneda	–4.9	–319	763
Caballito	125.0	463	807
Palermo	97.0	455	896
San Cristóbal	–165.4	–558	704
Total	17.0	27	793

Source: Authors' calculations, based on the Neighborhood Quality of Life Survey (NQLS).
Note: LS = life satisfaction; QoL = quality of life. Income compensation necessary for change from average to own neighborhood characteristics.

results but with a greater variability: the sample average compensation is $27, with neighborhood averages ranging from –$558 for San Cristóbal to $463 for Caballito. Panel (a) of figure 4.1 presents the distribution of these two valuations for all the households surveyed in Palermo and San Cristóbal. The average is higher for Palermo, which also has a greater dispersion. Although the mean and variance for both neighborhoods differ, both distributions appear to be normal.

Finally, table 4.11 computes the correlations between the four indexes computed for the NQLS data sets—two based on the hedonic price regressions and two based on the LS approach, including either objective variables only or all neighborhood characteristics. The correlations between indexes based on different methodologies are all positive and in the 0.153–0.248 range, indicating that the two methodologies are at least partially accounting for some common underlying level of QoL at the subcity level. This also is apparent in figure 4.1, which compares the distribution of QoL indexes from both methodologies for Palermo and San Cristóbal: although the values differ, it is remarkable that, for such differing methodologies, Palermo has a higher mean and more spread-out distribution, whereas San Cristóbal has a lower value and a less-dispersed index.

Conclusion

This chapter studied the level and determinants of QoL at the neighborhood level by means of two alternative methodologies (hedonic price regressions and LS valuation), using an original data source compiled for this study (the NQLS). The augmented hedonic price regressions highlighted

Figure 4.1 Distributor of QoL

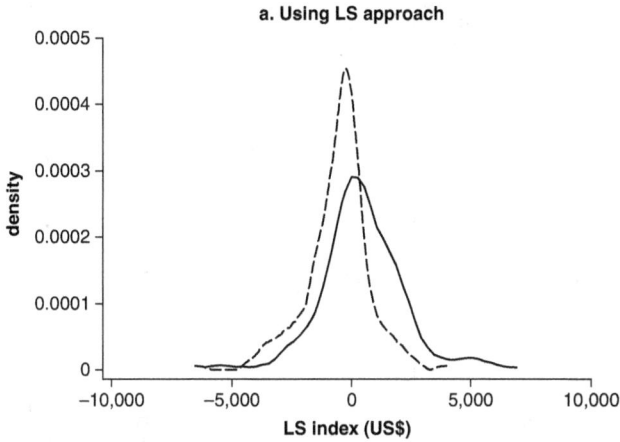

a. Using LS approach

Note: Monetized value of LS-based neighborhood QoL index; based on objective and subjective neighborhood characteristics.

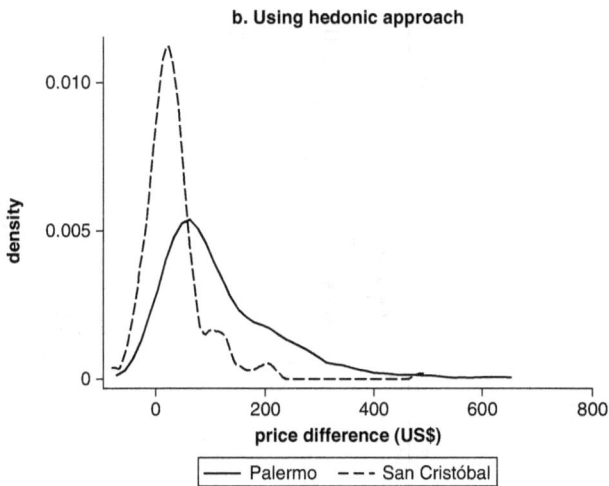

b. Using hedonic approach

Note: Distribution of implicit price differences for QoL indexes, by neighborhood.

Source: Authors' illustrations, based on the NQLS.

Table 4.11 Correlation between Hedonic and LS Indexes

	Hedonic regression		LS	
	Price difference, index based on objective characteristics	Price difference, index based on all characteristics	Income value, based on objective characteristics	Income value, based on all neighborhood characteristics
Hedonic regression				
Price difference, index based on objective characteristics	1.000			
Price difference, index based on all characteristics	0.765	1.000		
LS				
Income value, based on objective characteristics	0.248	0.209	1.000	
Income value, based on all neighborhood characteristics	0.153	0.210	0.334	1.000

Source: Authors' calculations, based on the Neighborhood Quality of Life Survey (NQLS).

the importance of factors related to local safety, cleanliness, peace and quiet, infrastructure maintenance, and transportation availability in the determination of rental prices within and between neighborhoods. This approach, however, produced some counterintuitive results—attributable to the fact that the observed relationships between prices and characteristics represent supply and demand factors simultaneously.

The subjective LS approach indicated the presence of a significant and robust relationship between satisfaction with one's neighborhood and satisfaction with one's life. A series of factors was associated with higher levels of neighborhood QoL satisfaction. One important aspect was the evaluation of the neighbors as a significant factor in neighborhood satisfaction. Other important factors pointed toward items susceptible to policy intervention, such as the availability of public transportation, the evaluation of safety, green areas, sidewalk maintenance, and cultural and sports activities.

A first conclusion from the empirical analysis is the existence of some multidimensional QoL factor associated with neighborhood characteristics, as witnessed by the similarity in the distribution of indexes for different methodologies and from different samples. Moreover, whether based on the reflection of local amenities and characteristics in property prices or on subjective levels of satisfaction, the two approaches suggest an important role for urban public policy making in improving QoL at the subcity level. Information on the significant variables in the analysis could be collected on a regular basis to monitor the evolution and impact of these urban public policy interventions.

Notes

1. In this chapter, the results and discussion will refer to AMBA as a heuristic term, which corresponds roughly to the definition of Gran Buenos Aires.

2. The Autonomous City of Buenos Aires has a statistical directorate that carries out a series of periodic data collection exercises (ranging from quarterly gatherings of real estate prices to annual household surveys), although these relatively abundant statistics are not all aggregated at the same level or for the same non-overlapping subcity units. Cruces, Ham, and Tetaz (2008) present a series of maps and a brief description of these different subcity units and their origins.

3. Gran Buenos Aires is divided into inner and outer rings or *cordones*. The first group of rings includes the affluent north corridor municipalities, whose population has a high educational attainment, on average. See DGEC (2006) for a definition of the inner and outer rings.

4. The four collection areas were selected to match, on average, the distribution of education for the City of Buenos Aires.

5. For further details on these areas and their characteristics, consult the report by Cruces, Ham, and Tetaz (2008).

6. For convenience, the rest of this chapter will refer simply to "neighborhoods," although the NQLS was carried out in these smaller areas within the actual neighborhoods.

7. These demographic indicators are labeled X in the ensuing analysis.

8. These housing characteristics are referred to as the HC variables in the regression analysis.

9. In the regression analysis below, the general life satisfaction variable is referred to as GS, the neighborhood QoL satisfaction variable is NS, and the other life domain satisfactions are referred to collectively as the DS variables.

10. These neighborhood evaluation variables correspond to the NE variables in the regression analysis below.

11. These subjective evaluations of neighborhood characteristics correspond to the SC variables in the regression analysis below.

12. These objective neighborhood characteristics correspond to the OC variables in the regression analysis below.

13. Cruces, Fernández, and Ham (2008) also reach this conclusion, using an alternate data source.

14. The regression in table 4.6 includes all the OC, NE, and SC variables; but only those that are significant at the standard levels are reported. Cruces, Ham, and Tetaz (2008) provide the full regression output, as well as estimations with neighborhood controls and the discussion of alternative specifications.

15. The problem is akin to the difficulties in identifying causal effects, or supply and demand equations. Some negative characteristics (for instance, traffic) might be correlated with more coveted areas: a positive relationship between traffic and prices will be reflecting the latter correlation, or a common causal factor (such as "desirability" exacerbating traffic problems and increasing housing demand). Although this is not an obstacle to computing QoL indicators (because traffic would be correlated with a more desirable neighborhood), it does affect the possibility of causal interpretation and thus of deriving policy implications. Cruces, Ham, and Tetaz (2008) discuss these potential endogeneity biases in detail.

16. The main advantage of COLS is that instrumental variables and 3SLS can be readily applied to the transformed variables, whereas it is cumbersome in nonlinear estimators like ordered probit.

17. The idea behind this model is that total life satisfaction can be decomposed into subcomponents. GS is thus a function of individual characteristics and of satisfaction in a series of life domains, such as work, personal economic situation, emotional life, and health, among others (Frey and Stutzer 2002). Using the same data, Cruces, Ham, and Tetaz (2008) show that in a regression of GS as a function of the X individual characteristics and the life satisfaction domains (summarized in table 4.2), all the domains have a positive and significant coefficient. Thus, neighborhood satisfaction is one of the life satisfaction domains.

18. The overidentification test from the estimation (not reported) of equation (4.2) in the system, instrumenting NS with the NE, SC, and OC variables, yields a p-value of the Hansen J statistic of 0.26. The exclusion restriction (null of no overidentification) cannot be rejected at standard levels, indicating that the instruments are correctly excluded from the second stage, the GS regression. These results do not differ significantly from the 3SLS estimation in table 4.9. The full instrumental variable results are reported in Cruces, Ham, and Tetaz (2008).

References

Blomquist, Glenn C. 2006. "Measuring Quality of Life." In *A Companion to Urban Economics*, ed. Richard Arnott and Daniel McMillen, 483–501. Malden, MA: Blackwell.

Cruces, Guillermo, Gonzalo Fernández, and Andrés Ham. 2008. "Mi Buenos Aires Querido: Urban Quality of Life and Real Estate Prices in the Metropolitan Area." Unpublished manuscript, Centro de Estudios Distributivos, Laborales y Sociales, Universidad Nacional de La Plata, Argentina.

Cruces, Guillermo, Andrés Ham, and Martín Tetaz. 2008. "Quality of Life in Buenos Aires Neighborhoods: Hedonic Price Regressions and the Life Satisfaction Approach." Latin American Research Network Working Paper R-559, Research Department, Inter-American Development Bank, Washington, DC.

DGEC (Dirección General de Estadísticas y Censos). 2006. *Anuario estadístico de la Ciudad de Buenos Aires 2005.* Buenos Aires, Argentina: Autonomous City of Buenos Aires Government.

Frey, Bruno, and Alois Stutzer. 2002. "What Can Economists Learn from Happiness Research?" *Journal of Economic Literature* 40 (2): 402–35.

Gyourko, Joseph, Matthew Kahn, and Joseph Tracy. 1999. "Quality of Life and Environmental Comparisons." In *Handbook of Regional and Urban Economics, Volume 3: Applied Urban Economics,* ed. Paul Cheshire and Edwin S. Mills, 1413–54. Amsterdam, The Netherlands: Elsevier Science.

Oswald, Andrew J. 1997. "Happiness and Economic Performance." *Economic Journal* 107 (445): 1815–31.

5

Quality of Life in Urban Neighborhoods of Bogotá and Medellín, Colombia

Carlos Medina, Leonardo Morales, and Jairo Núñez

This chapter estimates quality of life (QoL) in neighborhoods within Bogotá and Medellín, Colombia's largest cities. Those cities account for 27.0 percent of Colombia's urban population and 21.0 percent of the country's total population,[1] as well as 7.3 percent of the population of all South American cities with more than 1 million people. Those figures make the study of QoL in these cities relevant not only for the country, but also for the region as a whole.

Data from the two cities are used to describe key QoL indicators and to illustrate their spatial segregation at the census sector level. Although Cortés, Gamboa, and González (1999) have developed an atheoretical QoL index (Índice de Calidad de Vida) that combines factors related to access to water and sanitation services, school attendance, and housing features, this chapter extends the analysis in two dimensions. The first extension is incorporating other variables into the index, particularly those related to neighborhood characteristics and amenities. The second extension is using theory to derive weights to aggregate different QoL variables into one scalar indicator.

We thank the editors of this book for detailed comments on previous versions, and the other authors and participants in this project for helpful discussions. We also thank seminar participants at the Banco de la República in Bogotá and Medellín for their comments, and Francisco Lasso for assistance.

The estimation of hedonic models of house values shows the importance of the average level of education at the census sector level to determine house prices, in addition to other neighborhood attributes like access to services and crime indicators. The life satisfaction (LS) regressions show that, as usual, age and income are very important determinants of subjective well-being. Variables related to crime and neighborhood security are also quite significant. The indexes show a strong segregation pattern in each city, applying not only to socioeconomic characteristics (such as income and education), but also to neighborhood characteristics (such as access to public services and crime indicators). A major policy challenge is in improving the conditions of the poorest citizens while preventing segregation from deepening.

Data Used in the Study

Information at different levels of aggregation is available for both Bogotá and Medellín, with the greatest detail at the census sector level. In both cases, information for only the principal city itself is used, excluding the rest of the metropolitan area.

Data for Bogotá

Household-level data are drawn from the Encuesta de Calidad de Vida-Bogotá, collected by the Administrative Department of National Statistics in 2003.[2] This survey includes detailed information on living conditions in Bogotá, with more than 12,770 households interviewed across 19 subcity urban areas denominated *localidades* (see figure 5.1).[3] Within each *localidad*, households were randomly selected in a way that included households from each of the six different strata used in Colombia for targeting social spending.[4] Encuesta de Calidad de Vida data are complemented with information coming from census and official records, making it possible to divide Bogotá into more than 500 census sectors, each with an average of about 12,000 inhabitants.

Data for Medellín

Household-level data for Medellín are drawn from the Encuesta de Calidad de Vida-Medellín, conducted by the University of Antioquia in 2006. This survey has detailed information about living conditions of households in Medellín, with 21,787 households interviewed in 21 subcity areas: 16 *comunas* (shown in figure 5.1) and 5 *corregimientos*. Within each *comuna*, households were randomly selected in a way that would include each of the six different socioeconomic strata and would represent all neighborhoods in the city.[5] The survey is used to obtain *comuna*-level

Figure 5.1 Distribution of the ICV Index in *Localidades* of Bogotá (2003) and *Comunas* of Medellín (2006)

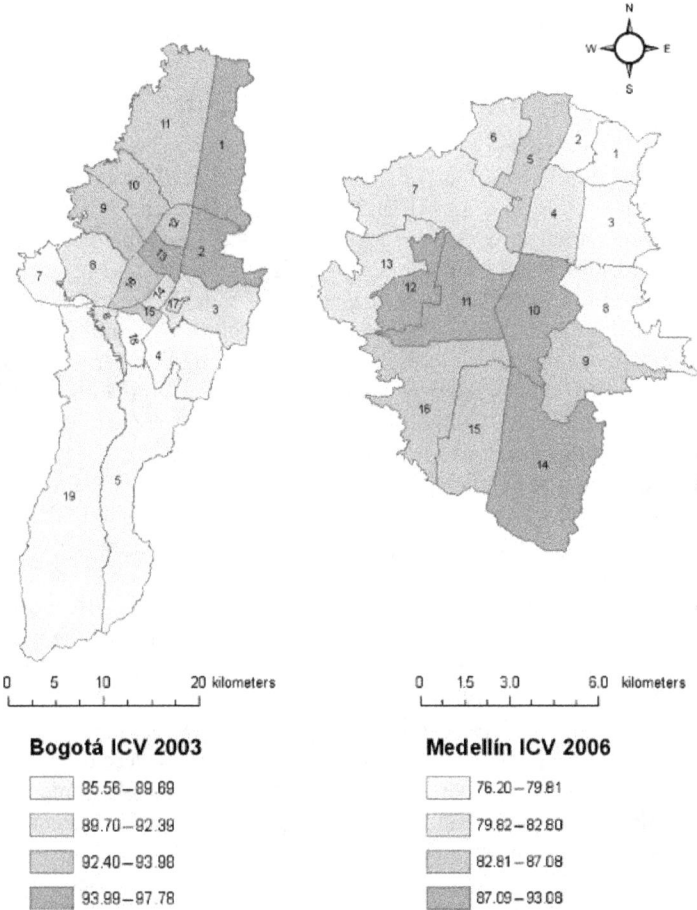

Bogotá ICV 2003

	85.56 – 89.69
	89.70 – 92.39
	92.40 – 93.98
	93.99 – 97.78

Medellín ICV 2006

	76.20 – 79.81
	79.82 – 82.80
	82.81 – 87.08
	87.09 – 93.08

Source: Authors' illustration, based on the ECV for Bogotá and Medellín.
Note: ECV = Encuesta de Calidad de Vida; ICV = Índice de Calidad de Vida. Bogotá *localidades*: 1 Usaquén, 2 Chapinero, 3 Santa Fé, 4 San Cristóbal, 5 Usme, 6 Tunjuelito, 7 Bosa, 8 Kennedy, 9 Fontibón, 10 Engativá, 11 Suba, 12 Barrios Unidos, 13 Teusaquillo, 14 Los Mártires, 15 Antonio Nariño, 16 Puente Aranda, 17 La Candelaria, 18 Rafael Uribe, 19 Ciudad Bolívar, 20 Sumapaz. Medellín *comunas*: 1 Popular, 2 Santa Cruz, 3 Manrique, 4 Aranjuez, 5 Castilla, 6 Doce de Octubre, 7 Robledo, 8 Villa Hermosa, 9 Buenos Aires, 10 La Candelaria, 11 Laureles-Estadio, 12 La América, 13 San Javier, 14 El Poblado, 15 Guayabal, 16 Belén. The figures shown in the legend correspond to the values of the ICV, which range from 0 to 100.

unemployment rates, with less than a 5 percent relative error, and to build key QoL indicators for each of nearly 200 polygons (subdivisions within Medellín). The additional use of census data and other official records makes it possible to divide Medellín into more than 150 sectors, each with an average of about 13,000 inhabitants.

Variables Related to QoL

A complete list of variables related to QoL and the grouping of those variables are found in annex 1 of Medina, Morales, and Núñez (2008), the working paper on which this chapter is based. The table describes the available variables and their sources for each city. Figure 5.1 shows the distribution by locality of the Índice de Calidad de Vida. Using principal component techniques to derive weights, that atheoretical QoL index combines different factors related to access to water and sanitation services, school attendance, and housing features (see Cortés, Gamboa, and González 1999; DNP 1997). High-QoL localities are concentrated in the northeast area of Bogotá and in the west and southeast areas of Medellín.

As indicated above, the analysis will be extended in two dimensions. First, additional variables—especially those related to neighborhood characteristics and amenities—will be incorporated into the QoL index. Second, implicit prices derived from hedonic regressions will be used as weights to construct the indexes. Alternatively, the marginal effect of these characteristics on self-reported life satisfaction will be used. The hedonic regressions for Bogotá use cadastral data on real estate prices, as well as square meters of land and built areas for each house. For Medellín, the 2006 survey asks renting households the amount they pay, and asks owners to estimate how much they would be paying if they were renting. This information is used as a dependent variable in that city's hedonic regressions.[6] Also available for each city is a complete set of geo-referenced data with key information on amenities across the city. Annex 1 of Medina, Morales, and Núñez (2008) describes some of the variables used. Descriptive statistics of the variables that were ultimately used in the empirical exercises are reported in annex 2 of Medina, Morales, and Núñez (2008).

Hedonic Approach to Inferring
Prices of Characteristics

Standard hedonic models are used to infer prices of housing characteristics and amenities, which will be used below to construct QoL indexes.[7] The general form of the equation is

$$\ln(P_{ij}) = \alpha_0 + \alpha_1 H_i + \alpha_2 A_j + u_{ij}, \tag{5.1}$$

where P_{ij} is either the value of the house or that of its rent, H_i is a vector of house i variables, and A_j is a vector of amenities in census sector j.

The relationships found in this section cannot be interpreted as causal in all cases. It nonetheless appears that reasonable estimates are obtained for most variables because the rich battery of data minimizes the omitted variables bias problem.

Implicit prices of housing characteristics and amenities can be gotten by linearizing the hedonic regressions, leading to linearized coefficients,

$$\alpha_X \overline{P}, \forall X, \tag{5.2}$$

which are used to obtain the monetary value of each of the i housing characteristics and j amenities, according to $\alpha_{1i} \overline{P} \cdot \overline{H}_i$ and $\alpha_{2j} \overline{P} \cdot \overline{A}_j$, respectively, where $\overline{P}$, $\overline{H}_i$, and $\overline{A}_j$ are average values of houses, house characteristic i, and amenity j, respectively. We now present separate results for Bogotá and Medellín.[8]

Results for Bogotá

Our data for Bogotá enable us to estimate hedonic equations using cadastral values of houses, which we can complement with prices reported by household owners. Table 5.1 presents the results of the hedonic regressions. The first panel of the table presents the results of estimating this equation, using the cadastral value; and the second panel increases the number of observations by including those households that could not be matched to cadastral data, but did report the value of their houses.

Overall, as shown in table 5.1, the estimation results are as expected. House values increase with better characteristics—such as their number of rooms; the presence of a garden, courtyard, garage, potable water service, and better flooring materials; and location in a better socioeconomic stratum. Clearly, house value increases with the size of its constructed area. Constructed area and area of land are available only for households that could be matched to cadastral data, and, as can be seen in the table, these variables substantially improve the fit of the regressions.

In regard to amenities, house values increase with variables at the census sector level—like the average level of education; distance to places of food supply; number of schools per capita; and, surprisingly, the average illiteracy rate.[9] House values are also higher in the absence of a ground transportation terminal, and with lower rates of variables that include (1) homicides and other violent crime, (2) educational inequality, (3) unemployment rates, and (4) shares of female heads of household. Shorter distances to universities are associated with higher house values.[10]

In contrast, we do not find the distance to the nearest TransMilenio bus rapid-transit station to be related to house values. This result reveals the difficulties in identifying the relationship between some of these

Table 5.1 Hedonic Regressions for Bogotá, 2003

Variable	Log of cadastral values[a]					Log of cadastral values or reported by households[b]				
	Coefficient	t	beta	Implicit price (US$)	Value (US$)	Coefficient	t	beta	Implicit price (US$)	Value (US$)
Number of rooms	0.0354	10.12	0.0519	661	2,264	0.0540	10.98	0.0772	1,043	3,570
House with piped gas service	n.a.	n.a.	n.a.	n.a.	n.a.	0.0993	3.05	0.0421	1,918	1,342
Household cooks with piped gas	n.a.	n.a.	n.a.	n.a.	n.a.	−0.0706	−2.27	−0.0311	−1,363	−898
Bad quality of garbage collection service	n.a.	n.a.	n.a.	n.a.	n.a.	−0.0920	−2.18	−0.0144	−1,776	−52
Bad quality of fixed phone line service	n.a.	n.a.	n.a.	n.a.	n.a.	−0.0768	−3.13	−0.0160	−1,483	−76
House with garden	0.0928	8.48	0.0436	1,732	742	0.1671	12.69	0.0779	3,228	1,382
House with courtyard	0.1160	3.75	0.0227	2,166	99	0.1554	4.16	0.0303	3,002	137
House with garage	0.0860	7.49	0.0368	1,606	487	0.0938	6.43	0.0408	1,811	550
House with terrace	n.a.	n.a.	n.a.	n.a.	n.a.	0.1700	11.71	0.0680	3,283	749
House	−0.0890	−6.33	−0.0417	−1,663	−685	−0.1825	−12.99	−0.0851	−3,525	−1,451

House with potable water service	0.3096	3.46	0.0234	5,783	5,728					
High-quality floor material	0.0401	2.86	0.0147	749	613	0.1062	5.70	0.0383	2,052	1,682
Stratum 2	0.2637	9.83	0.1190	4,925	1,658	0.2936	9.13	0.1305	5,671	1,909
Stratum 3	0.4468	13.47	0.2080	8,346	3,580	0.4894	12.41	0.2273	9,452	4,055
Stratum 4	0.6813	15.85	0.1871	12,724	1,259	0.6341	11.95	0.1803	12,246	1,212
Stratum 5	0.9161	16.87	0.1732	17,109	730	0.9011	13.41	0.1711	17,404	743
Stratum 6	1.1218	17.61	0.1714	20,951	632	1.1695	14.74	0.1911	22,587	681
Constructed area (square meters)	0.0037	10.38	0.4267	68	11,168	n.a.	n.a.	n.a.	n.a.	n.a.
Area of land (square meters)	-0.0003	-1.86	-0.0936	-4.74	-542	n.a.	n.a.	n.a.	n.a.	n.a.
Parks in neighborhood	n.a.	n.a.	n.a.	n.a.	n.a.	-0.1511	-8.04	-0.0496	-2,919	-441
House in area vulnerable to natural disasters	-0.0523	-2.86	-0.0126	-976	-71	-0.0901	-3.86	-0.0221	-1,741	-127
Factories in neighborhood	n.a.	n.a.	n.a.	n.a.	n.a.	0.0628	3.14	0.0179	1,212	125
Terminals of ground transportation in neighborhood	-0.0541	-2.72	-0.0087	-1,011	-39	-0.0883	-3.60	-0.0159	-1,706	-66

(continued)

Table 5.1 Hedonic Regressions for Bogotá, 2003 (continued)

Variable	Log of cadastral values[a]					Log of cadastral values or reported by households[b]				
	Coefficient	t	beta	Implicit price (US$)	Value (US$)	Coefficient	t	beta	Implicit price (US$)	Value (US$)
Land use is productive housing	n.a.	n.a.	n.a.	n.a.	n.a.	0.0877	6.19	0.0406	1,695	695
Class of soil is integral renovation	n.a.	n.a.	n.a.	n.a.	n.a.	0.0860	3.08	0.0126	1,661	42
Distance to nearest school[c]	-0.0002	-3.58	-0.0213	-3.01	-628	-0.0003	-5.07	-0.0381	-5.50	-1,149
Distance to nearest university	-0.00005	-6.76	-0.0470	-0.86	-1,315	-0.0001	-10.61	-0.0907	-1.74	-2,650
Distance to nearest place of public administration	-0.0001	-5.60	-0.0364	-1.05	-1,072	-0.0001	-6.59	-0.0587	-1.74	-1,784
Distance to nearest place of defense or justice	n.a.	n.a.	n.a.	n.a.	n.a.	0.0001	5.92	0.0488	0.97	1,688
Distance to nearest place of food provision	0.00002	4.00	0.0227	0.34	678	n.a.	n.a.	n.a.	n.a.	n.a.
Number of social welfare places per 1,000 population	n.a.	n.a.	n.a.	n.a.	n.a.	0.1473	5.80	0.0327	2,845	528

Number of cultural places per 1,000 population	-0.0974	-5.24	-0.0328	-1,818	-237	-0.1122	-6.63	-0.0366	-2,167	-282
Number of schools per 1,000 population	0.1361	4.35	0.0390	2,542	732	0.1901	8.10	0.0524	3,671	1,058
Lakes area (square meters) per 1,000 population	0.0000	6.19	0.0237	0.15	79	0.00001	3.92	0.0257	0.17	91
Crime rate (murders) per 100,000 population	-0.0395	-5.41	-0.0236	-738	-1,226	-0.0630	-6.51	-0.0359	-1,217	-2,023
Attacks	n.a.	n.a.	n.a.	n.a.	n.a.	-0.1127	-6.95	-0.0495	-2,176	-696
Gini coefficient of education	-0.3636	-2.60	-0.0352	-6,790	-2,406	-0.3244	-2.13	-0.0321	-6,265	-2,220
Number of attacks against life per 10,000 population	-0.0351	-4.69	-0.0237	-655	-262	n.a.	n.a.	n.a.	n.a.	n.a.
Population density	n.a.	n.a.	n.a.	n.a.	n.a.	0.0003	3.01	0.0179	5.53	306
Unemployment rate	-1.9299	-5.48	-0.0371	-36,045	-2,751	-3.5641	-8.92	-0.0700	-68,836	-5,253
Average years of education by census tract	0.0755	9.30	0.1552	1,411	14,420	0.0732	6.94	0.1530	1,413	14,449
Share of female heads of household	-2.1022	-6.00	-0.0484	-39,263	-3,771	-3.6747	-9.27	-0.0831	-70,973	-6,817

(continued)

Table 5.1 Hedonic Regressions for Bogotá, 2003 (continued)

Variable	Log of cadastral values[a]					Log of cadastral values or reported by households[b]				
	Coefficient	t	beta	Implicit price (US$)	Value (US$)	Coefficient	t	beta	Implicit price (US$)	Value (US$)
Illiteracy rate	0.4015	2.77	0.0171	7,499	610	0.7285	5.54	0.0310	14,070	1,144
Piped gas coverage	−0.2812	−5.38	−0.0365	−5,251	−4,217	−0.4042	−6.49	−0.0522	−7,807	−6,270
Constant	16.0133	96.06	n.a.	n.a.	n.a.	17.0915	95.68	n.a.	n.a.	n.a.
Observations (n)	8,868					10,832				
R^2	0.7963					0.5657				

Source: Authors' calculations, based on data from the ECV for Bogotá; the Administrative Cadastral Department of the District, Bogotá, 2004; the Central Directorate of the Judicial Police and Intelligence, Colombian National Police, 2000; Paz Pública, 2000; and Colombian population censuses, 1993 and 2005.

Note: n.a. = not applicable; ECV = Encuesta de Calidad de Vida. House: dummy variable equal to 1 if house, 0 otherwise (apartment and the like). High-quality floor material: floor material includes any marble, parquet, lacquered wood, carpet, floor tile, vinyl, tablet, or wood. Cultural place: Museums, theaters. Place of defense or justice: offices of defenders, jails, or garrisons; family commissaryships, solicitorships. Place of food provision: plazas, places of food supply. Place of public administration: embassies, consulates, comptrollerships, public utilities, ministries, superintendencies, and so forth. Social welfare places: infant shelters, communitarian centers, neighborhood houses, and so forth. Attacks: dummy variable equal to 1 if there have been attacks in the census sector by Fuerzas Armadas Revolucionarias de Colombia, Ejército de Liberación Nacional, or other groups. Definitions and descriptions of other variables are available in annex 1 of Medina, Morales, and Núñez (2008). The exchange rate in June 2003 was Col$2,827 per U.S. dollar.

a. Only includes households for which cadastral values are available.
b. Cadastral values if available, otherwise, the value reported by households surveyed.
c. All distances are in meters. The t-statistics are computed on the basis of robust standard errors corrected by clustering at the census sector level.

variables and the value of the house or its rent. Complementary exercises (not included here) show that the relationship between house values and distance to the nearest TransMilenio station is nonlinear. Prices of houses within 200 meters of a station are 5–7 percent lower—and prices of houses between 350 and 650 meters from the station are 1–4 percent higher—than are the prices of houses 1 kilometer or more from the nearest station.[11] The former result suggests a cost of being close to an important street or highway, the usual corridors of TransMilenio, whereas the later result quantifies the benefits of having access to transportation while living in a quieter and more residential neighborhood. Finally, because the relative importance of this variable was low in several exploratory exercises, it does not appear to be a key factor at the margin for Bogotá. A possible explanation is found in the 2003 QoL survey, in which fewer than 8 percent of respondents reported taking the TransMilenio to go to work, and about 50 percent reported using the traditional system. Moreover, the TransMilenio and the traditional transit systems are not integrated.[12]

In table 5.1, the relative importance of each of the control variables as determinants of house values can be read from the columns labeled "beta," which present standardized coefficients. According to the table, the constructed area is the variable that would imply the largest change in the house value, because an increase of 1.00 standard deviation (SD) in the constructed area would imply a rise of nearly 0.43 SD in the house value. The socioeconomic strata are also very important at the moment of determining house values. For example, increasing the share of stratum-4 houses in a specific census sector by 1.00 SD from its current level would imply an increase of 0.19 SD in the average value of its houses.[13] Similar magnitudes are found for socioeconomic strata 3, 5, and 6. However, increasing the average education of the census sector where the house is located would imply an increase of 0.16 SD in the house value. The most important variables, according to this criterion, would be the constructed area (a house variable), followed first by the socioeconomic stratum (estimated as a function of house and neighborhood variables), and then by the average education of the census sector (an amenity).[14]

In terms of their importance, the next variables are the area of land and the number of rooms. The area of land decreases house values by 9.4 percent of a SD, and the number of rooms increases the values 5.2 percent of a SD, when any of these variables is increased by 1.00 SD.[15]

The share of female household heads in the census sector, the distance to the nearest university, and the presence of a garden in the house affect the house value in the range of 4.3–4.8 percent of a SD. It is important to note that both the level and the inequality in the distribution of education (as measured by the Gini coefficient of education of the census sector) are relevant variables: an increase of 1 SD in the Gini coefficient of education of the census sector would decrease the value of the house 3.5 percent of its SD.

Similar results are obtained for an augmented sample including all households for which either the cadastral value of houses or their reported value is known. In this case, the most important variables in terms of explanatory power are socioeconomic strata, followed by the average education of the census sector, the distance to a center of higher education, whether the household lives in a house (as opposed to an apartment), the number of rooms, and the presence of a garden. The model does not include constructed area because that figure is not available for households that reported the value of their houses but could not be matched to cadastral data.[16]

The implicit prices of the variables and their monetary values, estimated according to equation (5.2) ("Implicit price" and "Value" columns in each panel of table 5.1), show that the largest monetary value capitalized in house value results from the average education in the census sector, followed by constructed area, the availability of potable water, and the share of female heads of household. Notice that the important monetary value of stratum 3—despite its lower implicit price, compared to the higher socioeconomic strata—is explained by the huge share of houses in that stratum (43 percent, versus 10 percent, 4 percent, and 3 percent in strata 4, 5, and 6, respectively).

Results for Medellín

Results of the hedonic regressions for Medellín are reported in table 5.2, which shows that house rents increase with the number of rooms and bathrooms in the house, and with access to fixed phone lines, piped gas, piped water, and Internet or satellite television. Values also increase if the housing unit is an apartment rather than a house, if there is a garage, and if floors and walls are made of good materials. Finally, rent values increase with socioeconomic stratum.

Looking at the amenities included in the regressions, we see that rents increase with variables at the census sector level, such as average education and per capita number of food supply places. Rent values decrease if the house is located in a place subject to environmental risks (flooding, landslides, and so forth). Distance to a subway or bus rapid-transit station is negatively related to house price, meaning that proximity implies a premium to house values.[17] House rents also increase with the distance to intermunicipal roads, the distance to public utilities and to places of cultural value.

The models estimated for Medellín are the same as those for Bogotá to quantify the importance of each of our control variables. As shown in table 5.2, changes in the socioeconomic strata are the ones that would affect the most house rents. Increasing the shares of stratum-3, -4, -5, and -6 houses in a specific census sector by 1.00 SD from the current levels would imply increases of 0.16, 0.19, 0.23, and 0.19 SD, respectively, in the average rent

Table 5.2 Hedonic Regressions for Medellin, 2006

	Rent paid + rent estimated[a]						Rent paid[b]					
Variable	Coefficient	t	beta	Implicit price (US$)	Value (US$)	Value (Col$)	Coefficient	t	beta	Implicit price (US$)	Value (US$)	Value (Col$)
Number of rooms	0.0674	22.46	0.1085	10	41	97,906	0.0717	14.74	0.1201	8.80	37	88,185
Number of bathrooms	0.0944	12.62	0.0781	14	20	46,942	0.1133	11.48	0.0838	14	20	47,724
House with fixed telephone line	0.1238	7.34	0.0242	18	17	40,751	0.1072	4.37	0.0249	13	13	29,883
House with piped gas service	0.0789	7.73	0.0376	11	3.51	8,286	0.0535	3.91	0.0246	6.57	2.01	4,762
Household cooks with piped gas	-0.0276	-3.49	-0.0141	-4.01	-1.62	-3,834	n.a.	n.a.	n.a.	n.a.	n.a.	n.a.
House with LPG service	0.0315	3.35	0.0160	4.57	1.78	4,197	0.0234	2.13	0.0132	2.87	1.12	2,637
House with Internet service	0.0719	7.24	0.0295	10	2.04	4,824	0.0634	4.22	0.0255	7.78	1.52	3,602
House with satellite television service	0.0447	5.94	0.0229	6.48	3.69	8,712	0.0383	3.32	0.0216	4.70	2.67	6,322
House	-0.0189	-2.51	-0.0098	-2.74	-1.37	-3,235	-0.0287	-2.73	-0.0162	-3.52	-1.76	-4,151
House with garage	0.1082	7.93	0.0433	16	2.86	6,764	0.1408	7.59	0.0532	17	3.15	7,455
High-quality floor material	0.1469	16.43	0.0633	21	16	38,997	0.1677	13.30	0.0786	21	16	37,702
High-quality wall material	0.1022	2.67	0.0111	15	15	34,531	n.a.	n.a.	n.a.	n.a.	n.a.	n.a.
House with potable water service	0.3633	1.90	0.0056	53	53	124,140	n.a.	n.a.	n.a.	n.a.	n.a.	n.a.

(continued)

Table 5.2 Hedonic Regressions for Medellín, 2006 (continued)

Variable	Rent paid + rent estimated[a]						Rent paid[b]					
	Coefficient	t	beta	Implicit price (US$)	Value (US$)	Value (Col$)	Coefficient	t	beta	Implicit price (US$)	Value (US$)	Value (Col$)
Kitchen is an additional room	0.1564	5.51	0.0213	23	22	52,598	0.1657	3.83	0.0270	20	20	47,177
Stratum 2	0.1046	5.93	0.0521	15	5.37	12,705	0.0751	3.47	0.0411	9.22	3.27	7,719
Stratum 3	0.3340	13.67	0.1618	48	15	36,612	0.2821	9.48	0.1523	35	11	26,180
Stratum 4	0.5760	19.28	0.1870	84	9.34	22,071	0.4847	13.21	0.1713	60	6.65	15,728
Stratum 5	0.7762	20.65	0.2305	113	10	23,765	0.6529	14.03	0.1915	80	7.16	16,928
Stratum 6	1.0358	19.63	0.1941	150	5.17	12,226	0.9056	12.80	0.1277	111	3.83	9,052
House in area vulnerable to natural disasters	-0.0613	-3.09	-0.0142	-8.89	-0.48	-1,144	-0.0973	-2.38	-0.0226	-11.95	-0.65	-1,539
Class of soil is urban	n.a.	n.a.	n.a.	n.a.	n.a.	n.a.	0.5543	5.82	0.0301	68.07	67.47	159,501
Class of soil is rural	n.a.	n.a.	n.a.	n.a.	n.a.	n.a.	0.4971	4.65	0.0226	61.04	0.38	894
Class of soil is residential	-0.0223	-2.06	-0.0091	-3.23	-2.60	-6,141	-0.0269	-1.94	-0.0122	-3.30	-2.65	-6,275
Distance to nearest cultural place[c]	0.00003	2.55	0.0159	0.005	3.32	7,837	n.a.	n.a.	n.a.	n.a.	n.a.	n.a.
Distance to nearest place of public administration	-0.00002	-1.45	-0.0120	-0.003	-3.21	-7,583	-0.00005	-3.64	-0.0322	-0.006	-6.99	-16,532

Distance to nearest subway or Metro-Plus station	−0.0001	−6.46	−0.0491	−0.008	−10	−23,845	0.0000	−4.86	−0.0467	−0.006	−7.66	−18,112
Distance to nearest place of refuge for children and the elderly	−0.00005	−5.23	−0.0443	−0.007	−8.22	−19,424	−0.00007	−6.21	−0.0701	−0.009	−10.42	−24,623
Distance to nearest marketplace	0.00002	4.17	0.0349	0.004	9.04	21,378	0.00002	2.13	0.0260	0.002	5.45	12,879
Distance to nearest place of recreation or sports	n.a.	n.a.	n.a.	n.a.	n.a.	n.a.	0.0000	−1.87	−0.0145	−0.003	−2.72	−6,435
Distance to nearest church/worship place	n.a.	n.a.	n.a.	n.a.	n.a.	n.a.	−0.0001	−1.60	−0.0094	−0.007	−2.99	−4,716
Distance to nearest place of vigilance	−0.00003	−2.14	−0.0154	−0.005	−3.60	−8,499	n.a.	n.a.	n.a.	n.a.	n.a.	n.a.
Distance to nearest place related to utility services	0.0001	3.61	0.0199	0.008	5.04	11,922	0.00003	2.51	0.0142	0.004	2.83	6,679
Distance to nearest place of help in case of disaster	0.00002	2.69	0.0306	0.003	6.80	16,080	n.a.	n.a.	n.a.	n.a.	n.a.	n.a.
Distance to nearest river or stream	−0.00002	−1.97	−0.0261	−0.003	−6.45	−15,243	−0.00002	−1.89	−0.0226	−0.002	−4.45	−10,523
Distance to nearest hill	n.a.	n.a.	n.a.	n.a.	n.a.	n.a.	0.00002	2.72	0.0221	0.003	5.12	12,115
Distance to nearest place identified with cultural heritage	n.a.	n.a.	n.a.	n.a.	n.a.	n.a.	0.0001	2.43	0.0349	0.006	6.52	15,402

(continued)

Table 5.2 Hedonic Regressions for Medellín, 2006 (continued)

Variable	Rent paid + rent estimated[a]						Rent paid[b]					
	Coefficient	t	beta	Implicit price (US$)	Value (US$)	Value (Col$)	Coefficient	t	beta	Implicit price (US$)	Value (US$)	Value (Col$)
Distance to nearest road connecting the city to neighboring cities	0.00001	2.03	0.0138	0.001	4.18	9,873	0.00001	1.97	0.0169	0.001	4.31	10,184
Distance to nearest university	-0.00003	-4.49	-0.0276	-0.005	-7.47	-17,670	-0.00004	-4.88	-0.0343	-0.005	-7.25	-17,142
Number of social welfare places per 1,000 population	n.a.	n.a.	n.a.	n.a.	n.a.	n.a.	-0.1619	-2.11	-0.0156	-20	-0.83	-1,954
Number of cultural places per 1,000 population	0.0987	1.64	0.0094	14	0.48	1,132	0.1795	2.97	0.0208	22	0.74	1,744
Number of places of public administration per 1,000 population	-0.0016	-0.18	-0.0005	-0.23	0.00	-7	0.0132	1.31	0.0077	1.62	0.02	52
Number of subway or Metro-Plus stations per 1,000 population	n.a.	n.a.	n.a.	n.a.	n.a.	n.a.	-0.0559	-1.15	-0.0090	-6.87	-0.14	-339
Number of marketplaces per 1,000 population	0.3535	2.33	0.0094	51	0.12	288	0.2948	2.16	0.0101	36	0.09	203

Number of places related to utility services per 1,000 population	n.a.	n.a.	n.a.	n.a.	n.a.	-0.0760	-1.66	-0.0076	-9.33	-0.28	-657
Population density	n.a.	n.a.	n.a.	n.a.	n.a.	0.00002	1.29	0.0043	0.00	0.14	320
Average years of education by census tract	0.0529	9.61	0.1111	7.67	71	167,527	0.0546	8.69	0.1156	6.70	62	146,481
Crime rate (murders) per 100,000 population	-0.0039	-6.20	-0.0336	-0.56	-6.06	-14,321	-0.0028	-3.41	-0.0258	-0.34	-3.67	-8,667
Constant	10.4345	n.a.	n.a.	n.a.	n.a.	10.3699	n.a.	n.a.	n.a.	n.a.		
Observations (n)	16,323					6,275						
R^2	0.7636					0.7246						

Source: Authors' calculations, based on data from the ECV of Medellín; Metroinformación, Department of Municipal Planning; and the Colombian 1993 and 2005 population censuses.

Note: n.a. = not applicable; ECV = Encuesta de Calidad de Vida; LPG = liquid propane gas. House: dummy variable equal to 1 if house, 0 otherwise (apartment and the like). High-quality floor material: floor material includes any marble, parquet, lacquered wood, carpet, floor tile, vinyl, tablet, or wood. Cultural place: museums, theaters. Place of vigilance: police station, Center of Immediate Attention, police departments. Place of food provision: plazas, places of food supply. Place of public administration: embassies, consulates, comptrollerships, public utilities, ministries, superintendencies, and so forth. Subway or Metro-Plus station: Medellín's massive transportation system, with Metro-Plus operating buses that travel on roads used exclusively by them. Definitions and descriptions of other variables are available in annex 1 of Medina, Morales, and Núñez (2008). The exchange rate in October 2006 was Col$2,364 per U.S. dollar.

a. Rent actually paid or value of rent that households estimate they would pay under lease.

b. Rent actually paid.

c. All distances are in meters.

for houses located in those census sectors. However, increasing the average education of the census sector, the number of rooms, and the number of bathrooms by 1.00 SD would imply house rent increases of 0.11, 0.11, and 0.08 SD, respectively. Finally, decreasing the distance to a subway or Metro-Plus station by 1.00 SD would increase house rents by 0.05 SD (that is, decreasing distance to the nearest station by 1 kilometer would increase house value by approximately 5 percent because the standard deviation of the rent is similar to its mean).

Again for Medellín as it was for Bogotá, most of the key determinants of house rents are amenities. Results do not change significantly when only renters—rather than a wider sample of households—are considered. The implicit price of the variables and their monetary values, estimated according to equation (5.2) ("Implicit price" and "Value" columns in each panel of table 5.2), show that the largest monetary value capitalized in house values results from the average education in the census sector, followed by the availability of potable water, the number of rooms, and the presence of a kitchen as an additional room. Despite its lower implicit price, stratum 3 again is explained by the larger share of houses in that stratum (32.0 percent, versus 11.0 percent, 9.0 percent, and 3.4 percent in strata 4, 5, and 6, respectively).

LS Approach to Constructing the QoL Index by Subcity Area

Looking at people's perceptions of their living conditions is an approach that increasingly is accepted among previously skeptical economists. As discussed in chapter 3 of this volume, several authors have argued in favor of studying happiness as a direct and plausible measure of utility.[18] Skepticism regarding the LS approach arose, in part, from a lack of evidence on the reliability of reported perceptions of well-being. Objective evidence described by Layard (2003) and others, however, suggests that individuals' perceptions indeed are reliable. Layard cites findings from neuroscience (Davidson 2000; Davidson, Jackson, and Kalin 2001) that show brain activity to be closely related to feelings reported by people, longitudinally for each individual and across people. These facts appear to support quantitative LS analysis based on the cardinality and interpersonal comparability assumptions implicit in the approach.

The following passages present the results of estimating a regression with specification similar to the hedonic approach, but using self-reported life satisfaction as the dependent variable. Chapter 3 already discussed a general specification for the LS equation. Included in these regressions are additional controls previously found to be related to life satisfaction, such as the age and health of the household head, household income, number of children in the household, and so forth.

The equation to be estimated is

$$LS_{ij} = \alpha_0 + \alpha_1 H_{ij} + \alpha_2 A_j + \alpha_3 h_{ij} + \rho \ln(y_{ij}) + u_{ij}, \tag{5.3}$$

where LS_{ij} is the measure of life satisfaction for household head i, who lives in census sector j; H_i is a vector of house variables of the household head's house; and A_j is a vector of amenities in census sector j. In this case, we also include other controls that vary at the household level: h_{ij} includes the age and age-squared of the household head, the number of children in the household, and the like; and y_{ij} is the per capita income of household i.[19] Implicit prices of housing characteristics and amenities can be determined by estimating the standard trade-off between any of the control variables X and income,

$$\frac{\partial LS}{\partial X} \bigg/ \frac{\partial LS}{\partial y} = \frac{\alpha_X \bar{y}}{\rho}, \forall X \tag{5.4}$$

The above relationship will be used to obtain the monetary value of each of the i housing characteristics, amenities, and household variables, according to $\alpha_{1i}\bar{y} \cdot \bar{H}_i / \rho$, $\alpha_{2j}\bar{y} \cdot \bar{A}_j / \rho$, and $\alpha_{2j}\bar{y} \cdot \bar{h}_j / \rho$, respectively.[20]

Results for Bogotá

Figure 5.2 illustrates the effects on reported life satisfaction of three variables related to welfare: old SISBEN, new SISBEN, and income decile.[21] Consistent with results reported elsewhere, self-reported life satisfaction is positively related to all three indicators in Bogotá.[22] The figure additionally suggests that the dispersion of life satisfaction increased between 1997 and 2003, so that worse-off people became relatively less happy.

Table 5.3 presents the regression results, which are very much in line with the cross-section models reviewed and obtained by Ferrer-i-Carbonell and Frijters (2004). For example, all models in the table suggest a U-shaped relationship between age and happiness. Household per capita income is positive, whereas the number of children aged 2–5 in the household is negative and significant.[23] In addition, widowed heads of household are happier. There is a positive relationship between objective health and happiness, based on measures including whether the household head suffers from any chronic disease, has been ill during the last 30 days, or has been hospitalized during the last 12 months. The happiness of the household head is not significantly explained by socioeconomic stratum after controlling for all covariates.

Table 5.3 further shows that variables related to the housing characteristics—such as number of rooms, access to piped gas, good quality of energy, and garbage collection services—positively affect happiness. That is also the case with some neighborhood features—such as easy

Figure 5.2 Life Satisfaction and Welfare, Bogotá, 1997 and 2003

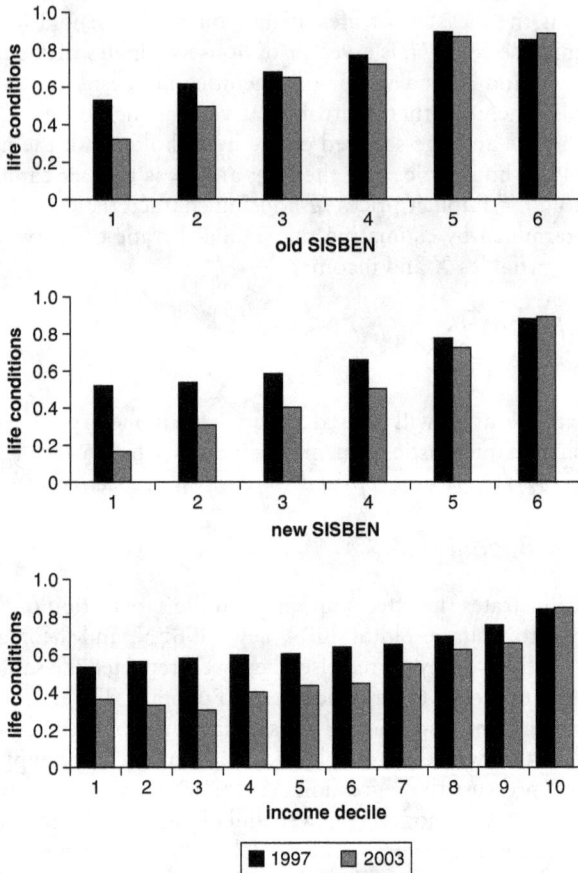

Source: Authors' calculations, based on Bogotá's 1997 and 2003 ECV.
Note: ECV = Encuesta de Calidad de Vida; SISBEN = System for the Selection of Beneficiaries of Social Programs.

access to parks and bars, amenities that increase self-reported life satisfaction. However, variables associated with crime—for instance, property crimes—significantly reduce happiness.

The relative importance of the variables can be inferred from the "beta" column in table 5.3. In this case, the linear and quadratic terms of age are the most important variables of the model, in the sense explained for the hedonic models. For example, a 1.00 SD increase in age (age-squared)

Table 5.3 LS Regressions for Bogotá, 2003

Variable	Coefficient	t	Marginal effect	Implicit price (US$)	Value (US$)	beta
Number of rooms	0.0814	6.18	0.0302	67	229	0.0808
House with piped gas service	0.1483	3.99	0.0556	123	86	0.0413
Bad quality of energy service	−0.2657	−2.43	−0.1024	−227	−5.4	−0.0267
Bad quality of garbage collection service	−0.2503	−2.73	−0.0963	−213	−6.3	−0.0273
Bad quality of fixed phone line service	−0.2153	−3.52	−0.0824	−182	−9.4	−0.0310
Parks in neighborhood	0.1019	1.83	0.0373	83	12	0.0178
High-quality floor material	0.1338	3.19	0.0504	112	91	0.0412
Stratum 2	−0.0096	−0.14	−0.0035	−7.86	−2.64	−0.0003
Stratum 3	−0.1039	−1.27	−0.0387	−86	−37	−0.0283
Stratum 4	−0.2054	−1.82	−0.0783	−173	−17	−0.0407
Stratum 5	−0.2013	−1.47	−0.0770	−170	−7.3	−0.0326
Stratum 6	0.0092	0.07	0.0034	7.56	0.23	−0.0273
Do you feel safe in your neighborhood?	0.4045	11.32	0.1532	339	234	0.1252
Number of attacks against wealth per 10,000 population	−0.0395	−2.31	−0.0147	−32	−10	−0.0246
Number of bars per 10,000 population	0.0420	2.90	0.0156	35	21	0.0269
Number of places selling drugs/narcotics per 10,000 population	0.0621	3.46	0.0230	51	25	0.0325

(continued)

Table 5.3 LS Regressions for Bogotá, 2003 (continued)

Variable	Coefficient	t	Marginal effect	Implicit price (US$)	Value (US$)	beta
Distance to nearest social welfare institution[a]	-0.0002	-2.18	-0.0001	-0.16	-45	-0.0268
Distance to places for recreation or sports	0.0000	2.31	0.0000	0.03	42	0.0209
Number of places of food provision per 1,000 population	0.5994	1.74	0.2225	493	2.01	0.0114
Number of churches/worship places per 1,000 population	-0.2207	-2.23	-0.0819	-181	-12	-0.0200
Number of places of defense or justice per 1,000 population	-0.1585	-2.08	-0.0588	-130	-2.62	-0.0132
Number of places of vigilance per 1,000 population	-0.3801	-2.87	-0.1411	-313	-9.40	-0.0181
Land use is productive housing	-0.0846	-2.12	-0.0315	-70	-29	-0.0308
Average education level by census tract	0.0422	2.72	0.0157	35	355	0.0626
Piped gas coverage	-0.5701	-3.96	-0.2116	-469	-376	-0.0494
Population density	-0.0005	-1.91	-0.0002	-0.38	-21	-0.0192
Log of household's per capita income	0.2723	11.79	0.1011	0.00035	224	0.2110
Household head with complete high school education	0.2009	3.29	0.0724	160	27	0.0569
Household head with incomplete college education	0.2761	4.69	0.0980	217	31	0.0598
Household head with complete college education	0.3103	4.32	0.1100	244	45	0.0665

Age	−0.0477	−7.60	−0.0177	−39	−1,848	−0.4503
Age squared	0.0004	6.22	0.0001	0.30	734	0.3495
Number of children in household	−0.0886	−1.99	−0.0329	−73	−14	−0.0230
Widowed household head	0.1160	2.06	0.0422	94	8.39	0.0216
Unemployed household head	−0.3809	−5.25	−0.1477	−327	−19	−0.0612
Household head has any kind of health insurance	0.2637	6.08	0.1004	222	181	0.0763
Household head has any chronic disease	−0.1671	−4.05	−0.0631	−140	−27	−0.0443
Household head was sick any time during last 30 days	−0.1879	−3.88	−0.0714	−158	−17	−0.0385
Household head was hospitalized any time during last 12 months	−0.1224	−2.03	−0.0463	−102	−7.31	−0.0208
Mean difference between age and education for people under 25	−0.0065	−1.64	−0.0024	−5.38	−26	−0.0095
Percentage of people under 25 attending a public school or college	−0.0922	−2.28	−0.0342	−76	−23	−0.0345
Household head's mother with complete elementary school education	0.0927	2.68	0.0341	76	19	0.0310
Household's per capita income × (number of children under 18)[b] ($000)	0.00028	4.49	0.000103	0.000	68.27	0.0192
Married × (number of children under 18)[b]	0.1493	5.19	0.0554	123	90	0.1085

(continued)

Table 5.3 LS Regressions for Bogotá, 2003 (continued)

Variable	Coefficient	t	Marginal effect	Implicit price (US$)	Value (US$)	beta
Household head with complete high school education × (number of children under 18)[b]	-0.0742	-1.97	-0.0275	-61	-10	-0.0221
Household head with college education × (number of children under 18)[b]	-0.1446	-3.32	-0.0537	-119	-32	-0.0288
Household head with college education × (number of children under 4)[b]	0.1880	2.40	0.0698	155	13	0.0266
Age of household head × (number of children under 18)[b]	-0.0033	-4.33	-0.0012	-2.69	-97	-0.0755
Constant	-2.5633	-6.99				
Observations (n)	12,621					
R^2	0.1853					

Source: Authors' calculations.

Note: LS = life satisfaction. High-quality floor material: floor material includes any marble, parquet, lacquered wood, carpet, floor tile, vinyl, tablet, or wood. Place of vigilance: police station, Center of Immediate Attention, police departments. Place of food provision: plazas, places of food supply. Place of defense or justice: offices of defenders, jails, or garrisons; family commissaryships, solicitorships. Definitions and descriptions of other variables are available in annex 1 of Medina, Morales, and Núñez (2008). Dependent variable = 1 if the answer to the question, "Currently, living conditions in your households are:" is "very good" or "good"; and = 0 if the answer is "fair" or "bad."

a. All distances are in meters.

b. The variable was constructed as the product of an interaction (multiplication) of two variables.

would imply a 0.45 (0.35) SD decrease (increase) in happiness. Income is the second most important variable, with a 1.00 SD increase in the log of per capita income implying a 0.21 SD increase in happiness. Feeling safe in the neighborhood is in third place (0.12 SD). Another interesting result is that a 1.00 SD increase in the interaction variable that implies a household composed of a married couple (or a couple living in partnership) living with children under age 18 makes happiness increase by 0.11 SD. Although the average education of the census tract is still an important variable, it has a much more modest importance than it did in the hedonic model based on property values.

Results for Medellín

Data on life satisfaction for Medellín come from a survey conducted by the Centro Nacional de Consultoría during the fourth quarter of 2007. The survey was done among a subsample of nearly 1,900 households from the 2006 Medellín household survey. The complete questionnaire and the methodology used to collect it can be found in Medina, Morales, and Núñez (2008). The question used to elicit the response (item 19 of that questionnaire) is identical to the question used in the 2003 Bogotá survey.

Figure 5.3 illustrates the relationships between happiness and income and between happiness and socioeconomic stratum. The former relationship is U-shaped; the latter one is increasing, resembling the relationship between income and happiness in Bogotá.

A regression model similar to that for Bogotá was estimated. As shown in table 5.4, the linear and quadratic terms of the age of the household head variables are negatively and positively related to happiness, respectively. Household per capita income is positively related to happiness, and the number of children aged 0–18 in the household is negatively related (and does not vary by either the age or the education level of the household head). Perhaps it is surprising that no relationship is found between happiness and objective good health, measured as whether the household head was ill during the last 30 days or hospitalized in the last 12 months; the survey does not provide information on chronic disease. In contrast to Bogotá, socioeconomic stratum in Medellín still contributes to household head happiness, with households in higher strata being happier. Housing features like satellite television service and high-quality flooring material also have a positive effect on life satisfaction.

As in Bogotá, age in Medellín is the most important variable in determining happiness—a finding that is consistent with the U-shaped pattern set forth in table 5.4. The demographic composition of the household is very important in Medellín. For example, a higher number of children under 18 reduces happiness; but, all things being equal, happiness increases when at least one child is living in the household with his or her mother. These

Figure 5.3 Life Satisfaction and Welfare, Medellín, 2006

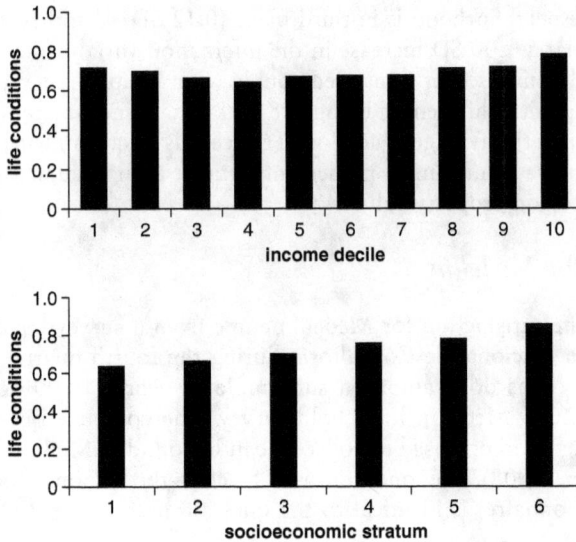

Source: Authors' calculations, based on Medellín's 2006 ECV.
Note: ECV = Encuesta de Calidad de Vida.

results reflect both the costs of raising children under 18 and the reduction of those costs when the mother lives with them. Socioeconomic stratum and the household head's education and marital status (happier if married or widowed) are also among the most important variables. Household per capita income is less important in Medellín than in Bogotá.

Indexes of QoL Based on the Hedonic and LS Models

Results of census sector–level QoL indexes are presented, based on hedonic and LS estimates for Bogotá and Medellín. Because several of the variables included in these models come from those cities' household surveys (which, by design, do not allow us to make inferences at the census sector level), we estimate the values of these variables at the census sector level nonparametrically; and then we use these means by census sector to estimate their respective indexes.[24]

Figure 5.4 shows the distribution of the estimates of QoL indexes for Bogotá and Medellín, respectively weighted using the implicit prices

Table 5.4 LS Regressions for Medellín, 2006

Variable	Coefficient	t	Marginal effect	Implicit price (US$)	Value (US$)	beta
Number of rooms	0.0365	1.35	0.0125	311	1,316	0.0415
Satellite television service	0.1904	2.31	0.0655	1,632	928	0.0664
High-quality floor material	0.1756	1.77	0.0614	1,530	1,185	0.0576
Stratum 3	0.2342	2.54	0.0779	1,942	621	0.0796
Stratum 4	0.6448	4.19	0.1835	4,574	511	0.1216
Stratum 5	0.6167	3.13	0.1752	4,367	390	0.1034
Stratum 6	0.8775	3.25	0.2193	5,465	188	0.0783
Distance to nearest cultural place[a]	0.0001	1.77	0.00004	1.05	749	0.0481
Distance to nearest place of public administration	0.0002	2.74	0.0001	1.43	1,620	0.0613
Distance to nearest road connecting the city to neighboring cities	0.0000	−1.91	−0.00001	−0.33	−1,467	−0.0602
Number of prisons per 1,000 population	2.7019	3.56	0.9208	22,955	69	0.0384
Number of cultural places per 1,000 population	0.5402	1.40	0.1841	4,589	154	0.0337
Number of hospitals or medical centers per 1,000 population	−0.6895	−3.05	−0.2350	−5,858	−364	−0.0752
Number of places related to utility services per 1,000 population	0.3633	0.76	0.1238	3,086	92	0.0189
Number of places for help in case of disaster per 1,000 population	3.2814	2.85	1.1183	27,877	101	0.0368

(continued)

Table 5.4 LS Regressions for Medellín, 2006 (continued)

Variable	Coefficient	t	Marginal effect	Implicit price (US$)	Value (US$)	beta
Class of soil is rural	-1.1154	-5.00	-0.4230	-10,543	-65	-0.0301
Class of soil is residential	-0.2080	-2.18	-0.0682	-1,701	-1,368	-0.0573
Unemployment rate	-1.6462	-1.15	-0.5610	-13,986	-1,083	-0.0338
Population density	0.0001	0.67	0.00003	0.86	48	0.0079
Age	-0.0444	-3.13	-0.0151	-377	-19,444	-0.4706
Age squared	0.0003	2.44	0.0001	2.49	7,357	0.3461
Log of household's per capita income	0.0133	2.17	0.0045	0.00042	113	0.0441
Household head with complete elementary school education	0.1425	1.43	0.0479	1,193	344	0.0596
Household head with incomplete high school education	0.1317	0.67	0.0436	1,086	134	0.0259
Household head with complete high school education	0.2298	1.76	0.0752	1,875	416	0.0775
Household head with incomplete college education	0.0841	0.37	0.0282	703	122	0.0422
Household head with complete college education	0.2871	1.49	0.0911	2,272	273	0.0605
Number of children under 18	-0.2165	-2.57	-0.0738	-1,839	-1,370	-0.1591
Married household head	0.2171	2.63	0.0738	1,838	818	0.0769
Widowed household head	0.2525	2.32	0.0815	2,032	294	0.0645

Household head has any kind of health insurance	0.3811	2.35	0.1405	3,502	3,326	0.0524
Mother or father unemployed or inactive × (number of children under 5)[b]	−0.1834	−2.27	−0.0625	−1,558	−238	−0.0593
Percentage of people under 25 who attend a public school or college	−0.1445	−1.98	−0.0492	−1,227	−483	−0.0463
Household head with complete primary education × (number of children under 18)[b]	0.1459	1.35	0.0497	1,240	244	0.0741
Household head with complete high school education × (number of children under 18)[b]	0.0756	0.70	0.0258	642	129	0.0373
Household head with college education × (number of children under 18)[b]	0.1409	1.22	0.0480	1,197	284	0.0592
Children living with their mother in household	0.3733	4.06	0.1331	3,317	2,446	0.1071
Constant	0.6533	1.45				
Observations (n)			1,890			
Pseudo R^2			0.122			

Source: Authors' calculations.

Note: LS = life satisfaction. *High-quality floor material:* floor material includes any marble, parquet, lacquered wood, carpet, floor tile, vinyl, tablet, or wood. *Cultural place:* museums, theaters. Definitions and descriptions of other variables are available in annex 1 of Medina, Morales, and Núñez (2008). Dependent variable = 1 if the answer to the question, "Currently, living conditions in your households are:" is "very good" or "good"; and = 0 if the answer is "fair" or "bad."

a. All distances are in meters.

b. The variable was constructed as the product of an interaction (multiplication) of two variables.

Figure 5.4 Distribution of QoL Indexes, by Household,
Bogotá (2003) and Medellín (2006)

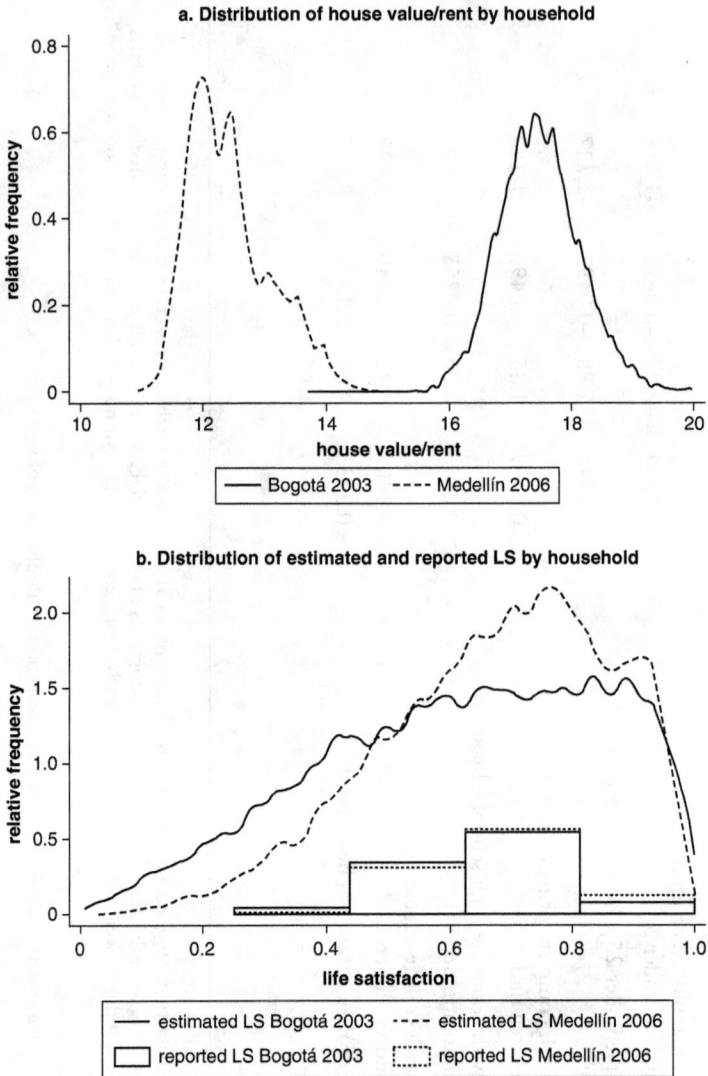

a. Distribution of house value/rent by household

b. Distribution of estimated and reported LS by household

Source: Authors' calculations.

determined by hedonic and LS approaches. The distribution of the hedonic-weighted QoL index for Bogotá contains more extreme values and is more dispersed than is the distribution for Medellín. However, LS-weighted QoL indexes show that, on average, household heads from Medellín enjoy a higher level of QoL, and that this indicator is less hetero-geneous than in Bogotá.

Figure 5.5 shows the distribution of these indexes at the census sector level rather than at the household level. Panel (a) of the figure shows the distribution of the hedonic-weighted QoL index. In contrast to figure 5.4,

Figure 5.5 Distribution of QoL Indexes, by Census Sector, Bogotá (2003) and Medellín (2006)

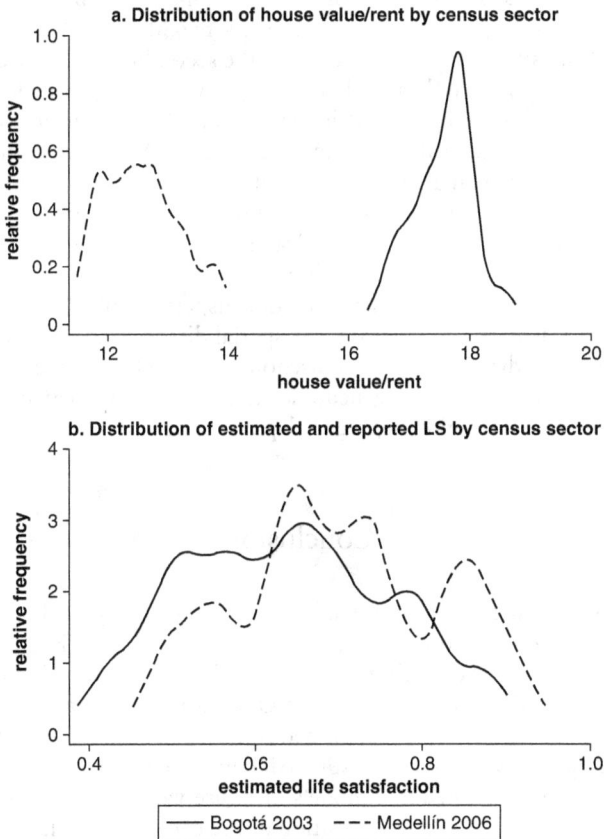

a. Distribution of house value/rent by census sector

b. Distribution of estimated and reported LS by census sector

Bogotá 2003   --- Medellín 2006

Source: Authors' calculations.

Medellín's curve is now more dispersed. This suggests that much of Medellín's dispersion could be explained by differences between rather than within census sectors, compared with Bogotá. Panel (b) shows the distribution of the LS-weighted QoL index at the census sector level. As previously suggested by figure 5.4, QoL indexes, on average, are higher and less dispersed in Medellín than in Bogotá.

Tables 5.5 through 5.8 present QoL indexes in monetary values for each locality within the two cities. These values are the sum of the monetary values of (1) amenities; (2) housing characteristics; and for the index based on life satisfaction, (3) household characteristics. The indexes are expressed in pesos so that their differences represent the necessary compensation for moving from one locality to the other.

To some extent, the results resemble the order shown in figure 5.1; but there are interesting differences as well. For example, when hedonic weighting is used, Barrios Unidos shows the highest QoL value, in part because of the high monetary value of its neighborhood amenities. In figure 5.1, however, Barrios Unidos is in the second tier. Likewise, the use of hedonic weighting indicates that moving someone from one location in Bogotá to another with the next-lower ranking would require compensation of more than $1,500. The same exercise for Medellín, using a flow (rent paid) rather than a stock (house value), indicates that compensation with a net present value of about $2,500 would be required.[25] The LS model, on the other hand, implies dramatically lower compensations of $100 in Bogotá and $800 in Medellín.[26]

A final issue of interest is the spatial dispersion of QoL indexes by subcity area. Figure 5.6 illustrates the spatial distribution of QoL, including the spatial distribution of household per capita income. There are important similarities among hedonic, LS, and atheoretical indexes, all of which reveal a highly segregated pattern of high- versus low-QoL neighborhoods.

Conclusion

Using data from Bogotá and Medellín to describe key QoL indicators, this chapter extends previous analysis in two dimensions. First, variables related to neighborhood characteristics and amenities are incorporated into the QoL index. Second, different QoL variables are aggregated into one scalar indicator. In particular, hedonic and LS regressions are run to derive implicit monetary values for each component of the QoL index.

The estimation of hedonic models of house values showed the importance of the average level of education at the census sector level to determine house prices, in addition to such other neighborhood attributes as access to services and crime indicators. Various studies have analyzed the importance of the average level of education in a neighborhood at

Table 5.5 Hedonic-Weighted QoL Index for Localities in Bogotá, 2003
Col$

	Amenities		Stratum		Amenities + Stratum		Housing		Total	
1	Barrios Unidos	8,371,543	Chapinero	43,132,797	Chapinero	47,367,804	Los Mártires	71,708,020	Barrios Unidos	103,920,558
2	Usaquén	7,608,590	Usaquén	37,289,294	Usaquén	44,897,885	Antonio Nariño	71,032,885	Chapinero	101,263,532
3	Suba	5,930,696	Teusaquillo	32,471,591	Barrios Unidos	37,111,045	Puente Aranda	68,825,474	Usaquén	100,638,299
4	Teusaquillo	4,474,754	Barrios Unidos	28,739,502	Teusaquillo	36,946,345	Barrios Unidos	66,809,513	Antonio Nariño	95,649,052
5	Chapinero	4,235,006	Suba	28,709,570	Suba	34,640,265	Tunjuelito	64,463,287	Los Mártires	94,376,609
6	Antonio Nariño	1,126,135	Fontibón	26,271,372	Fontibón	25,195,235	La Candelaria	61,833,116	Teusaquillo	93,370,211
7	Los Mártires	-827,634	Los Mártires	23,496,224	Antonio Nariño	24,616,166	Fontibón	61,423,024	Suba	89,635,952
8	Fontibón	-1,076,137	Antonio Nariño	23,490,031	Los Mártires	22,668,590	Engativá	57,353,334	Puente Aranda	88,972,817
9	Engativá	-1,861,510	Puente Aranda	23,462,228	Engativá	21,244,515	Teusaquillo	56,423,866	Fontibón	86,618,259
10	Puente Aranda	-3,314,885	Engativá	23,106,025	Puente Aranda	20,147,343	Usaquén	55,740,414	Engativá	78,597,849
11	Kennedy	-4,264,068	Kennedy	20,833,379	Kennedy	16,569,312	Bosa	55,279,541	Tunjuelito	74,499,366
12	Tunjuelito	-7,635,458	Rafael Uribe	17,673,727	Tunjuelito	10,036,078	Kennedy	55,243,638	Kennedy	71,812,949
13	La Candelaria	-9,817,124	Tunjuelito	17,671,536	Rafael Uribe	7,720,447	Suba	54,995,687	La Candelaria	65,724,009
14	Bosa	-9,865,556	Santa Fé	17,220,651	Bosa	4,261,242	Rafael Uribe	54,868,463	Rafael Uribe	62,588,910
15	Rafael Uribe	-9,953,280	San Cristóbal	14,839,514	La Candelaria	3,890,893	Chapinero	53,895,728	Bosa	59,540,783
16	San Cristóbal	-14,259,901	Bosa	14,126,798	San Cristóbal	579,613	San Cristóbal	53,280,809	San Cristóbal	53,860,422
17	Ciudad Bolívar	-18,009,783	La Candelaria	13,708,017	Santa Fé	-3,537,536	Santa Fé	50,248,407	Santa Fé	46,710,871
18	Usme	-18,190,350	Usme	10,892,814	Usme	-7,297,536	Ciudad Bolívar	47,668,137	Ciudad Bolívar	38,068,795
19	Santa Fé	-20,758,188	Ciudad Bolívar	8,410,441	Ciudad Bolívar	-9,599,341	Usme	44,028,074	Usme	36,730,538

Source: Authors' calculations.

149

Table 5.6 LS-Weighted QoL Index for Localities in Bogotá, 2003

Col$

#	Housing	Stratum	Amenities	Stratum + amenities	Household	Total	Total without socioeconomic status
1	Usaquén 1,301,422	Usme −17,844	Chapinero 1,096,164	Chapinero 885,846	Chapinero 149,588	Chapinero 2,404,008	Chapinero 2,193,690
2	Puente Aranda 1,256,835	Ciudad Bolívar −25,251	Teusaquillo 1,054,115	La Candelaria 863,427	Usaquén −121,107	Usaquén 2,115,113	Usaquén 1,856,494
3	Engativá 1,253,779	Bosa −41,879	Usaquén 934,797	Santa Fé 723,147	Teusaquillo −1,011,178	Teusaquillo 1,257,450	Teusaquillo 843,462
4	Antonio Nariño 1,228,016	San Cristóbal −58,882	La Candelaria 930,378	Usaquén 676,179	Suba −1,515,775	Suba 446,784	Suba 180,104
5	Teusaquillo 1,214,513	La Candelaria −66,951	Barrios Unidos 889,425	Teusaquillo 640,127	Barrios Unidos −1,697,620	Barrios Unidos 350,106	Barrios Unidos 16,669
6	Suba 1,208,587	Tunjuelito −107,834	Santa Fé 840,414	Barrios Unidos 555,987	La Candelaria −1,896,160	La Candelaria −108,694	La Candelaria −214,454
7	Kennedy 1,176,343	Santa Fé −117,267	Suba 753,972	Suba 487,292	Santa Fé −1,916,088	Santa Fé −147,503	Engativá −339,344
8	Barrios Unidos 1,158,301	Rafael Uribe −124,951	Antonio Nariño 649,685	Engativá 416,381	Fontibón −1,997,088	Fontibón −238,170	Santa Fé −424,515
9	Chapinero 1,158,255	Kennedy −178,818	Engativá 647,031	Antonio Nariño 409,227	Engativá −2,009,505	Puente Aranda −307,247	Antonio Nariño −532,165
10	Fontibón 1,141,009	Chapinero −210,318	Fontibón 617,909	Los Mártires 335,403	Puente Aranda −2,151,593	Engativá −314,148	Fontibón −554,607
11	Tunjuelito 1,089,697	Engativá −230,650	Los Mártires 574,403	Fontibón 323,914	Antonio Nariño −2,191,849	Antonio Nariño −457,258	Puente Aranda −696,669
12	Rafael Uribe 1,083,073	Los Mártires −239,000	Puente Aranda 437,500	Usme 307,145	Los Mártires −2,252,832	Los Mártires −619,104	Los Mártires −858,103
13	Los Mártires 1,059,325	Puente Aranda −239,410	Usme 324,989	San Cristóbal 261,539	Kennedy −2,264,543	Kennedy −808,076	Kennedy −986,894
14	Bosa 995,148	Antonio Nariño −240,458	San Cristóbal 320,421	Puente Aranda 198,089	Tunjuelito −2,370,955	Tunjuelito −989,482	Tunjuelito −1,097,316
15	Ciudad Bolívar 970,962	Usaquén −258,619	Tunjuelito 291,776	Tunjuelito 183,942	Rafael Uribe −2,504,815	Rafael Uribe −1,238,694	Rafael Uribe −1,363,645
16	Usme 933,514	Suba −266,680	Kennedy 280,125	Kennedy 101,306	Bosa −2,507,114	San Cristóbal −1,350,009	San Cristóbal −1,408,890
17	San Cristóbal 916,575	Fontibón −293,995	Rafael Uribe 183,048	Rafael Uribe 58,098	Ciudad Bolívar −2,549,417	Usme −1,405,277	Usme −1,423,121
18	La Candelaria 818,278	Barrios Unidos −333,438	Bosa 39,052	Bosa −2,827	San Cristóbal −2,587,005	Bosa −1,472,913	Bosa −1,514,792
19	Santa Fé 768,427	Teusaquillo −413,988	Ciudad Bolívar −50,423	Ciudad Bolívar −75,674	Usme −2,663,780	Ciudad Bolívar −1,628,878	Ciudad Bolívar −1,654,129

Source: Authors' calculations.

Table 5.7 Hedonic-Weighted QoL Index for Localities in Medellín, 2006
Col$

	Amenities		Stratum		Amenities + stratum		Housing		Total		Castaño (2005)
1	El Poblado	235,851	El Poblado	316,131	El Poblado	551,982	El Poblado	605,202	El Poblado	1,157,184	El Poblado
2	Laureles-Estadio	199,523	Laureles-Estadio	245,726	Laureles-Estadio	445,249	Laureles-Estadio	573,057	Laureles-Estadio	1,018,305	Laureles-Estadio
3	Belén	181,981	La América	174,745	La América	354,887	La América	519,697	La América	874,584	La América
4	La América	180,143	La Candelaria	149,481	La Candelaria	327,546	Belén	513,300	Belén	839,329	Belén
5	La Candelaria	178,065	Belén	144,048	Belén	326,029	La Candelaria	483,262	La Candelaria	810,808	La Candelaria
6	Guayabal	160,269	Guayabal	121,203	Guayabal	281,471	Guayabal	483,086	Guayabal	764,558	Guayabal
7	Robledo	114,412	Castilla	102,883	Castilla	213,639	Castilla	449,378	Castilla	663,017	Castilla
8	Buenos Aires	113,042	Buenos Aires	89,312	Buenos Aires	202,354	Buenos Aires	449,314	Buenos Aires	651,668	Robledo
9	Castilla	110,756	Aranjuez	80,625	Aranjuez	178,205	Aranjuez	435,436	Aranjuez	611,614	Aranjuez
10	San Javier	104,417	Robledo	60,713	Robledo	175,125	Robledo	433,409	Robledo	610,561	Buenos Aires
11	Aranjuez	97,580	San Javier	57,524	San Javier	161,941	Doce de Octubre	430,830	San Javier	587,189	Doce de Octubre
12	Villa Hermosa	82,332	Doce de Octubre	52,425	Villa Hermosa	133,577	San Javier	425,248	Doce de Octubre	557,931	San Javier
13	Doce de Octubre	74,676	Villa Hermosa	51,245	Doce de Octubre	127,101	Manrique	416,650	Villa Hermosa	543,592	Manrique
14	Manrique	73,021	Manrique	43,897	Manrique	116,917	Villa Hermosa	410,015	Manrique	533,568	Villa Hermosa
15	Santa Cruz	69,551	Santa Cruz	34,629	Santa Cruz	104,180	Santa Cruz	394,288	Santa Cruz	498,468	Santa Cruz
16	Popular	22,741	Popular	27,206	Popular	49,947	Popular	376,142	Popular	426,089	Popular

Source: Authors' calculations.

Table 5.8 LS-Weighted QoL Index for Localities in Medellín, 2006

Col$

	Housing	Stratum	Amenities	Stratum + amenities	Household	Total	Castaño (2005)
1 El Poblado	11,048,093 El Poblado	11,854,197 El Poblado	-903,927 La América	10,386,203 El Poblado	-8,997,374 Belén	12,145,483 El Poblado	El Poblado
2 Laureles-Estadio	10,707,786 Laureles-Estadio	10,355,856 Laureles-Estadio	-1,467,994 El Poblado	7,793,033 Laureles-Estadio	-9,288,814 El Poblado	7,382,149 Laureles-Estadio	Laureles-Estadio
3 La América	10,018,424 La América	7,941,392 La América	-1,611,504 San Javier	7,037,464 La América	-11,174,688 La América	5,881,200 La América	La América
4 Belén	9,631,911 La Candelaria	7,290,867 Robledo	-1,849,516 Belén	2,850,570 Laureles-Estadio	-11,118,670 Belén	3,485,107 Belén	Belén
5 La Candelaria	9,281,231 Belén	6,338,172 Belén	-2,373,913 Doce de Octubre	2,766,052 Guayabal	-12,286,548 La Candelaria	-630,834 Guayabal	La Candelaria
6 Guayabal	9,219,740 Guayabal	5,228,231 Guayabal	-2,462,179 Guayabal	1,219,233 La Candelaria	-12,493,884 Castilla	-1,786,084 La Candelaria	Guayabal
7 Castilla	8,710,647 Castilla	4,004,240 Castilla	-2,562,824 Laureles-Estadio	450,906 Castilla	-12,510,473 Robledo	-3,625,064 Castilla	Castilla
8 Buenos Aires	8,028,077 Buenos Aires	3,358,701 Buenos Aires	-3,487,602 Belén	158,173 San Javier	-12,598,714 San Javier	-5,012,887 Robledo	Robledo
9 Doce de Octubre	7,941,994 Aranjuez	2,828,426 Aranjuez	-3,608,793 Manrique	-139,890 Robledo	-12,616,625 Guayabal	-5,052,471 Buenos Aires	Buenos Aires
10 Robledo	7,637,476 San Javier	2,062,411 San Javier	-3,846,067 Castilla	-1,136,728 Doce de Octubre	-12,854,022 Buenos Aires	-6,702,126 Aranjuez	Aranjuez
11 Aranjuez	7,533,632 Robledo	1,709,626 Robledo	-4,322,524 Aranjuez	-1,494,099 Aranjuez	-13,383,684 Manrique	-6,904,632 Doce de Octubre	Doce de Octubre
12 San Javier	7,095,337 Villa Hermosa	1,512,887 Villa Hermosa	-4,519,245 Villa Hermosa	-2,078,687 Buenos Aires	-13,507,391 Doce de Octubre	-7,620,614 San Javier	San Javier
13 Manrique	6,571,716 Doce de Octubre	1,237,185 Doce de Octubre	-5,437,388 Buenos Aires	-2,895,530 Manrique	-13,660,148 Aranjuez	-9,707,497 Manrique	Manrique
14 Villa Hermosa	6,241,057 Manrique	713,263 Manrique	-5,657,676 Popular	-3,006,357 Villa Hermosa	-13,685,052 Villa Hermosa	-10,450,352 Villa Hermosa	Villa Hermosa
15 Santa Cruz	5,410,419 Popular	n.a. Popular	-6,071,634 La Candelaria	-5,657,676 Popular	-13,793,202 Santa Cruz	-14,539,590 Santa Cruz	Santa Cruz
16 Popular	4,423,730 Santa Cruz	n.a. Santa Cruz	-6,156,808 Santa Cruz	-6,156,808 Santa Cruz	-13,963,263 Popular	-15,197,209 Popular	Popular

Source: Authors' calculations.

Note: n.a. = not applicable.

Figure 5.6 Quintiles of Hedonic, LS, and Atheoretical QoL Indexes and Average Per Capita Income, Bogotá and Medellín

Bogotá

QH Index

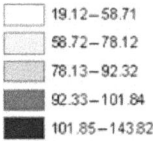

☐	19.12–58.71
☐	58.72–78.12
▨	78.13–92.32
▨	92.33–101.84
■	101.85–143.82

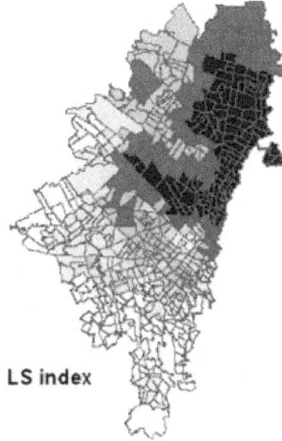

LS index

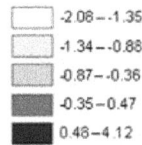

☐	-2.08 – -1.35
☐	-1.34 – -0.88
▨	-0.87 – -0.36
▨	-0.35 – 0.47
■	0.48 – 4.12

Per capita Income

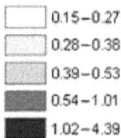

☐	0.15–0.27
☐	0.28–0.38
▨	0.39–0.53
▨	0.54–1.01
■	1.02–4.39

Atheoretical

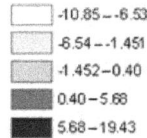

☐	-10.85 – -6.53
☐	-6.54 – -1.451
▨	-1.452 – 0.40
▨	0.40 – 5.68
■	5.68 – 19.43

(continued)

Figure 5.6 Quintiles of Hedonic, LS, and Atheoretical QoL Indexes and Average Per Capita Income, Bogotá and Medellín *(continued)*

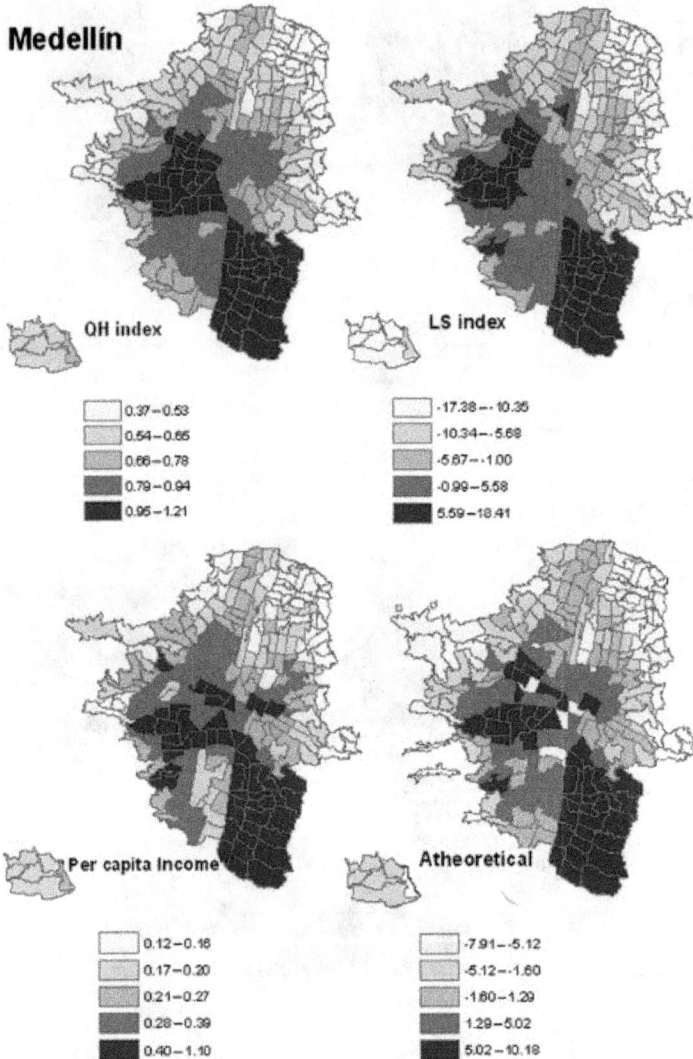

Medellín

QH index

| 0.37–0.53 |
| 0.54–0.65 |
| 0.66–0.78 |
| 0.79–0.94 |
| 0.95–1.21 |

LS index

| -17.36 – -10.35 |
| -10.34 – -5.68 |
| -5.67 – -1.00 |
| -0.99 – 5.58 |
| 5.59 – 18.41 |

Per capita income

| 0.12–0.16 |
| 0.17–0.20 |
| 0.21–0.27 |
| 0.28–0.39 |
| 0.40–1.10 |

Atheoretical

| -7.91 – -5.12 |
| -5.12 – -1.60 |
| -1.60 – 1.29 |
| 1.29 – 5.02 |
| 5.02 – 10.18 |

Source: Authors' calculation.

Note: LS = life satisfaction; QH = quality of life index based on the hedonic model.; QoL = quality of life. Figures of the QoL and household per capita income are in millions.

the moment when people are choosing where to live. Average education level is often taken as a proxy for socioeconomic status that is considered by households for location purposes, as assumed by Bayer, Fang, and McMillan (2005). It is also a source of complementarities and various externalities that are anticipated by households to affect their members' current and future socioeconomic outcomes, as studied by Bayer, Fang, and McMillan (2005), Benabou (1996a, b), Borjas (1995, 1998), Conley and Topa (2002), Cutler and Glaeser (1997), Kremer (1997), and Topa (2001), among others. To the extent that households that differ in education are likely to differ in other dimensions as well (not only class, but also habits, culture, race, and so forth), average education level is also linked to a form of social capital, as suggested by Helliwell and Putnam (2007). Finally, the education level is likely to be linked to segregation by neighborhood tipping—a process that establishes cut-off levels beyond which people would rather leave the neighborhood than stay there—as formerly modeled by Schelling (1969, 1972).

Several other findings arise as well. In the LS regressions, as usual, age and income are very important determinants of subjective well-being. At the same time, variables related to crime and neighborhood security are very significant. The estimated QoL indexes show strong segregation patterns in each city. Households are not only spatially segregated according to socioeconomic characteristics (income, education, and the like), but also are segregated in terms of neighborhood characteristics like access to public services and crime indicators.

From a policy perspective, the evidence suggests that addressing current socioeconomic stratification in a way that reaches the poorest people while preventing segregation from deepening may represent the most important challenge in improving the QoL in Colombia's main cities.

Some policies oriented to derive more information about the conditions and dynamics of QoL within cities could include the following:

1. Establish a system to monitor QoL within cities. There already are efforts in this direction, such as a program begun by several nongovernmental organizations to monitor socioeconomic indicators in Bogotá. The program has been replicated in Medellín and other cities.[27] This monitoring network collects data from several secondary sources and conducts its own surveys to assess satisfaction with local government. The programs additionally promote debates and meetings with the local administration and participants from industry, commerce, and academia. These programs' most valuable asset is their independent and technical approach to local issues. Institutions like this should move ahead and look for a much more detailed monitoring of local issues. The local administrations of Bogotá and Medellín have advanced substantially in the generation of information to enable these institutions and academia to analyze the local

situation, and they have made it possible for researchers to generate additional information of the type used here.

2. Some procedures could be improved to produce better and more timely information, particularly standardizing data. Whereas Bogotá's Living Standards Measurement Survey is conducted by the Administrative Department of National Statistics, Medellín's Living Standards Measurement Survey is collected by local firms. That distinction prevents comparison with other cities and regions.

3. Because much can be learned from hedonic models, such as those used here, producing detailed updated cadastral data becomes crucial. Although the national government relies on cadastral data from the Agustin Codazzi Geographic Institute, three regions composed of two departments (among them, Antioquia, where Medellín is located) and Bogotá have assumed responsibility for their own data. There remains room for improvement in this area, however—possibly more so in the case of Antioquia. The Codazzi Institute previously has provided assistance to these cities' efforts, and it can continue to do so to make cadastral data available for further analysis.

4. Easily collected data on life satisfaction could be substituted for typically scarce cadastral data for several purposes. Nonetheless, LS questions must be kept comparable across surveys.

5. Because census data can be used to build detailed indicators of QoL and other topics, local authorities should continue to make administrative records available to analysts. The ultimate beneficiaries of analysts' findings are those authorities themselves, along with the public. Multilateral organizations likewise may find ways to make available to researchers and analysts the data from multiple sources, including well-known sources such as Gallup polls, the Living Standards Measurement Survey, and employment surveys. Making data widely available over time can prevent policy making and program evaluation from depending on the capacity and specific interests of institutions that currently provide or have exclusive access to information.

Notes

1. Estimates are based on Colombia's 2005 population census.
2. The survey was conducted between June 6 and July 23. Household members 18 years and older were directly interviewed.
3. Bogotá is divided into 20 *localidades*—19 urban and 1 rural.
4. Urban areas are split into six socioeconomic strata, the first of which has the lowest QoL levels. Households in different socioeconomic strata are usually very different, although Medina and Morales (2007) show that, in most of the cases in Bogotá, houses on both sides of a boundary between two socioeconomic strata become more similar the closer they are to their common boundary.

5. The socioeconomic stratification is a spatial system used in Colombia to target subsidies to domiciliary public utility services. To determine the socioeconomic stratum to which a house belongs, an agency of the central government designs a methodology that is applied by each municipality. The methodology considers both information about the house (constructed square meters, number of rooms, number of bathrooms, material of floors and walls, and the like) and about its neighborhood (quality of streets, public parks, access to transportation, and so forth) to estimate a score. These socioeconomic strata are ranked from 1 (most deprived conditions) to 6 (least deprived conditions).

6. For Bogotá, house values also are available from the survey of households owning houses in which they live. Rent prices are available for households living as tenants (question: how much do you pay?) and for those living in their own houses (question: how much would you pay if your house was rented?).

7. For more details on hedonic regressions, see Rosen (1974).

8. For an analysis that compares the two cities, see Medina, Morales, and Núñez (2008).

9. Clearly, this coefficient should be negative, and the coefficient of piped gas coverage should be positive rather than negative. These results suggest they might be capturing the presence of unobserved characteristics not accounted for in the regression.

10. Some exploratory exercises (not reported) show that there are nonlinearities in the relationship between distance to school and house value that imply that prices initially increase and then decrease with distance to schools. The finding suggests that households like to have schools in proximity, but not too close to bear such costs as those arising from traffic congestion.

11. Mendieta and Perdomo (2007) also find a positive effect of being closer to a TransMilenio station, although one of much higher magnitude.

12. Echeverry et al. (2005) point to the lack of integration of the traditional and TransMilenio transit systems as one of the most important factors of quantifying negative spillovers of TransMilenio.

13. Because the shares of households in all socioeconomic strata must always add up to 1.00, think of having a marginal change of 0.43 times a very small fraction of a 1.00 SD of the house price caused by a change of the same very small fraction of a 1.00 SD in the share of households in stratum 4, compensated with a reduction of the same magnitude in the share of households in stratum 1, and maintaining equal the shares of households in the other strata.

14. An opulent house would rarely be classified as poor, nor would a modest house located in a prosperous neighborhood.

15. The negative relationship with the area of land, given that the area of construction is already controlled for, might be signaling that houses are located in poorer areas within socioeconomic strata.

16. For rents (results not reported), the most important variable is the number of rooms, followed by the socioeconomic stratum, the average education of the census sector, and whether the household has gas available for cooking.

17. Medellín's bus rapid-transit system is called Metro-Plus. Although it was under construction at the time of the survey, households knew where its stations would be located.

18. For a survey on this topic, see Frey and Stutzer (2002) or van Praag (2007). The terms *life satisfaction* and *happiness* are used interchangeably here because previous work by Blanchflower and Oswald (2004) and Di Tella, MacCulloch, and Oswald (2001) has found the terms' implications to be similar.

19. Note that the question used is different from the one traditionally included in the European Social Survey (namely, "All things considered, how satisfied are you with your life as a whole nowadays? Please answer using this card, where

0 means extremely dissatisfied and 10 means extremely satisfied.") or in the German Socio-Economic Panel ("In conclusion, we would like to ask you about your satisfaction with your life in general, please answer according to the following scale: 0 means completely dissatisfied and 10 means completely satisfied: How satisfied are you with your life, all things considered?").

20. You will find similar applications in Di Tella and MacCulloch (2007) and Ferrer-i-Carbonell and van Praag (2002).

21. Old and new SISBEN (System for the Selection of Beneficiaries of Social Programs) are proxy means tests used to target social public expenditure in Colombia.

22. For example, see Frey and Stutzer (2002), Layard (2003), and the references therein.

23. A deeper analysis of the role of children can be found in Medina, Morales, and Núñez (2008).

24. To estimate indexes by census sector, we identify the location of the 200 neighbors closest to the centroid of each census sector (either located in that specific census sector or located elsewhere); and, on that basis, we define a bandwidth for each census sector with which we construct biweight kernels. We found similar results when using the nearest 400 neighbors.

25. This figure is 12 times the amount of an annual perpetuity at the 10 percent discount rate. A discount rate of 15 percent would imply a present value of $1,700, very similar to the one for Bogotá.

26. It is a bit surprising that the negative average obtained for the indexes based on LS models is more negative in Medellín than in Bogotá. According to our approach, it would imply that individuals are pricing negative characteristics in a magnitude they cannot afford to fully compensate with their reported incomes. This fact suggests a gap between the way household heads consider what characteristics should be worth and what they are actually willing to pay to get them.

27. These are the programs known as Bogotá Cómo Vamos and Medellín Cómo Vamos. They are part of a wider cities-monitoring network called Red de Ciudades.

References

Bayer, Patrick, Hanming Fang, and Robert McMillan. 2005. "Separate When Equal? Racial Inequality and Residential Segregation." Working Paper 11507, National Bureau of Economic Research, Cambridge, MA.

Benabou, Roland. 1996a. "Equity and Efficiency in Human Capital Investment: The Local Connection." *Review of Economic Studies* 63 (2): 237–64.

————. 1996b. "Heterogeneity, Stratification, and Growth: Macroeconomic Implications of Community Structure and School Finance." *American Economic Review* 86 (3): 584–609.

Blanchflower, David G., and Andrew J. Oswald. 2004. "Well-Being over Time in Britain and the USA." *Journal of Public Economics* 88 (7–8): 1359–86.

Borjas, George J. 1995. "Ethnicity, Neighborhoods, and Human-Capital Externalities." *American Economic Review* 85 (3): 365–90.

————. 1998. "To Ghetto or Not to Ghetto: Ethnicity and Residential Segregation." *Journal of Urban Economics* 44 (2): 228–53.

Castaño, Elkin. 2005. "Evolución de las Condiciones de Vida y Reestimación del Indicador de Calidad de Vida para la Ciudad de Medellín." Departamento Administrativo de Planeación de Medellín – Centro de Estudios de Opinión, Universidad de Antioquia.

Conley, Timothy G., and Giorgio Topa. 2002. "Socio-Economic Distance and Spatial Patterns in Unemployment." *Journal of Applied Econometrics* 17 (4): 303–27.

Cortés, Darwin C., Luis Fernando Gamboa, and Jorge I. González. 1999. "ICV: Hacia una medida de estándar de vida." *Coyuntura Social* 21 (November): 159–80.

Cutler, David M., and Edward L. Glaeser. 1997. "Are Ghettos Good or Bad?" *Quarterly Journal of Economics* 112 (3): 827–72.

Davidson, Richard J. 2000. "Affective Style, Psychopathology, and Resilience: Brain Mechanisms and Plasticity." *American Psychologist* 55 (11): 1196–214.

Davidson, Richard J., Daren Jackson, and Ned Kalin. 2001. "Emotion, Plasticity, Context, and Regulation: Perspectives from Affective Neurosciences." *Psychological Bulletin* 126 (6): 890–906.

DNP (Departamento Nacional de Planeación). 1997. "Índice de Condiciones de Vida Urbano-Rural." Social Mission, Bogotá, Colombia.

Di Tella, Rafael, and Robert MacCulloch. 2007. "Happiness, Contentment and Other Emotions for Central Banks." Working Paper 13622, National Bureau of Economic Research, Cambridge, MA.

Di Tella, Rafael, Robert MacCulloch, and Andrew J. Oswald. 2001. "Preferences over Inflation and Unemployment: Evidence from Surveys of Happiness." *American Economic Review* 91 (1): 335–41.

Echeverry, Juan Carlos, Ana María Ibáñez, Andrés Moya, and Luis Carlos Hillón. 2005. "The Economics of TransMilenio, a Mass Transit System for Bogotá." *Economía* 5 (2): 151–88.

Ferrer-i-Carbonell, Ada, and Paul Frijters. 2004. "How Important Is Methodology for the Estimates of the Determinants of Happiness?" *Economic Journal* 114 (497): 641–59.

Ferrer-i-Carbonell, Ada, and Bernard M.S. van Praag. 2002. "The Subjective Costs of Health Losses Due to Chronic Diseases: An Alternative Model for Monetary Appraisal." *Health Economics* 11 (8): 709–22.

Frey, Bruno, and Alois Stutzer. 2002. "What Can Economists Learn from Happiness Research?" *Journal of Economic Literature* 40 (2): 402–35.

Helliwell, John F., and Robert D. Putnam. 2007. "Education and Social Capital." *Eastern Economic Journal* 33 (1): 1–19.

Kremer, Michael. 1997. "How Much Does Sorting Increase Inequality?" *Quarterly Journal of Economics* 112 (1): 115–39.

Layard, Richard. 2003. "Happiness: Has Social Science a Clue?" Lionel Robbins Memorial Lecture, London School of Economics, March 3–5.

Medina, Carlos, and Leonardo Morales. 2007. "Stratification and Public Utility Services in Colombia: Subsidies to Households or Distortions on Housing Prices?" *Economía* 7 (2): 41–86.

Medina, Carlos, Leonardo Morales, and Jairo Núñez. 2008. "Quality of Life in Urban Neighborhoods in Colombia: The Cases of Bogotá and Medellín." Borradores de Economía 536, Banco de la República, Bogotá, Colombia.

Mendieta, Juan Carlos, and Jorge Andrés Perdomo. 2007. "Especificación y estimación de un modelo de precios hedónicos espacial para evaluar el impacto de TransMilenio sobre el valor de la propiedad en Bogotá." Centro de Estudios sobre Desarrollo Económico document 22, Facultad de Economía, Universidad de los Andes, Bogotá, Colombia.

Rosen, Sherwin. 1974. "Hedonic Prices and Implicit Markets: Product Differentia-
tion in Pure Competition." *Journal of Political Economy* 82 (1): 34–55.

Schelling, Thomas C. 1969. "Models of Segregation." *American Economic Review*
59 (2): 488–93.

———. 1972. "A Process of Residential Segregation: Neighborhood Tipping."
In *Racial Discrimination in Economic Life*, ed. Anthony H. Pascal, 157–84.
Lexington, MA: Lexington Books.

Topa, Giorgio. 2001. "Social Interactions, Local Spillovers and Unemployment."
Review of Economic Studies 68 (2): 261–95.

van Praag, Bernard M.S. 2007. "Perspectives from the Happiness Literature and
the Role of New Instruments for Policy Analysis." *CESifo Economic Studies*
53 (1): 42–68.

6

Pricing Amenities in Urban Neighborhoods of Costa Rica

Luis J. Hall, Juan Robalino,
and Róger Madrigal

More than 60 percent of Costa Rica's population lives in cities (INEC 2000), and those people face challenges particular to highly concentrated population areas. To identify the demands of people living in urban areas, this chapter uses census data and a life satisfaction (LS) survey. Also examined are how people value amenities in urban neighborhoods and their general life satisfaction.

Following Blomquist, Berger, and Hoehn (1988) and Gyourko, Kahn, and Tracy (1999), this chapter shows how neighborhood amenities and public goods influence the pricing of neighborhoods. The chapter additionally uses detailed census data on housing characteristics and introduces neighborhood amenities using geographic information systems. These data permit detailed and precise calculations of neighborhood amenities and improved controls for unobservable effects. For instance, instead of

This chapter was developed as part of the Latin American Research Network Project "Quality of Life in Urban Neighborhoods in Latin America and the Caribbean." The research would not have been possible without financial support from the Inter-American Development Bank Research Network and the support of the Environment for Development Initiative at Centro Agronómico Tropical de Investigación y Enseñanza (CATIE), where this research was hosted. Additionally, we thank Andrea Collado and the Central American Center of Population at the University of Costa Rica for their outstanding work in the application of the survey. We thank Diego Chaverri and Laura Villalobos for their excellent research assistance. Finally, we thank the advisory committee, Eduardo Lora, Andrew Powell, Pablo Sanguinetti, and Bernard M.S. van Praag, for their valuable advice and support throughout this project; and all the other Latin American research teams for their constructive and helpful comments. All errors are our own.

determining whether there is a fire department within the neighborhood, the distance from the nearest fire department to the respondent's home is considered. Data of this type are also available for health variables (such as distance to clinics and hospitals) and education characteristics (such as distance to neighboring schools).

Wages and rent differentials across neighborhoods also can be used to estimate price amenities. Within San José's metropolitan area, only rent differentials are considered (as in Linneman 1980); however, the estimation of price amenities outside San José also considers wage differentials (as in Blomquist, Berger, and Hoehn 1988). This distinction is made because wages within San José do not reflect differences in price amenities, as people are able to live in one neighborhood and work in another. People in urban areas outside San José, however, tend to work in the area where they live and are restricted by a smaller labor market.

The relative importance of housing and neighborhood amenities in determining rents is calculated following Linneman (1980), and neighborhood amenities are found to explain 39 percent of the standardized variation of rents. These price estimates are used to compute an index with results similar to those of previous studies (MIDEPLAN 2007). Some neighborhoods present consistently good profiles of both housing characteristics and amenities; other districts fare well in one dimension, but poorly in another. This fact suggests that indirect policy measures could reduce inequality in urban areas by improving neighborhood amenities. Other factors considered include geographic differences in the valuation of amenities and the relationship between wages and the pricing of amenities.

To provide more detailed discussions of neighborhood amenities, additional research for this chapter included a survey on the quality of life (QoL) in the metropolitan area of San José, gathering data on other factors driving the QoL and on individuals' subjective valuations of their life satisfaction. The latter has garnered attention in the literature (see Di Tella and MacCulloch 2006; Kahneman and Krueger 2006; and van Praag and Ferrer-i-Carbonell 2004). Among subjective variables, housing and safety satisfaction are the key determinants of life satisfaction. This chapter thus enables policy makers at both national and local levels to identify disadvantaged urban areas and determine the most effective interventions. The findings presented also might help individuals and firms make more informed decisions concerning their locations and what they should demand from the local and central governments.

Data and Descriptive Statistics

Data were drawn from several sources: the 2000 Housing and Population Census, the 2003 Multipurpose Household Survey, and geographic information systems' neighborhood amenity variables. This section describes these data sets in detail.

2000 Housing and Population Census Data

The unit of analysis is a household. In the 2000 census, 1,034,893 households were counted across Costa Rica. Of those households, 605,821 households (58.53 percent) were located in urban areas and peripheral urban areas (for formal definitions of "urban" and "peripheral urban" areas, see INEC 2000). Census tracts are divided into urban, peripheral urban, rural, and sparse rural areas, according to the classification that appears in the census.

The census tract represents the smallest geographic division available, and districts are composed of census tracts. Counties are composed of districts; and provinces, in turn, are composed of counties. The analysis focuses on the urban and peripheral urban census tracts of two areas: (1) the metropolitan area defined as the greater metropolitan area of San José (GAM), including the metropolitan area of San José (AMSJO); and (2) other urban areas of Costa Rica.

Table 6.1 shows the population and population density of these urban areas. Most residents live in GAM; and AMSJO is the most densely populated urban area. Regardless of location, however, each census tract has approximately 250 people because those tracts are designed to facilitate census interviews.

Of the 605,821 households in urban areas, only 20 percent rent their homes. People in San José tend to rent their houses more often than do people in other urban areas (table 6.1). Hall, Madrigal, and Robalino (2008) suggest that there is spatial segregation in the distribution of rents, though statistical tests are needed to confirm this hypothesis.

The 2000 census additionally contains a series of housing and household characteristics. Table 6.1 shows the average household size for each of the areas under analysis. The size of households across Costa Rica does not vary significantly within urban areas, nor does the average number of rooms and bedrooms. The share of houses in poor condition is higher outside GAM than inside GAM. Electricity and water access are widespread in all urban areas, although these services have better coverage inside GAM.

The number of rooms and water access are used as a proxy for housing conditions in AMSJO. A high concentration of houses with a higher number of rooms is found in the east and west sections of AMSJO. Smaller houses are found in the south, and medium-size houses are found in the north. Water access in AMSJO, however, is uniformly distributed (see Hall, Madrigal, and Robalino 2008).

2003 Multipurpose Household Survey Data

Because individuals might be willing to accept a lower (higher) wage for living in a neighborhood that generates amenities (disamenities), wage behavior is important for determining the implicit price of neighborhood

Table 6.1 Urban Characteristics

Characteristic	AMSJO	GAM	Urban areas outside GAM	All urban areas
Population (2000 census)				
Population (n)	975,175	1,653,854	595,442	2,249,296
Population per km^2 (n)	6,129	4,796	1,963	3,470
Average population per CT (n)	251	253	238	249
Household characteristics				
Households (n)	264,530	439,976	165,845	605,821
Households renting (n)	63,191	91,938	29,227	121,165
Households renting (%)	23.9	20.9	17.6	20.0
Housing characteristics				
Average household size	3.92	3.99	3.90	3.97
Average number of bedrooms	2.59	2.16	2.45	2.56
Average number of rooms	5.09	5.14	4.73	5.03
House condition: good (%)	65.5	67.8	59.3	65.5
House condition: regular (%)	20.9	19.6	23.8	20.8
House condition: poor (%)	7.4	6.6	8.9	7.2
Access to electricity (%)	99.9	99.8	99.3	99.7
Access to water (%)	91.3	91.3	87.5	90.2
Labor market (2003)				
Head of household unemployment rate (%)	2.52	2.57	3.93	3.04

(continued)

Table 6.1 Urban Characteristics *(continued)*

Characteristic	AMSJO	GAM	Urban areas outside GAM	All urban areas
Head of household monthly wages (colones)	188,725	178,616	133,661	166,177
Education				
Primary school finished (%)	90.6	88.9	77.2	84.1
Secondary school finished (%)	40.3	39.2	27.4	34.3
Diploma (%)	5.8	6.0	4.2	5.2
Bachelor's degree (%)	6.7	5.8	3.7	4.9
Postgraduate studies (%)	2.8	2.8	0.8	2.0
Labor affiliations[a]				
Unions (%)	4.7	4.8	8.0	6.1
Cooperatives (%)	9.5	9.5	14.7	11.6
Solidarity associations (%)	13.4	14.1	8.5	11.8
Socioeconomic status of CT				
High (%)	42.6	38.3	43.8	39.8
Medium (%)	41.2	50.2	36.7	46.5
Low (%)	16.2	11.4	19.6	13.7

Source: Authors' compilation.

Note: AMSJO = metropolitan area of San José; CT = census tract; GAM = greater metropolitan area of San José, including AMSJO; km^2 = square kilometer.

a. It may add up to more than 100 percent because some of the workers may belong to more than one organization.

characteristics. The 2003 Multipurpose Household Survey is used to obtain labor market information.

Heads of household are considered, under the assumption that they make location decisions based on the goal of maximizing their welfare. Only employed heads of households are considered so that the survey may focus on people who have to work in a specific place and whose remuneration only comes from selling their labor. Table 6.1 shows their unemployment rates and wage levels. Unemployment is lower inside GAM, and lower still inside AMSJO. Likewise, wages are higher in GAM, and even higher in AMSJO.

Labor force characteristics. Also shown in table 6.1 are the characteristics of the labor force. People in AMSJO are more educated than people in the rest of the urban areas, and they are less likely to belong to a union or cooperative. These findings reveal the importance of controlling for a variety of explanatory variables of wage differentials.

Neighborhood data. Information was obtained at the census-tract level; and neighborhood variables are divided into social neighborhood characteristics, environmental (dis)amenities, and public goods:

- *Social neighborhood characteristics*—An important set of neighborhood characteristics is related to neighborhood composition. The following characteristics clearly affect housing location decisions and rents:
  - *Socioeconomic status*—A census tract's socioeconomic status is defined on the basis of a series of individuals' socioeconomic characteristics. Table 6.1 shows the share of census tracts in each socioeconomic stratum. Although areas outside the metropolitan area contained tracts of relatively lower socioeconomic status, high and medium socioeconomic levels do not show any clear patterns.
  - *Political participation*—District-level information on the percentage of individuals who voted in the 2002 election might reflect how politically active neighbors are.
- *Environmental (dis)amenities*—This group includes variables related to contamination and environmental risk. Because rivers are associated with high levels of contamination and odors within urban areas of Costa Rica, the distance from the centroid of each census tract to the closest river is calculated. Physical and natural characteristics of neighborhoods were also computed for this study, using tract-level data for average precipitation, average slope of the terrain, and geographic information on the risk of flood and volcanic eruption. Finally, the distance from each census tract to the epicenter of every earthquake greater than 3.0 on the Richter scale that occurred from 2000 to 2004 is calculated. (This variable serves as a proxy for expectation of earthquakes.)
- *Public goods*—The following public goods affect neighborhood QoL:
  - *Roads*—Besides their obvious role as infrastructure, roads can serve as a proxy for contamination. For each census tract, the lengths of primary, secondary, and neighborhood roads were determined; and the density of each type of road was calculated.
  - *Educational facilities*—The distances from each tract to the closest primary school and secondary school were calculated.

- *Fire departments*—The distance from each census tract to the closest fire department was used as a measure of neighborhood fire protection.
- *Health facilities*—The distance from the centroid of the census tract to the closest facility was calculated.
- *Recreation areas*—The distances to national parks, biological reserves, and national monuments from each census tract were computed.
- *Safety*—Given the wide variety in the types of crimes, a county-level index of safety developed for Costa Rica by the United Nations Development Programme in 2004 was used.

That highly detailed information is used to calculate prices of neighborhood amenities.

Pricing Amenities, Using Hedonic Analysis

Wages and rents are simultaneously determined, and both are affected by neighborhood amenities. Following Blomquist, Berger, and Hoehn (1988), the implicit price of the amenity is composed of (1) the sum of the land expenditure differential and (2) the negative of the wage differential. Changes in rents and wages are considered because when the amount of an amenity in neighborhood k increases, people will move into the neighborhood—leading to an increase in housing demand and therefore an increase in rents. However, the supply of labor will increase and wages will also decrease. People will move in until what they pay extra (increase in housing expenditures plus decrease in wages) equals the benefit of the additional amount of the amenity. The change of housing expenditures in equilibrium is represented by h_k (dp_k / da_k), where h_k represents the amount of housing consumed by the household, and (dp_k / da_k) represents the change in the equilibrium prices of housing as a result of the change in the amenity. The change in equilibrium wages produced by the change in the amenity is represented by (dw_k / da_k). Therefore, the implicit price of amenity k can be written as

$$f_k = h_k(dp_k/da_k) - dw_k/da_k. \tag{6.1}$$

To determine those two components, changes in housing expenditures and wages with the amount of amenities are estimated.

The Box-Cox search procedure is used to determine the functional form of the hedonic equations for rents and wages. Formally, both coefficients λ (within the range from –0.2 to 1.4)[1] and δ (that could only take the value of either 0 or 1) are estimated in the equation,

$$\frac{Y^\lambda - 1}{\lambda} = b_0 + \sum_{i=1}^{n} b_i \frac{X^\delta - 1}{\delta} + \varepsilon, \tag{6.2}$$

where the dependent variable Y is estimated first for rents and second for wages, and where X represents the set of explanatory variables.

The data set provides rent information only for people who actually rent the house or for people who are currently working. This is treated as an endogenous selection mechanism that may bias estimations, producing inadequate amenity prices. Following Heckman (1979), sample selection is corrected. Following standard practice in labor economics, correction is also made for self-selection bias in the wage equation in relation to labor participation decisions.

It also is assumed that neighborhoods have different land and labor markets. This assumption is plausible in estimating the prices of city amenities, but less so for neighborhood amenities; workers may live in one neighborhood with the amenities they prefer and work in a different neighborhood. If this is true, amenity price will be captured solely by the housing market. The empirical analysis thus examines within-city effects using only the housing market, and across-city effects using both housing and labor markets.

Results and Amenity Prices for AMSJO

The "b" column of table 6.2 presents the estimates of b from equation (6.1), and the "Monthly price" column presents the estimated implicit price. The price is obtained by transforming the coefficient, using

$$b' = b((\bar{y})^{(1-\lambda)}),\qquad\qquad(6.3)$$

following Blomquist, Berger, and Hoehn (1988), where $\bar{y}$ is the sample mean monthly rent (and wages for the following sections). This is how much an average household benefits from using an additional unit of the amenity for a month. The "Mean" column of the table presents each specific amenity's mean contribution to the AMSJO neighborhoods; and the "25%," "50%," and "75%" columns show the contributions of each of the amenities by quartiles (the first, second, and third quartiles, respectively).

Maximizing the log likelihood finds that δ equals 1 and that λ equals 0.1006. These results are similar to what Blomquist, Berger, and Hoehn (1988) found ($\delta = 1$ and $\lambda = 0.2$).

Most of the coefficients in the "b" column are statistically significant. Regarding the sign of the coefficient, all of the statistically significant coefficients produce the expected signs. A higher number of rooms leads to higher rents, implying that the price of each additional room is positive. This price represents how much an additional room is valued by the average household. If the floors, walls, roofs, and ceilings are in good condition, the price of the house also increases. The type of water source and sewerage also has a significant effect on price, which decreases when water is not supplied by the national water company (Acueductos y Alcantarillados) and when the

Table 6.2 Rent Regression with Selection Correction for AMSJO

Amenities	b	Monthly price[a]	Component of the index			
			Mean	25%	50%	75%
Housing characteristics						
Number of bedrooms	0.55***	9,500	24,886	22,439	24,887	27,382
Number of rooms (no bedrooms)	0.33***	5,791	14,707	12,535	14,146	16,297
Floor (good)	0.24***	4,198	3,043	2,448	3,205	3,798
Walls (good)	0.44***	7,644	5,414	4,320	5,662	6,857
Walls of blocks	0.82***	14,083	9,691	7,041	10,026	13,351
Roof (good)	0.32***	5,614	3,957	3,186	4,101	4,940
Ceiling (good)	0.43***	7,534	6,152	5,560	6,918	7,401
Water source: community organization	−0.36***	−6,235	−199	0	0	0
Water source: rain	−0.82**	−14,189	−11	0	0	0
Water source: well	0.13	2,291	3	0	0	0
Water source: river	−0.89***	−15,287	−16	0	0	0
Sewer: septic tank	−0.10***	−1,856	−603	−1,349	−179	−30
Sewer: latrine	−0.21*	−3,609	−44	0	0	0
Sewer: other	−0.33***	−5,728	−48	0	0	0
No sewer	0.09	1,555	7	0	0	0
Exclusive bathroom for the household	0.48***	8,339	8,116	8,339	8,339	8,081
Electricity supplied not by CNFL	−0.24***	−4,206	0	0	0	0
No electricity supplied	−0.70**	−12,059	−16	0	0	0
Total housing characteristics contribution			75,072	70,211	75,779	81,716
Housing relative importance (%)	60.8					
Neighborhood characteristics						
Safety index	0.46***	7,953	4,077	2,226	3,976	5,328
Slope degrees	−0.01***	−177	−1,309	−1,644	−837	−380

(continued)

Table 6.2 Rent Regression with Selection Correction for AMSJO
(continued)

Amenities	b	Monthly price[a]	Component of the index			
			Mean	25%	50%	75%
Precipitation (mm³)	−0.12**	−2,154	−4,478	−4,308	−4,308	−4,308
Risk of being affected by an eruption	−0.13**	−2,316	−2,024	−2,316	−2,316	−2,316
Log distance to national parks (km)	−1.25***	−21,589	−57,751	−53,840	−59,005	−61,543
Log distance to clinics (km)	0.01	175	42	−42	46	140
Log distance to secondary schools (km)	0.02	364	−161	−296	−128	13
Log distance to primary schools (km)	0.00	59	−49	−71	−42	−20
Log distance to rivers (km)	0.06***	1,054	−1,035	−1,665	−887	−250
Log distance to fire departments (km)	0.05**	968	638	244	730	1,174
Log distance to Sabana Park (km)	−0.54***	−9,419	−17,997	−15,497	−19,493	−22,064
Log distance to Peace Park (km)	1.35***	23,273	65,655	62,467	65,594	68,625
Length of primary roads (km)	−0.46***	−7,974	−146	0	0	0
Length of secondary roads (km)	0.23***	4,098	180	0	0	0
Length of urban-neighborhood roads (km)	0.57***	9,785	4,691	1,689	3,028	4,826
Tract qualified as poor	−0.35***	−6,133	−1,092	0	0	0
Total neighborhood characteristics contribution			−10,444	−12,271	−11,117	−8,170

(continued)

Table 6.2 Rent Regression with Selection Correction for AMSJO *(continued)*

Amenities	b	Monthly price^a	Component of the index			
			Mean	25%	50%	75%
Neighborhood amenities relative importance (%)	39.2					
Other parameters						
Constant	16.081***					
Selection Parameter	–0.224					
Lambda	0.101					

Source: Authors' compilation.

Note: AMSJO = metropolitan area of San José; CNFL = Compañía Nacional de Fuerza y Luz; km = kilometer; mm³ = cubic millimeter. To obtain these values, estimated prices were multiplied by quantities of the amenity. Price amenities are measured at the mean prices in 2000, when C 308 = \$1.

a. The price was calculated following Blomquist, Beger, and Hoehn (1988). Price = $b*$(average of Y)$^{\wedge}(1-\lambda)$, where b is the estimated coefficient from the best functional form and Y is the dependent variable. The dummy left out for sewer is being connected to a sewer network. The dummy left out for water source is being supplied by the national water company.

*p < .10 **p < .05 ***p < .01.

source of the water is rain or a river. A house's price additionally decreases if it is not connected to a sewer network, having instead only a septic tank or latrine. As expected, the source of electricity also affects rent levels. Houses covered by the national electric company (Compañía Nacional de Fuerza y Luz) are more valued.

Intuitive results are found for most neighborhood factors. The safety indicator price suggests that safer neighborhoods have higher rents. However, steep terrain, high precipitation levels, and high volcanic eruption risk reduce values. People value living close to national parks, whereas proximity to rivers (highly polluted in the city) negatively affects rents. Primary roads are negatively valued in San José because they are associated with contamination and noise; but secondary, urban, and neighborhood roads are positively valued. It is surprising to find that proximity to primary and secondary schools has a negative (but statistically insignificant) effect, and proximity to fire departments is negatively valued (perhaps because of associated noise). Finally, rents decrease significantly if the census tract is classified as being of a low socioeconomic stratum.

Following Linneman (1980), the relative importance of housing and neighborhood amenities in determining rents is calculated as the ratio of the sum of the absolute beta coefficients for neighborhood amenities to the same sum for all the amenities included in the regression. The beta coefficients are a measure of the standardized impact of a variable, and are defined as $b_i (\sigma_I / \sigma_y)$. Neighborhood amenities explain 39.15 percent of the standardized variation of housing rents, which shows the importance of neighborhood amenities within San José.

Also examined is the distribution of the value of housing and neighborhood characteristics. For housing characteristics, the mean and the median differ by less than 1 percent; and the distances from the median to the first quartile and third quartile are similar, indicating a symmetric distribution. For neighborhood characteristics, however, the mean is 10 percent higher than the median, which implies that more than 50 percent of the neighborhoods are worse-off than the mean neighborhood characteristics. In addition, there is a wider gap between the median neighborhood and the neighborhood in the top quartile than between the median neighborhood and the neighborhood in the lowest quartile, indicating that some neighborhoods are significantly better off than most others in the metropolitan area. These results suggest that neighborhood characteristics create a regressive effect on welfare distribution.

Neighborhood Rankings for AMSJO

The value of the endowment of amenities offered by each district can be calculated by taking the vector of amenities. This value is taken as the QoL index to rank the districts considered. Three rankings are estimated: the first considers housing as well as neighborhood characteristics, the second considers only neighborhood characteristics, and the third considers only housing characteristics. Formally, the index is defined as

$$QLI_k = \sum_{i=1}^{I} f_i a_{ki}, \tag{6.4}$$

where f refers to the price of the amenity (uniform across urban cities, equilibrium value); a refers to the quantity of amenity i in urban neighborhood k; and I is the number of housing characteristics, neighborhood amenities, or both. The index is obtained for each census tract. For purposes of illustration, however, the index is aggregated at the district level by averaging the indexes of its constituent census tracts (so that districts easily can be identified by a name rather than a number).

Among the 51 districts in AMSJO, the value of the index based on housing and neighborhood characteristics ranges from $143 to $370, and the value of the index based on neighborhood characteristics ranges from –$67 to $27. Finally, the index based on housing characteristics ranges from $183 to $343.

Table 6.3 presents overall rankings of urban districts in AMSJO as well as decompositions into neighborhood and housing characteristics. The

Table 6.3 Ranking of Districts by Housing and Neighborhood Characteristics

District name	Housing and neighborhood characteristics		Neighborhood characteristics		Housing characteristics	
	Rank	Value	Rank	Value	Rank	Value
Sanchez	1	370	1	27	1	343
San Rafael	2	285	2	9	8	275
Mata Redonda	3	275	10	−23	2	299
Carmen	4	264	11	−24	3	287
San Vicente	5	258	8	−20	6	277
Anselmo Llorente	6	254	13	−28	4	281
San Isidro	7	245	3	−5	23	250
San Pedro	8	238	20	−32	10	271
San Juan	9	237	16	−30	11	267
Sabanilla	10	237	35	−39	7	276
Colima	11	236	12	−27	14	263
Escazú	12	235	4	−11	26	246
Gravillas	13	235	25	−36	9	271
San Francisco de Dos Ríos	14	231	44	−47	5	278
San Antonio	15	228	30	−37	12	265
Patalillo	16	228	5	−15	28	242
Curridabat	17	226	33	−38	13	264
Mercedes	18	225	29	−37	15	262
San Rafael	19	224	14	−28	20	252
Calle Blancos	20	222	19	−32	17	254
Granadilla	21	222	18	−31	19	252
Pavas	22	220	9	−20	29	240
Mata de Platano	23	220	22	−34	18	254
Zapote	24	216	41	−45	16	260
Ipis	25	215	17	−30	27	246
Damas	26	212	26	−36	25	248
Guadalupe	27	211	37	−40	22	251

(continued)

Table 6.3 Ranking of Districts by Housing and Neighborhood Characteristics *(continued)*

District name	Housing and neighborhood characteristics		Neighborhood characteristics		Housing characteristics	
	Rank	Value	Rank	Value	Rank	Value
San Antonio	28	211	7	−19	35	230
Desamparados	29	207	39	−42	24	249
Hatillo	30	205	42	−46	21	251
Catedral	31	196	38	−41	31	238
San Rafael Arriba	32	194	31	−38	33	232
Leon XIII	33	193	24	−35	37	228
Merced	34	192	27	−37	36	228
San Rafael Abajo	35	189	43	−46	32	235
San Sebastián	36	188	45	−51	30	239
Uruca	37	181	21	−33	41	214
San Francsico	38	181	34	−39	39	220
Purral	39	180	23	−35	40	215
Salitrillos	40	176	6	−17	50	192
San Miguel	41	172	32	−38	44	210
Alajuelita	42	172	48	−59	34	230
Hospital	43	169	40	−42	42	211
San Jocesito	44	166	46	−54	38	220
San Felipe	45	165	36	−40	46	205
Cinco Esquinas	46	164	28	−37	48	200
Patarrá	47	154	15	−29	51	183
San Juan de Dios	48	148	50	−62	45	210
Tirrases	49	144	51	−67	43	211
Concepción	50	143	49	−61	47	204
Aserrí	51	143	47	−57	49	199

Source: Authors' compilation.
Note: Table presents estimates of equilibrium prices per month in 2000 dollars.

order is as expected. In particular, very rich urban neighborhoods (such as Sanchez, San Rafael, and Mata Redonda) appear at the top, and extremely poor urban neighborhoods (such as Salitrillos, Patarrá, and Concepción) appear lower in the rankings.

The data nonetheless provide some unexpected results. For example, Mata Redonda ranks 2nd in housing characteristics, but 10th in neighborhood amenities; Escazú ranks 26th in housing characteristics, but 4th in neighborhood amenities. Those findings suggest that public policy might be able to increase the welfare of people living in districts with low-value neighborhood characteristics.

Pricing Amenities in Different Urban Areas

Hedonic pricing methods again are used to test whether amenities are valued differently across urban areas. GAM is considered first, using results for both AMSJO and GAM.[2] The results are presented in table 6.4. Whereas safety, slope, and precipitation coefficients are very similar in both areas, volcanic eruption risk in GAM has a significantly greater effect than in AMSJO. The effect of national parks changes significantly in terms of both coefficient and prices. People in AMSJO place a significantly higher value on living close to a national park than do people in GAM. People inside AMSJO might be more restricted in their access to green areas, and therefore tend to value proximity to a national park more highly.

Distance to primary and secondary schools is insignificant in both areas. People in GAM tend to negatively value proximity to clinics, whereas such distances do not seem to matter in AMSJO. The sign of the coefficient for the distance to San José's Sabana Park is the same in both areas. However, the effect of proximity to the park is significantly lower in GAM.

The negative effects of primary roads are reduced significantly when GAM is considered. Although primary roads are associated with noise and pollution, they could facilitate transportation for areas farther from downtown. Secondary roads lose value, although small urban neighborhood roads have very similar coefficients.

Table 6.5 considers all urban areas in Costa Rica, measuring the prices of amenities by their effects on labor markets. As discussed above, amenities affect the amount of workers in an urban area; in turn, that affects wages. For example, when all urban areas are considered, the safety index seems not to correlate with rents. However, safety is significantly correlated with lower wages, meaning that people would have to accept lower wages to live in a safe neighborhood. This effect is significantly higher in urban areas.

However, amenities also could affect the location of firms, in turn affecting wages. Even though slopes seem irrelevant for rents when all urban areas are considered, they significantly affect the equilibrium wage. Because firms might tend to locate on plains, people actually may end up paying (through a reduction in their wages) for living in places with steep slopes.

In urban areas, the risk of being affected by a volcanic eruption decreases rents in a fashion similar to what was found previously. Wages, however, are not significantly affected. Flood risk significantly reduces wages as

Table 6.4 Regression Results and Price Amenities with Selection Decision for AMSJO and GAM

Amenities	AMSJO		GAM	
	b	*Price*	*b*	*Price*
Safety index	0.46***	7,953	0.52***	6,801
Slope degrees	−0.01***	−177	−0.01***	−165
Precipitation (mm^3)	−0.12**	−2,154	−0.10***	−1,283
Risk of being affected by an eruption	−0.13**	−2,316	−0.23***	−2,980
Log distance to national parks (km)	−1.25***	−21,589	−0.66***	−8,582
Log distance to clinics (km)	0.01	175	0.05***	678
Log distance to secondary schools (km)	0.02	364	0.00	−58
Log distance to primary schools (km)	0.00	59	−0.01	−68
Log distance to rivers (km)	0.06***	1,054	0.09***	1,201
Log distance to fire departments (km)	0.05**	968	0.07***	881
Log distance to Sabana Park (km)	−0.54***	−9,419	−0.54***	−7,025
Log distance to Peace Park (km)	1.35***	23,273	0.43***	5,663
Length of primary roads (km)	−0.46***	−7,974	−0.18***	−2,384
Length of secondary roads (km)	0.23***	4,098	0.08	1,092
Length of urban-neighborhood roads (km)	0.57***	9,785	0.39***	5,105
Tract qualified as poor	−0.35***	−6,133	−0.39***	−5,140
Relative importance of negative amenities (%)	39.15		29.7	
Lambda	0.1006		0.1217	

Source: Authors' compilation.

Note: AMSJO = metropolitan area of San José; GAM = greater metropolitan area of San José, including AMSJO; km = kilometer; mm^3 = cubic millimeter. Housing characteristics controlled. Prices are presented in 2000 colones, when C 308 = $1. The estimated coefficient has been specified to two decimal places.

*$p < .10$ **$p < .05$ ***$p < .01$.

Table 6.5 Regression Results and Price Amenities with Selection Decision

Amenities	All urban areas			Urban areas outside GAM		
	Monthly rents	Monthly wage	Price	Monthly rents	Monthly wage	Price
Safety index	-0.03	-25.24***	23,393	-0.03	-39.32***	30,079
Slope degrees	0.00	-0.40***	329	-0.01***	-0.46***	268
Precipitation (mm^3)	-0.09***	-0.96	-668	0.01	-1.33	1,112
Risk of being affected by an eruption	-0.22***	1.12	-5,380	0.15***	-3.52	3,993
Risk of being affected by flows	-0.06**	-7.67*	5,540	-0.09**	-13.17***	9,435
Log distance to earthquakes (km)	-0.06***	0.57	-856	0.16***	0.87**	657
Log distance to national parks (km)	-0.28***	-1.39*	-2,691	-0.17***	-1.76***	-37
Log distance to clinics (km)	0.03***	-2.91**	3,085	-0.01	-5.71	4,334
Log distance to secondary schools (km)	0.03***	-1.55	1,826	-0.05***	0.22	-592
Log distance to primary schools (km)	0.02***	-3.07*	3,192	0.10***	-2.35	2,616
Log distance to rivers (km)	0.07***	0.33	754	0.07***	-1.55	1,796

(continued)

Table 6.5 Regression Results and Price Amenities with Selection Decision *(continued)*

Amenities	All urban areas			Urban areas outside GAM		
	Monthly rents	Monthly wage	Price	Monthly rents	Monthly wage	Price
Log distance to fire departments (km)	0.02***	4.05***	3,853	−0.06***	−3.66***	2,332
Length of primary roads (km)	0.07*	−1.13	1,912	0.56***	−0.85	5,280
Length of secondary roads (km)	0.06	1.89	−1,194	0.27***	2.73*	118
Length of small urban-neighborhood roads (km)	0.24***	−1.16***	4,659	0.12***	−1.02***	1,811
Tract qualified as poor	−0.28	−4.25***	−1,334	−0.37***	−5.87**	1,458
Relative importance of negative amenities (%)	22.71	12.01		27.73	17.28	
Lambda	0.09	0.41		0.11	0.41	

Source: Authors' compilation.

Note: AMSJO = metropolitan area of San José; GAM = greater metropolitan area of San José, including AMSJO; km = kilometer; mm³ = cubic millimeter. We used a GAM dummy for all urban areas. We did not consider a GAM dummy when calculating the relative importance of neighborhood amenities for all urban areas for comparison reasons. The wage effect was deflated to 2000 colones (C 308 = $1). Housing characteristics controlled.

*p < .10 **p < .05 ***p < .01.

well as rents, so that people who want to live in a flood-prone place would actually have to pay to do so. Markets thus can be seen as reacting to risks and reducing the negative impact of this type of natural disaster.

It is surprising to note that distance from earthquake sites has a negative coefficient. This means that the farther from an earthquake, the lower the rents. If, for example, house structures are resistant to earthquakes in GAM, the effect of earthquakes might be zero and the coefficient may be capturing some unobservable effect. However, when we look at urban areas outside GAM, the negative effect of earthquakes is shown to be significant.

The effects of roads also are interesting. Primary roads have a positive effect on rents in all urban areas, especially in those outside GAM. The positive effect of primary roads—reducing transportation costs—is greater than the negative effects of pollution and noise cited in AMSJO, with an increase in price from C 1,912 to C 5,280. The implicit price of an abundance of secondary roads also increases when only areas outside GAM are considered (from having a negative value of C 1,194 to having a positive value of C 118). Small urban neighborhood roads become less important in urban areas outside GAM.

Finally, as expected, being in a poor neighborhood decreases rents (even more so outside GAM); but it also decreases wages. This negative effect on wages is larger outside GAM, switching the sign of the price (from having a negative value of C 1,334 to having a positive value of C 1,458). An average household will end up paying for living in a poor neighborhood because of the lower wage level they will be able to access.

It also would be interesting to include other amenities—such as garbage collection, provision of social events, proximity to coasts, and performance measures of health and education—to improve the precision of the index.

The LS Approach

Research for this section included a survey on life satisfaction issues and QoL. The sample of 748 individuals is representative of AMSJO for socioeconomic strata (low, medium, and high) and for counties. For a detailed explanation of the survey, see Hall, Madrigal, and Robalino (2008).

The survey included a question on subjective valuation of QoL: "In general, on a scale of 1 to 10, with 1 being the lowest score and 10 the highest score, how high or low is your quality of life?" Figure 6.1 shows the distribution of responses, with a mean of approximately 8.15 and a standard deviation of 1.39.

Table 6.6 breaks down responses by county, finding considerable dispersion in the valuation of QoL across counties. The QoL subjective valuation ranges from 7.67 to 8.68, almost one unit for the averages. Expressing the standard deviation in mean terms, the relative variation ranges from 0.11 to 0.21 mean units.

Figure 6.1 Distribution of the Subjective Valuation of Life Satisfaction

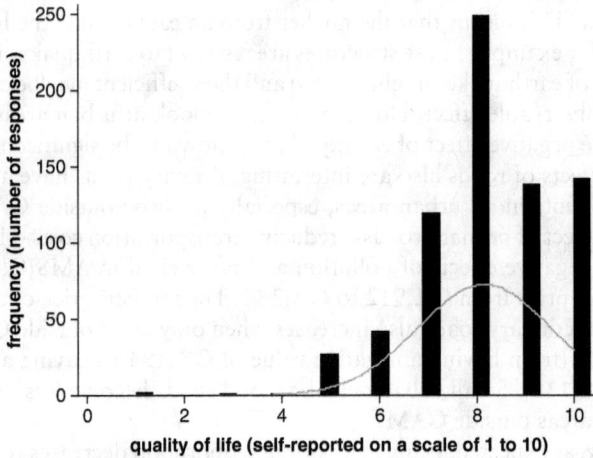

Source: Authors' illustration.

Additional survey questions involved housing, safety, health, and neighborhood satisfaction. The responses are studied using formal methods proposed by van Praag and Ferrer-i-Carbonell (2004). Individual regressions and explanatory variables presented for each component of life satisfaction are found in Hall, Madrigal, and Robalino (2008). Overall QoL is explained using these four components, and tables 6.7 and 6.8 summarize the results. Finally, overall QoL is explained using the same explanatory variables as in each of the four individual satisfaction domains.

Housing, health service, safety, and neighborhood satisfaction are then used as explanatory variables for overall QoL. A variable, Z, obtained from a first components analysis of these four elements, is used to disentangle potential endogenous effects (see van Praag and Ferrer-i-Carbonell 2004 for details). All of the variables are positively associated with overall QoL valuation, and all but neighborhood satisfaction are statistically significant (see table 6.7). Table 6.8 uses predicted values of these four components obtained from the previous four regressions; and, under these conditions, shows that health satisfaction, in particular, becomes insignificant.

Finally, variables previously used to explain each of the satisfaction domains are now used to explain overall QoL, with results presented in Table 6.9. The presence of gangs decreases QoL, and life satisfaction is increased by the quality of policing. Housing characteristics have an important impact on overall valuation of life.

Table 6.6 Descriptive Statistics of the Subjective Valuation of QoL, by County

Statistic	San José	Escazú	Desamparados	Aserrí	Goicochea	Alajuelita	Coronado	Tibás	Moravia	Montes de Oca	Curridabat	Total
Observations (n)	180	40	155	62	89	67	15	51	13	37	36	745
Mean of QoL response	8.06	8	8.01	8.11	8.27	8.06	7.67	8.61	8.38	8.68	8.42	8.15
Standard deviation	1.61	1.4	1.42	1.24	1.28	1.4	1.63	1.02	0.96	1	1.3	1.39
Standard deviation/mean	0.2	0.17	0.18	0.15	0.15	0.17	0.21	0.12	0.11	0.12	0.15	0.17

Source: Authors' compilation.
Note: QoL = quality of life.

Table 6.7 LS Regression Explained by Other Subjective Valuations, Model COLS

Variable	Coefficient
Housing satisfaction	0.19***
Safety satisfaction	0.09**
Health facilities satisfaction	0.08**
Neighborhood satisfaction	0.07
Z (first component analysis)	–0.14
Constant	5.35***
Observations (n)	635
Log likelihood	–1,083

Source: Authors' compilation.
Note: COLS = cardinal ordinary least squares; LS = life satisfaction.
**$p < .05$ ***$p < .01$.

Table 6.8 LS Regression Explained by Predicted Subjective Valuations, Model COLS

Variable	Coefficient
Housing satisfaction	0.31***
Safety satisfaction	0.11*
Health facilities satisfaction	–0.04
Neighborhood satisfaction	0.6
Z (first component analysis)	0.24***
Constant	4.55***
Observations (n)	633
Log likelihood	–1,064

Source: Authors' compilation.
Note: COLS = cardinal ordinary least squares; LS = life satisfaction.
*$p < .10$ ***$p < .01$.

Conclusion

Wages and rent differentials across neighborhoods were used to estimate price amenities. For AMSJO, the price of safety is positive—that is, safer neighborhoods are more valuable. Average slopes negatively affect the value of the neighborhood: on average, the steeper a neighborhood is, the lower its value. Precipitation has a negative effect on the value of a house; and people value significantly less those areas with a high risk of being affected by volcanic eruption.

Table 6.9 LS Regression Explained by Objective Variables, Model COLS

Variable	Coefficient
Sex (male = 1)	−0.01
ln (age)	2.42
ln (age squared)	−0.35
ln (children in the household + 1)	0.01
Log of income	0.03
Log of number of people in the household	−0.21
Number of rooms	0.03
Robbed in the last six months	0.01
Presence of vandalism	−0.09
Presence of auto theft	0.09
Presence of dangerous driving	−0.08
Presence of dangerous-looking individuals	0.14
Presence of gangs	−0.36***
Police quality	0.20*
Safety index	−0.24
Time to clinic	−0.01
Needed medical attention	−0.13
Reported not receiving adequate attention	−0.26
Time to reach a park	0
Distance to fire departments (km)	0.00*
Distance to primary schools (km)	0
Distance to secondary schools (km)	0
Distance to clinics (km)	0
Length of primary roads (km)	0.00**
Length of secondary roads (km)	0
Length of neighborhood and urban roads (km)	0
Distance to national parks (km)	0
Average slope	0
Floor made of cement	−0.32*
Floor made of wood	−0.41*
Rented house	−0.33**
	(continued)

Table 6.9 LS Regression Explained by Objective Variables,
Model COLS *(continued)*

Variable	Coefficient
Constant	4.31
Observations (n)	671
Log likelihood	–1,122

Source: Authors' compilation.
Note: COLS = cardinal ordinary least squares; km = kilometer; LS = life
satisfaction. Dummy left out for type of floors is ceramic floor.
$*p < .10 **p < .05 ***p < .01$.

Additionally, people value living close to national parks. Proximity
to rivers negatively affects the level of rents—perhaps reflecting people's
reaction to the highly contaminated rivers inside the city. The presence of
primary roads is negatively valued; however, the presence of urban and
neighborhood roads is positively valued within San José.

Neighborhood amenities explain 39 percent of the standardized variation of rents. The distribution of the contributions of housing and neighborhood characteristics to the level of rents was also considered. For
housing characteristics, the mean and the median are very similar (less
than 1 percent difference). This is not the case for neighborhood characteristics. First, the mean is 10 percent higher than the median, which
implies that more than 50 percent of neighborhoods are worse off than the
mean neighborhood characteristics. Second, there is a wider gap between
the median neighborhood and the neighborhood in the top quartile than
between the median neighborhood and the neighborhood in the lowest
quartile. This is evidence that some neighborhoods are significantly better
off than most of the neighborhoods in the metropolitan area—suggesting
that neighborhood characteristics create a regressive effect on welfare
distribution.

Perhaps it is surprising that districts like Mata Redonda rank very
highly in housing characteristics, but poorly in neighborhood amenities;
whereas districts like Escazú rank poorly in housing characteristics, but
highly in neighborhood amenities. These findings reveal the potential
of indirect policy measures to reduce inequality in urban areas through
improvement of neighborhood amenities.

Wages represent an important and possibly underappreciated component of implicit price amenities. In fact, 12 percent and 17 percent of the
standard deviation of the wage can be explained by environmental amenities in all urban areas and in urban areas outside GAM, respectively.
For some disamenities—such as the risk of being affected by floods—
firms' avoidance of certain areas plays so important a role that prices of
the amenities switch sign when wage effects are considered. Individuals

actually would end up paying to live in an area with a risk of being affected by a flood because wages are significantly lower in such an area. This finding implies that the decisions firms make regarding their locations might reduce the effect of disasters because probabilities of these disasters change and firms change location (provided full information is available).

Differences in how people value amenities also are found to be important. Prices change in different areas, according to differences in demand. For instance, in more sparse urban areas, distance to national parks becomes less important; distance to primary roads, however, becomes more important.

Further regressions on aspects of QoL, as well as overall valuation of QoL, yield the expected results. However, results change when predicted (instead of real) values of those domains are used: health satisfaction, for instance, becomes insignificant. On that basis, housing and safety satisfaction appear to be the key components in determining life satisfaction.

Finally considered are the variables that make up the domains used to explain QoL. Although income seems to be insignificant, it appears that the factors affecting QoL are being controlled for, and those factors must be purchased. In other words, income alone might not generate QoL, but the goods bought by that income do generate it.

Whether the LS approach and hedonic price approach are comparable remains under discussion. One method might be better for estimating prices of specific goods than the other method. The better uses might depend on the type of good, whether the assumptions of the hedonic price method hold (labor and housing market conditions), and whether the assumptions of the LS approach hold. Here, the use of both methods finds housing and safety characteristics to be highly valued in Costa Rica.

The findings of this study will enable policy makers at both the national and local levels to identify which urban areas are disadvantaged, and to determine what actions will be most effective for improving the QoL there. The information generated may help individuals and firms make more informed decisions concerning where to live or locate and what to demand as a community from local and central governments.

Notes

1. Note that choosing this functional form is more general than just taking the logs. We are allowing the data to show us if taking the logs ($\lambda = 0$) is better than other specifications ($\lambda \neq 0$).

2. In this analysis, only the rent regression was considered because when we look at one city, anyone living within GAM can access any job position in GAM. So, amenity prices will be reflected only in the housing market, not in the labor market. Consistent with this argument, neighborhood amenities did not have any effect on wages when only considering observations within GAM or AMSJO.

References

Blomquist, Glenn C., Mark C. Berger, and John P. Hoehn. 1988. "New Estimates of Quality of Life in Urban Areas." *American Economic Review* 78 (1): 89–107.

Di Tella, Rafael, and Robert MacCulloch. 2006. "Some Uses of Happiness Data in Economics." *Journal of Economic Perspectives* 20 (1): 25–46.

Gyourko, Joseph, Matthew Kahn, and Joseph Tracy. 1999. "Quality of Life and Environmental Comparisons." In *Handbook of Regional and Urban Economics, Volume 3: Applied Urban Economics*, ed. Paul Cheshire and Edwin S. Mills, 1413–54. Amsterdam, The Netherlands: Elsevier Science.

Hall, Luis J., Róger Madrigal, and Juan Robalino. 2008. "Quality of Life in Urban Neighborhoods in Costa Rica." Research Network Working Paper R-563, Research Department, Inter-American Development Bank, Washington, DC.

Heckman, James J. 1979. "Sample Selection Bias as a Specification Error." *Econometrica* 47 (1): 153–62.

INEC (Instituto Nacional de Estadísticas y Censos). 2000. Censo de población y vivienda del año 2000. INEC, San José, Costa Rica.

Kahneman, Daniel, and Alan B. Krueger. 2006. "Developments in the Measurement of Subjective Well-Being." *Journal of Economic Perspectives* 20 (1): 3–24.

Linneman, Peter. 1980. "Some Empirical Results on the Nature of the Hedonic Price Function for the Urban Housing Market." *Journal of Urban Economics* 8 (1): 47–68.

MIDEPLAN (Ministerio de Planificación Nacional y Política Económica). 2007. "Índice de Desarrollo Social 2007." MIDEPLAN, San José, Costa Rica.

van Praag, Bernard M.S., and Ada Ferrer-i-Carbonell. 2004. *Happiness Quantified: A Satisfaction Calculus Approach*. New York: Oxford University Press.

7

Influence of Individual, Urban, and Civil Society Spheres on Quality of Life in Metropolitan Lima, Peru

Lorena Alcázar and Raúl Andrade

Quality of life (QoL) is increasingly being examined using social and political variables other than consumption that may have an effect on individuals' levels of satisfaction or well-being. The related literature has focused mostly on cities in developed countries, discussing such determinants of life satisfaction as personal achievement, health, perceived safety, personal relationships, community membership, and future security.[1]

In recent decades, many Latin American cities have experienced rapid growth accompanied by social problems, including inadequate basic services, poor provision of public goods, increases in crime and in drug consumption and dealing, lack of urban planning and organization, and poor transportation. For example, Lima, the capital of Peru, has experienced rapid, chaotic, and unequal growth, mainly through waves of migration; its population has grown almost tenfold in the last five decades.

Measuring individuals' QoL in cities like Lima is both an interesting challenge from an academic perspective and a crucial input for policy

The authors thank Eduardo Lora, Andrew Powell, Pablo Sanguinetti, and Bernard M.S. van Praag for their very valuable comments on previous drafts of this chapter. They are also grateful to the Latin American centers participating in this project for comments and suggestions in the start-up and preliminary drafts discussion seminars. Juan Manuel del Pozo and Luis Escobedo provided excellent research assistance for the project.

making. Moreover, disentangling the effects of different factors on an individual's perceived QoL is important for policy making. Individuals may increase their QoL by making individual decisions related to variables that are under their control (hereafter called the *individual sphere*), such as income-generating activities. But an individual's QoL also may be influenced by such services as security against crime or efficient transportation systems provided by local authorities (hereafter called the *urban sphere*). Finally, how people interact with their neighbors may be a source of satisfaction with QoL (hereafter called the *civil society/trust sphere*). Studying the contributions of these three spheres will provide important insights concerning the determinants of QoL in cities undergoing rapid growth.

This chapter thus has three main objectives: (1) to provide estimates of QoL indicators and indexes for urban neighborhoods of metropolitan Lima; (2) to construct QoL indexes for three districts of Lima, identifying their main driving forces (socioeconomic versus other urban and social capital dimensions); and (3) to evaluate how the individual, urban, and civil society/trust spheres influence the constructed QoL index and how that influence differs across the three districts.

The core information used for the study has been collected through a survey in three districts of metropolitan Lima: La Victoria, Los Olivos, and Villa El Salvador. The collected data permit the computation of QoL indexes, combining multiple factors into a one-dimensional measure by combining information on self-reported life satisfaction. When the overall QoL index is constructed, the contributions of different dimensions to the index are evaluated.

Context

With almost 8.5 million inhabitants, Lima has experienced a long period of intensive growth. Its population accounted for 13 percent of Peru's population in 1940 and for 30 percent by 2005. The city also has expanded in territory, developing a very large periphery. Despite the territorial expansion, the population density in Lima is 219 people per square kilometer; in contrast, the average density for Peru is 15 people per square kilometer (CAPECO 2006, 13). This growth is mainly the result of migration from rural areas, starting in 1920 (Gonzales de Olarte 1992).

The metropolitan area of Lima is composed of 43 districts in a territory of 2,800 square kilometers. However, some of the districts in the peripheral area of Lima are predominantly rural, and some districts located near the coast are mostly seasonal residence districts. The urban agglomeration of these districts is not articulated with the complexity of metropolitan Lima. For this reason, only information from the 33 districts forming the conurbation of Lima is considered in this study. The average population in the districts belonging to the conurbation of metropolitan Lima is 203,473 inhabitants. The three districts considered here have higher than the average population for the districts of Lima, but they are of different relative sizes among them. Villa El Salvador has 402,140 inhabitants, compared with 208,184 in La Victoria and 313,613 in Los Olivos.

Districts' socioeconomic conditions can be examined by considering how many people belong to each different socioeconomic level (SEL). The levels range in descending order from A to E, and are based on an index of households' information on combined income, labor market activities, assets ownership, and dwelling characteristics (see figure 7.1). Among the districts considered here, Villa El Salvador has Lima's lowest percentage of people in SELs A and B (0.1 percent), whereas 20.7 percent of people in Los Olivos and 32.6 percent of people in La Victoria belong to those two strata. Concerning the lowest SELs (D or E), Villa El Salvador has 68.3 percent (Lima's third-highest proportion), compared with 37.4 percent in Los Olivos and 14.0 percent in La Victoria. A complete listing of the districts' SELs is found in table 7.1.

Regarding the related indicators of average income per capita and education, metropolitan Lima as a whole shows an average income per capita of S/.688 per month (approximately $230). In Villa El Salvador and Los Olivos, the amount is lower than average ($203 and $219, respectively); it is higher in La Victoria ($281). As expected, the level of educational attainment is positively correlated with the level of wealth in the districts. In the three districts under analysis, the percentage of heads of household with higher education is 43 percent in Los Olivos, 34 percent in La Victoria, and 21 percent in Villa El Salvador.

Indicators regarding other dimensions of QoL (discussed in greater detail in Alcázar and Andrade 2008) include crime, municipal revenue and spending per capita, number of health centers per 1,000 inhabitants, and number of beneficiaries of the Glass of Milk Program (which works to improve nutrition among poor people) per 1,000 inhabitants. An overview of all these indicators shows a highly unequal distribution of wealth among districts. In general, districts in central areas are significantly richer than districts on the periphery. Although most variables related to wealth and income (for example, level of education, health services) are highly correlated among the districts of Lima, other indicators—such as crime rates—are not so correlated.

In many ways, the districts considered are representative of Lima. Los Olivos and Villa El Salvador, like most districts on the periphery, grew as a result of Andean migration to Lima. In contrast, centrally located La Victoria is one of the oldest districts. Examining these three districts also permits geographic comparison. Los Olivos and Villa El Salvador are typically considered part of the periphery, whereas La Victoria clearly represents the center. Better access to public services and transportation, as well as a greater number of police officers and general hospitals, should be found in La Victoria. As shown in table 7.2, this relationship generally exists, even though La Victoria's SEL profile is very similar to that of Los Olivos.

Figure 7.1 Distribution of Population, by Socioeconomic Level, Metropolitan Lima

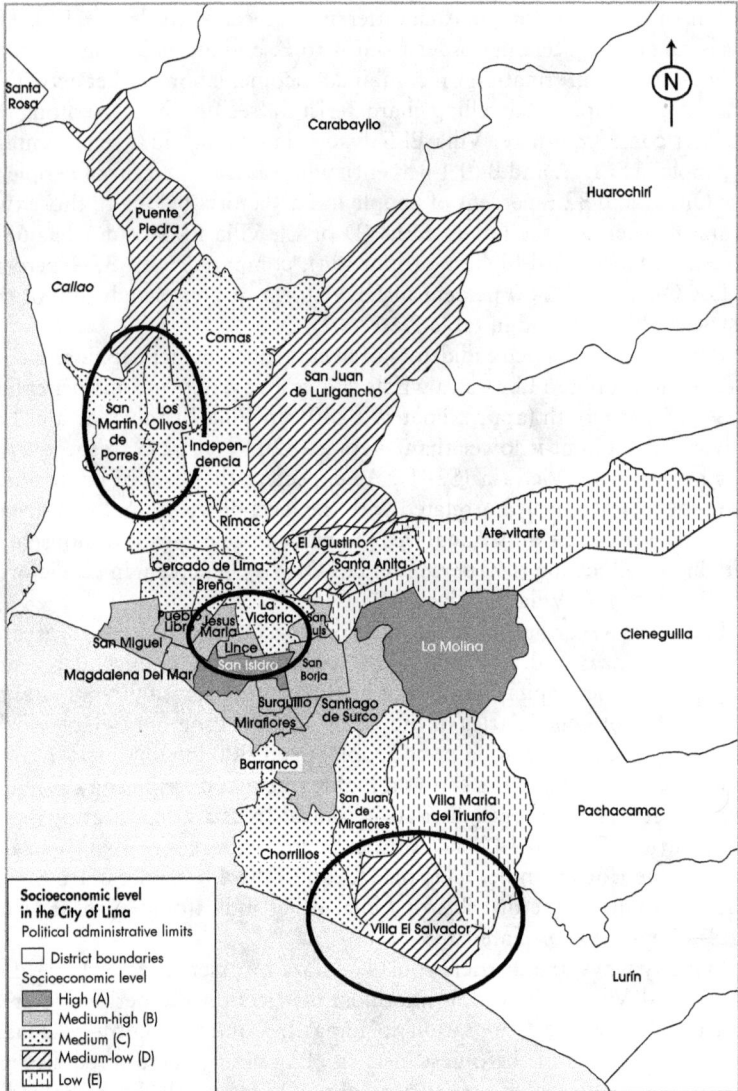

Source: Alcázar and Andrade 2008.

Table 7.1 Socioeconomic Levels of Populations in Districts under Analysis, 2005

Socioeconomic level	Lima	Los Olivos	La Victoria	Villa El Salvador
Population (n)	7,691,333	313,613	208,184	402,140
Level A (%)	3.4	0.1	0.3	0
Level B (%)	12.5	20.6	32.3	0.1
Level C (%)	35.3	41.8	53.4	31.6
Level D (%)	30.6	31.1	11.9	48.0
Level E (%)	18.2	6.3	2.1	20.3

Source: Ipsos APOYO Opinión y Mercado poll and the 2005 Peruvian census.

Table 7.2 Indicators for Districts under Analysis
Percent

Indicator	Los Olivos	La Victoria	Villa El Salvador
Households with water supply	93.0	81.0	78.0
Children not attending school	4.1	3.3	4.5
Households with at least one unsatisfied basic need[a]	28.4	21.9	48.4
Dwellings with infrastructure deficiencies	7.0	1.6	29.4

Source: National Statistical Institute.

a. This indicator is measured as the proportion of households in at least one of the following situations: the materials of house walls, roofs, and floors are not of an appropriate material; there are more than three people per room; there is no sewerage service; at least one child between 6 and 17 years of age is not going to school; or there are three non–income earners per each income earner (when head of households has completed primary education or less).

Including Los Olivos and Villa El Salvador also permits a comparison of different urban development schemes. Los Olivos belongs to north Lima—an area of the city that, during the last 15 years, has come to be considered very important in terms of economic expansion (especially in financial and commercial services). This area's population consists largely of small industrialists and entrepreneurs. In contrast, the districts of the south, especially Villa El Salvador, have a tradition of collective action based on the organization of economic activities by the state and local governments. Districts like Los Olivos are considered representative of the market model of development; Villa El Salvador is considered representative of a model based on collective economy, where issues related to civil society and trust are thought to be key.

Overview of the Survey

The survey conducted for this study had three main goals: (1) to collect objective information on QoL indicators by measuring aspects related to urban and neighborhood characteristics, such as access to green areas, presence of crime, public and social participation, and access to public services; (2) to collect information on perceptions of access to and quality of public goods; and (3) to ask respondents to rank different characteristics and services (dimensions of QoL) in terms of the importance that these dimensions have for them. The survey also collected information (based on surveyors' direct observation) about the characteristics of the blocks where surveyed households were located.

The survey considered the following 10 topics[2]:

1. household income and socioeconomic conditions
2. housing characteristics
3. safety (including crime, drugs, police, and so forth)
4. health care and health facilities
5. education and education facilities
6. green areas
7. cleaning conditions of streets
8. commuting and transportation
9. recreational activities
10. public participation and social interaction.

Regarding the sample design, four important features should be noted:

1. The universe of the study comprised the heads of households (or partners) of both sexes who reside in the districts of La Victoria, Los Olivos, and Villa El Salvador.
2. The sampling method considered stratification by SELs, with computerized random selection of blocks and systematic selection of dwellings within each block.
3. The sample size was 604 surveys, distributed evenly among the three districts.
4. The margin of error is ±4, assuming a confidence level of 95 percent, the greatest dispersion of results ($p = 0.5$), and a complete probabilistic selection of the interviewees.

As shown in table 7.3, because these three districts are relatively poor, most surveyed individuals belong to SELs C (44 percent) and D (42 percent). Of the total sample, 54 percent declared themselves to be head of the household, and 38 percent were male. Finally, the average age of respondent was 43, ranging from 18 to 86 years of age.

Methodology

QoL is a concept that needs to be measured using indicators of a variety of dimensions other than income and socioeconomic conditions. When objective measures of indicators of different dimensions are available, a key issue is how to combine these indicators into a single QoL index. This study assumes that QoL is a linear combination of these objective indicators. That is, QoL can be approximated by a weighted average of the indicators.

In particular, let there be K indicators representing the individual sphere, J indicators representing the urban sphere, and N indicators representing the civil society/trust sphere. Let H_k be the kth indicator of the individual sphere ($k = 1, \ldots, K$); let D_j be the jth indicator of the urban sphere ($j = 1, \ldots, J$); and T_n be the nth indicator of the civil society/trust sphere ($n = 1, \ldots, N$).

Table 7.3 Characteristics of the Sample

Characteristic	Total (n)	Percent
All surveys	604	100
Surveys by district		
La Victoria	201	33
Los Olivos	201	33
Villa El Salvador	202	33
Surveys by socioeconomic level		
Levels A/B	85	14
Level C	267	44
Level D	252	42
Surveys by gender		
Females	376	62
Males	228	38

Source: Authors' compilation.

The aggregated QoL index at the individual level will be[3]

$$QoL = \sum_{k=1}^{K} \hat{\alpha}_k H_k + \sum_{j=1}^{J} \hat{\beta}_j D_j + \sum_{n=1}^{N} \hat{\phi}_n T_n. \tag{7.1}$$

Key components in equation (7.1) are the weights $\hat{\alpha}_k, \hat{\beta}_j,$ and $\hat{\phi}_n$ for $k = 1, \ldots, K, j = 1, \ldots, J,$ and $n = 1, \ldots, N$, respectively. They are critical in computing QoL as the weighted average of the indicators.

Computation of the weights is based on the methodological insights provided by the literature on life satisfaction. This literature is based on empirical studies focusing on the measurement of well-being and happiness, and on their relationships with utility (Baker and Palmer 2006; Frey and Stutzer 2002; Oswald 1997; Tiliouine, Cummins, and Davern 2006; van Praag and Baarsma 2005; van Praag and Ferrer-i-Carbonell 2008; van Praag, Frijters, and Ferrer-i-Carbonell 2003) and different economic and social indicators (Cattaneo et al. 2007; Di Tella and MacCulloch 2006; Easterlin 1974; Frey, Luechinger, and Stutzer 2004). Intuitively, the idea is to exploit the association between a measure of utility defined as self-reported life satisfaction or happiness (Frey, Luechinger, and Stutzer 2004), and indicators at the household and district levels. The statistical influence of each indicator on self-reported life satisfaction will be computed by means of regression analysis, as the following equation shows:

$$s_{id} = c + \delta X_{id} + \sum_{j=1}^{J} \beta_{jd} D_{jd} + \sum_{n=1}^{N} \phi_{nd} T_{jd} + \sum_{k=1}^{K} \alpha_{ki} H_{ki} + v_{id}, \tag{7.2}$$

where self-reported life satisfaction is denoted by S_{id}, and X_{id} is a list of control variables. The rest of the variables are defined as shown in equation (7.1).[4] Computing this regression yields estimates of the parameters β, ϕ, and α, which will then be used to construct the index using equation (7.1).

Two issues specific to this study methodology are important to mention:

1. Regarding the life satisfaction approach, as the dependent variable in regression (7.2) we used a categorical variable taking only integer values between 1 and 10 (responses to the question asking for a ranking of overall satisfaction with QoL). Thus, an ordered logit specification is methodologically appropriate. However, we also present ordinary least squares (OLS) estimates, given that results are easier to interpret and weights can be obtained directly because there is only one potential outcome to predict. In the case of the ordered logit specification, given that there are 10 categories, there are 10 possible outcomes and we would have to compute 10 outcome-specific sets of weights.

2. An alternative method to deal with the categorical dependent variable is based on taking advantage of its implicit cardinality properties. This is obtained by transforming the categorical variable, assuming that it follows a standard normal distribution, and estimating the resulting model by OLS. This method, called cardinal OLS (COLS) is presented in detail in van Praag and Ferrer-i-Carbonell (2008). Alternative estimates found through this method are also presented.

Regarding the explanatory variables—the QoL indicators—given the wide scope of this study, many indicators are conceptually important to consider. However, including so many explanatory variables in the regression may not be desirable because most of the indicators may be highly correlated. Two alternative approaches were used to deal with this issue. First, we selected only the objective variables that have a statistically significant association between the dimensions to which they belong and the dimension-specific level of satisfaction (approximately 20 objective variables). Second, we computed dimension-specific regressions (presented in the next section), and then used the estimated dimension-specific predicted values as independent variables in the overall QoL regression (a method that yields 10 indicators, 1 for each dimension).

QoL Regressions

The first measure of QoL provided by the survey is given by the direct answers to the following question: "On a scale from 1 to 10, where 1 is totally unsatisfied and 10 is totally satisfied, how satisfied are you with your overall quality of life?" The mean value of this measure, self-reported QoL, is 6.05 (with a standard deviation of 2.10). When it is conditioned by the districts (shown in the upper panel of figure 7.2), the district with the highest QoL is Villa El Salvador (6.27); it is followed by La Victoria (6.17) and Los Olivos (5.73). This result is somewhat surprising because, as discussed above, Villa El Salvador has the largest proportion of poor population and greater needs than the other districts studied.

The lower panel of figure 7.2 shows the distribution of self-reported QoL in the overall sample and in each district, with the greatest dispersion in Villa El Salvador. This distribution means that although there is a peak in self-reported satisfaction in Villa El Salvador at the value 8 (compared with approximately 5–6 in La Victoria and Los Olivos), there are also more people reporting lower values. In Los Olivos, there is also an important accumulation of frequencies below the middle of the scale (5), and La Victoria's distribution is skewed toward the higher portion of the scale.

Figure 7.2 Self-Reported Satisfaction with QoL, by District, Mean, and Distribution

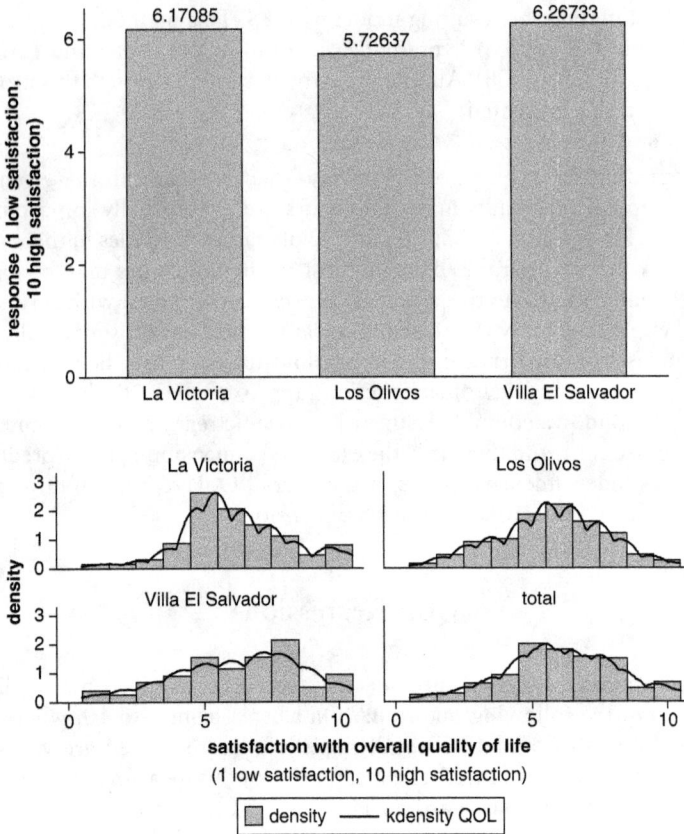

Source: Authors' estimations.
Note: QoL = quality of life.

Figure 7.3 shows self-reported QoL conditioned on SELs. Clearly, belonging to higher SELs is associated with greater QoL. It should be noted that there appears to be an inconsistency between this finding and the aforementioned district-based results because Villa El Salvador is the district with the highest proportion of its population in the lowest SELs. According to figure 7.3, it should be the district with lower self-reported QoL. This inconsistency suggests that this subjective measure is partly related to aspects of daily life that are not observed and, therefore, not considered as prior determinants of QoL by the researcher.

Figure 7.3 Self-Reported Satisfaction with Overall QoL, by Socioeconomic Level

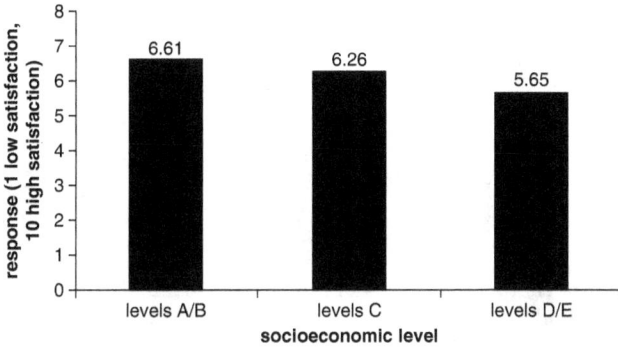

Source: Authors' estimations.
Note: QoL = quality of life.

Explanatory Variables: QoL Indicators

Each of the tables in this section considers a different QoL indicator. The tables present three specifications for each dimension, in accordance with the discussion in the methodology section: column (1) presents the results using an ordered logit specification, column (2) uses OLS, and column (3) uses COLS. A later section will select some of these objective indicators to find their statistical association with the overall self-reported QoL measure.

Individual sphere. As noted above, the dimensions in the individual sphere include income, housing infrastructure, health, and education. Table 7.4 presents the results concerning the income dimension. The dependent variable is the reported "satisfaction with family income." As the table shows, variables traditionally associated with life satisfaction are statistically significant. Satisfaction with income decreases with age, and it does so at a positive rate. Also, having a partner is statistically positively correlated with income satisfaction; the proportion of children is negatively correlated with income satisfaction. Specifically, the proportion of children between 6 and 18 years of age has a coefficient that is negative and statistically significant.

The four objective indicators are significant for all specifications. Family per capita income, being employed (either in an independent or dependent regimen), and having proportionally more economically contributing members of the household positively correlate with satisfaction with family

Table 7.4 Self-Reported Satisfaction with Income

Explanatory variable	(1) Ordered logit	(2) OLS	(3) COLS
Sex of respondent	0.2278 (0.1599)	0.2105 (0.1845)	0.0672 (0.0603)
Age of respondent	−0.0858*** (0.0319)	−0.0883** (0.0361)	−0.0304** (0.0118)
Age of respondent^2	0.0008** (0.0003)	0.0009** (0.0004)	0.0003** (0.0001)
Completed secondary education	0.1765 (0.1777)	0.1548 (0.20448)	0.0311 (0.0668)
Proportion of children between 0 and 5 years	−1.1193 (0.7814)	−1.2270 (0.9045)	−0.4113 (0.2954)
Proportion of children between 6 and 18 years	−1.4710** (0.6166)	−1.7086** (0.7057)	−0.5650** (0.2305)
Respondent has a partner	0.3387* (0.1807)	0.4005* (0.2086)	0.1221* (0.0681)
Familial income per capita	0.9299*** (0.1471)	1.0574*** (0.1654)	0.3308*** (0.0540)
Number of independent workers	0.8030*** (0.2475)	0.9087*** (0.2878)	0.3049*** (0.0940)
Number of dependent workers	1.0797*** (0.2332)	1.1662*** (0.2619)	0.3938*** (0.08553)
Rate of economic dependence	0.5590** (0.2554)	0.6447** (0.2966)	0.2129** (0.0969)
La Victoria	—	—	—
Los Olivos	−0.5256*** (0.1812)	−0.6770*** (0.2113)	−0.2139*** (0.0690)
Villa El Salvador	−0.3299* (0.1827)	−0.4237** (0.2121)	−0.1156* (0.0693)
Constant		0.4191 (1.3060)	−1.2243*** (0.4266)
Observations (n)	582	582	582
R^2		0.16	0.15

Source: Authors' calculations.
Note: — = not available; COLS = cardinal ordinary least squares; OLS = ordinary least squares. Standard errors appear in parentheses.
*p < .10 **p < .05 ***p < .01.

income. Finally, the coefficients related to district effects are negative and statistically significant.

Table 7.5 shows regressions for satisfaction with dwelling infrastructure. House ownership is significant and associated with approximately 0.76 additional points on the 1–10 scale, according to OLS results. Among the objective indicators shown in the table, water from a public network and adequate roof and wall materials increase satisfaction with dwelling conditions. District effects are not significant.

Table 7.6 presents results on health. Source of water again is included in this table, given that connection with a public water network is associated with controlling contagion. Other objective indicators considered are the time needed to reach the nearest health center and its location (in or out of the district). The results suggest that the availability of services in

Table 7.5 Self-Reported Satisfaction with House Infrastructure

Explanatory variable	(1) Ordered logit	(2) OLS	(3) COLS
Owns house	0.6078***	0.7710***	0.2781***
	(0.1689)	(0.2058)	(0.0731)
Water from public network in the house	0.8127***	1.0621***	0.3717***
	(0.2590)	(0.3178)	(0.1129)
Roof is made of appropriate material	0.5794***	0.7073***	0.2520***
	(0.1889)	(0.2319)	(0.0824)
Walls are made of appropriate material	0.8650***	1.0546***	0.3415***
	(0.1891)	(0.2296)	(0.0816)
La Victoria	—	—	—
Los Olivos	0.0854	0.0776	0.0198
	(0.1846)	(0.2301)	(0.0817)
Villa El Salvador	0.2417	0.2357	0.0942
	(0.2008)	(0.2455)	(0.0872)
Constant		3.7974***	–0.2248
		(0.9119)	(0.3239)
Observations (n)	604	604	604
R^2		0.20	0.18

Source: Authors' calculations.

Note: — = not available; COLS = cardinal ordinary least squares; OLS = ordinary least squares. Standard errors appear in parentheses. The following control variables were included in the regression, but their results are not reported: sex, age, age^2, educational level, whether respondent has a partner, proportion of children between 0 and 5 years and between 6 and 18 years, and whether the respondent is employed.

*p < .10 **p < .05 ***p < .01.

Table 7.6 Self-Reported Satisfaction with Health

Explanatory variable	(1) Ordered logit	(2) OLS	(3) COLS
Water from public network in the house	0.2855 (0.2597)	0.3449 (0.2917)	0.1105 (0.0941)
Time to the nearest health center	−0.1458 (0.1091)	−0.1688 (0.1241)	−0.0674* (0.0400)
Attends health center in the district	1.3230*** (0.3070)	1.4680*** (0.3526)	0.4142*** (0.1137)
La Victoria	—	—	—
Los Olivos	0.1064 (0.1854)	0.0310 (0.2120)	−0.0124 (0.0684)
Villa El Salvador	−0.0662 (0.1848)	−0.0713 (0.2100)	−0.0112 (0.0677)
Constant		6.1138*** (0.9712)	0.5430* (0.3132)
Observations (n)	584	584	584
R^2		0.08	0.07

Source: Authors' calculations.

Note: — = not available; COLS = cardinal ordinary least squares; OLS = ordinary least squares. Standard errors appear in parentheses. The following control variables were included in the regression, but their results are not reported: sex, age, age^2, educational level, whether respondent has a partner, proportion of children between 0 and 5 years and between 6 and 18 years, and whether the respondent is employed.

   $*p < .10$ $**p < .05$ $***p < .01$.

the district, rather than the location of services actually used, is important for satisfaction.

The correlation between objective variables and respondents' satisfaction with their children's quality of education is reported in table 7.7. First, the number of household members in school is positively and significantly correlated with satisfaction with the quality of education. Second, the number of children in the household attending public schools is significant and negatively correlated with satisfaction, possibly reflecting the extremely low quality of the Peruvian public education system.

Urban sphere. As noted above, the dimensions of this sphere include crime and safety, cleaning conditions of the streets, presence of parks and green areas, and the transportation system. Table 7.8 reports on satisfaction with neighborhood safety conditions. Three indicators—having been a victim of a robbery or an attempted robbery (both within the last month)

Table 7.7 Self-Reported Satisfaction with Quality of Education

Explanatory variable	(1) Ordered logit	(2) OLS	(3) COLS
Log of children at school	1.0745* (0.5616)	1.3136** (0.6313)	0.5279** (0.2358)
Log of children in public school	−1.1057*** (0.2427)	−1.2583*** (0.2684)	−0.4584*** (0.1003)
Time to get to school	−0.1563 (0.1653)	−0.0968 (0.1866)	−0.0654 (0.0697)
Number of family members studying in the district	−0.5787* (0.3245)	−0.4970 (0.3586)	−0.2174 (0.1340)
La Victoria	—	—	—
Los Olivos	−0.3072 (0.2237)	−0.3949 (0.2539)	−0.1919** (0.0949)
Villa El Salvador	0.0686 (0.2296)	0.1239 (0.2558)	0.0393 (0.0956)
Constant		8.3747*** (1.2720)	1.4848*** (0.4752)
Observations (n)	396	396	396
R^2		0.12	0.12

Source: Authors' calculations.

Note: — = not available; COLS = cardinal ordinary least squares; OLS = ordinary least squares. Standard errors appear in parentheses. The following control variables were included in the regression, but their results are not reported: sex, age, age^2, educational level, whether respondent has a partner, proportion of children between 0 and 5 years and between 6 and 18 years, and whether the respondent is employed.
$*p < .10 **p < .05 ***p < .01$.

and the presence of gangs in the neighborhood—are negatively correlated with satisfaction.

Table 7.9 reveals satisfaction with the cleaning conditions of the streets, and shows that daily cleaning has a positive influence. A positive assessment of conditions by the surveyor is also associated with satisfaction. These results suggest that street cleaning—not merely trash collection—is important. Location in Los Olivos also has a positive effect.

Results on satisfaction with parks and green areas are shown in table 7.10, and most of the variables considered are significant. Green areas in good condition have a positive impact on satisfaction, as does the interviewer's perception of those areas. It is surprising to note that satisfaction increases with time needed to go to the park, which means that living farther from the park enhances satisfaction. This result may reflect the fact

Table 7.8 Self-Reported Satisfaction with Neighborhood Safety
Conditions

Explanatory variable	(1) Ordered logit	(2) OLS	(3) COLS
Victim of a theft	−0.5043** (0.2326)	−0.5079** (0.2582)	−0.1315* (0.0786)
Victim of attempted robbery	−1.2664*** (0.2731)	−1.2750*** (0.2952)	−0.3847*** (0.0898)
Gangs exist in the neighborhood	−0.7014*** (0.2288)	−0.9221*** (0.2514)	−0.3142*** (0.0765)
La Victoria	—	—	—
Los Olivos	0.1473 (0.1811)	0.1346 (0.2020)	0.0274 (0.0615)
Villa El Salvador	0.2820 (0.1846)	0.2954 (0.2023)	0.0803 (0.0616)
Constant		6.0559*** (0.7917)	0.4462* (0.2409)
Observations (n)	588	588	588
R^2		0.10	0.10

Source: Authors' calculations.

Note: — = not available; COLS = cardinal ordinary least squares; OLS = ordinary least squares. Standard errors appear in parentheses. The following control variables were included in the regression, but their results are not reported: sex, age, age^2, educational level, whether respondent has a partner, proportion of children between 0 and 5 years and between 6 and 18 years, and whether the respondent is employed.

   *p < .10 **p < .05 ***p < .01.

that most parks in these districts are poorly maintained and may displease nearby residents.

Of the findings for public transportation presented in table 7.11, only district effects are significant: living in Los Olivos and Villa El Salvador positively influences satisfaction with transportation when compared with living in La Victoria. Because transportation is mostly a municipal phenomenon, other indicators lose their power when district effects are included. When district effects are excluded, however, the quality of roads and the time to commute to work have a positive impact. The latter surprising result suggests a relationship with individuals' decisions regarding where to work.

Civil society/trust sphere. Dimensions belonging to the civil society/ trust sphere are recreational activities and trust in neighbors. Results for satisfaction with recreational activities are presented in table 7.12.

Table 7.9 Self-Reported Satisfaction with Cleaning Conditions of the Streets

Explanatory variable	(1) Ordered logit	(2) OLS	(3) COLS
Trash is picked up daily	0.6355 (0.5094)	1.0095 (0.6417)	0.3167 (0.2052)
Streets are cleaned daily	2.3318*** (0.3653)	3.0646*** (0.4310)	0.9482*** (0.1378)
Good cleaning condition (observation)	0.3073* (0.1611)	0.4839** (0.1911)	0.1568** (0.0611)
La Victoria	—	—	—
Los Olivos	1.4480*** (0.3394)	1.8758*** (0.4222)	0.5596*** (0.1350)
Villa El Salvador	0.1254 (0.3422)	0.4299 (0.4299)	0.1454 (0.1375)
Constant		3.2111*** (0.9518)	−0.3726 (0.3043)
Observations (n)	601	601	601
R^2		0.21	0.19

Source: Authors' calculations.

Note: — = not available; COLS = cardinal ordinary least squares; OLS = ordinary least squares. Standard errors appear in parentheses. The following control variables were included in the regression, but their results are not reported: sex, age, age^2, educational level, whether respondent has a partner, proportion of children between 0 and 5 years and between 6 and 18 years, and whether the respondent is employed.

*p < .10 **p < .05 ***p < .01.

Respondents who attend movies or engage in sporting activities report greater satisfaction, and municipal participation in offering recreational activities increases satisfaction. When district effects are considered, living in Los Olivos positively influence satisfaction in this dimension, relative to La Victoria; living in Villa El Salvador negatively influences satisfaction, relative to La Victoria.

Finally, regarding satisfaction with civil participation and trust (table 7.13), only two variables have a positive impact. Although involvement in participatory budgeting is not associated with satisfaction, trust in neighbors has a positive influence. Finally, the variable related to the number of times that the respondent shared a recreational activity with a neighbor other than a relative also is significant, suggesting that social interaction is a key indicator. As for district effects, living in Villa El Salvador positively influences satisfaction, relative to living in La Victoria; living in Los Olivos decreases it.

Table 7.10 Self-Reported Satisfaction with Parks and
Green Areas

Explanatory variable	(1) Ordered logit	(2) OLS	(3) COLS
Time to the park	0.4334*** (0.0712)	0.5083*** (0.0827)	0.1563*** (0.0258)
Green areas in good condition (observation)	1.4374*** (0.2395)	1.6851*** (0.2735)	0.5010*** (0.0853)
La Victoria	—	—	—
Los Olivos	0.5838*** (0.1791)	0.6593*** (0.2129)	0.1891*** (0.0664)
Villa El Salvador	−0.3225* (0.1877)	−0.4056* (0.2199)	−0.1245* (0.0686)
Constant		3.3613*** (0.8410)	−0.2779 (0.2622)
Observations (n)	603	603	603
R^2		0.20	0.19

Source: Authors' calculations.

Note: — = not available; COLS = cardinal ordinary least squares; OLS = ordinary least squares. Standard errors appear in parentheses. The following control variables were included in the regression, but their results are not reported: sex, age, age^2, educational level, whether respondent has a partner, proportion of children between 0 and 5 years and between 6 and 18 years, and whether the respondent is employed.

$*p < .10$ $**p < .05$ $***p < .01$.

Regression Results Regarding Overall QoL

This section presents the results of estimations of the statistical associations between self-reported QoL and different sets of explanatory variables. First, objective indicators (selected because of their significance from among those used in the regressions for each dimension of QoL presented in the previous section) are used as regressors. Second, the predicted dependent variables for each dimension (computed using the regression results presented in the "QoL Regressions" section) are used as indicators of life satisfaction in each of the dimensions. The idea behind this procedure is that self-reported QoL—a general measure of satisfaction with QoL—can be determined by satisfactions in different areas, represented by the dimensions within the individual, urban, and civil society/ trust spheres.

Objective indicators. Given the large number of indicators used in the 10 dimensions (for which results are presented in tables 7.4–7.13), a first

Table 7.11 Self-Reported Satisfaction with Transportation System

Explanatory variable	(1) Ordered logit	(2) OLS	(3) COLS
Time to commute to work	0.0675 (0.0594)	0.0823 (0.0749)	0.0300 (0.0237)
Time to the nearest bus stop	–0.1867 (0.1570)	–0.2710 (0.1896)	–0.0949 (0.0599)
Roads are in good condition (observation)	0.1325 (0.1633)	0.2889 (0.1976)	0.1060* (0.0624)
La Victoria	—	—	—
Los Olivos	1.6390*** (0.2030)	1.9134*** (0.2318)	0.5596*** (0.0732)
Villa El Salvador	1.3052*** (0.1929)	1.6127*** (0.2313)	0.4806*** (0.0730)
Constant		5.4584*** (0.9859)	0.4490 (0.3112)
Observations (n)	562	562	562
R^2		0.16	0.15

Source: Authors' calculations.

Note: — = not available; COLS = cardinal ordinary least squares; OLS = ordinary least squares. Standard errors appear in parentheses. The following control variables were included in the regression, but their results are not reported: sex, age, age^2, educational level, whether respondent has a partner, proportion of children between 0 and 5 years and between 6 and 18 years, and whether the respondent is employed.

*$p < .10$ **$p < .05$ ***$p < .01$.

step is to select which indicators will be included in regressions to explain overall QoL. Three main criteria were used. First, in most of the cases, only those indicators proven to be statistically significant were considered. Second, if two or more indicators were conceptually similar or excessively collinear, only one was chosen. Finally, because some indicators were measured with more reliability than others, indicators considered more reliable were selected. Table 7.14 shows the final selected objective indicators for all the dimensions and their descriptive statistics.

Table 7.15 presents results using the selected objective indicators as explanatory variables. Columns (1) and (2) show the results for the ordered logit estimation. In column (1), only control variables are included (the same set used for the results per dimension) to see how they correlate with life satisfaction before the inclusion of the objective indicators. Objective indicators are included in columns (2)–(4). Columns (3) and (4) use OLS and COLS estimators, respectively.

Table 7.12 Self-Reported Satisfaction with Recreational Activities

Explanatory variable	(1) Ordered logit	(2) OLS	(3) COLS
Respondent goes to movie shows	0.6169** (0.2735)	0.4254* (0.2437)	0.0986 (0.0724)
Respondent does sport activities	1.0500*** (0.2764)	0.9678*** (0.2384)	0.2479*** (0.0710)
Municipality offers movie shows	0.9089** (0.4129)	0.9575** (0.3709)	0.3352*** (0.1108)
Municipality organizes sport activities	0.4308 (0.2801)	0.2833 (0.2540)	0.1273* (0.0756)
Municipality offers sports activities	1.0350*** (0.2927)	0.9948*** (0.2590)	0.2396*** (0.0768)
La Victoria	—	—	—
Los Olivos	0.5449*** (0.2079)	0.4545** (0.1778)	0.1227** (0.0520)
Villa El Salvador	–0.5643*** (0.1957)	–0.4567*** (0.1728)	–0.1317*** (0.0506)
Constant		4.2899*** (0.6757)	–0.08850 (0.1977)
Observations (n)	508	508	508
R^2		0.19	0.19

Source: Authors' calculations.

Note: — = not available; COLS = cardinal ordinary least squares; OLS = ordinary least squares. Standard errors appear in parentheses. The following control variables were included in the regression, but their results are not reported: sex, age, age², educational level, whether respondent has a partner, proportion of children between 0 and 5 years and between 6 and 18 years, and whether the respondent is employed.
 *$p < .10$ **$p < .05$ ***$p < .01$.

The ordered logit specification with only control variables shows that the independent variables that are statistically significant are age of respondent (age and age-squared), if respondent has a partner, and family income per capita. Having a partner and family income per capita positively affect the self-reported QoL. In the case of age, the result is similar to that found in previous sections: QoL decreases with age at a positive rate (recall that the sample includes individuals between 18 and 64 years of age). These results hold when we include objective variables in columns (2)–(4).

In the ordered logit specification (column [2]), the variable representing daily cleaning of streets shows a positive and significant coefficient. In addition, indicators of civil participation and trust are positively and

Table 7.13 Self-Reported Satisfaction with Civil Society/Trust

Explanatory variable	(1) Ordered logit	(2) OLS	(3) COLS
Recreational activities with neighbors	0.2245* (0.1292)	0.2299* (0.1285)	0.0624 (0.0388)
Involvement in participatory budgeting	0.1674 (0.4522)	0.1116 (0.4565)	0.0414 (0.1378)
Trust in the neighbors	0.4122*** (0.0394)	0.3854*** (0.0339)	0.1146*** (0.0102)
La Victoria	—	—	—
Los Olivos	−0.3823** (0.1828)	−0.4101** (0.1802)	−0.1311** (0.0544)
Villa El Salvador	0.2490* (0.1211)	0.2772* (0.1409)	0.0611* (0.0324)
Constant		2.3329*** (0.7341)	−0.5753*** (0.2216)
Observations (n)	586	586	586
R^2		0.25	0.24

Source: Authors' calculations.

Note: — = not available; COLS = cardinal ordinary least squares; OLS = ordinary least squares. Standard errors appear in parentheses. The following control variables were included in the regression, but their results are not reported: sex, age, age^2, educational level, whether respondent has a partner, proportion of children between 0 and 5 years and between 6 and 18 years, and whether the respondent is employed.
  *$p < .10$ **$p < .05$ ***$p < .01$.

significantly related to self-reported QoL, and are statistically significant. Finally, of the district effects, the dummy variable indicating that the respondent lives in Villa El Salvador is significant and positive. Because the reference is La Victoria, this result suggests that there are other district characteristics that raise QoL in Villa El Salvador, relative to La Victoria. These results hold for columns (3) and (4).

Predicted satisfaction, by dimension. Table 7.16 shows results of using each dimension's predicted values of satisfaction as explanatory variables (shown in "hat" in the table). Regarding the individual sphere and the self-reported QoL, predicted satisfaction with income is significant and positively correlated with self-reported QoL in column (3). In addition, the predicted satisfaction with dwelling infrastructure is significant and positively correlated with life satisfaction in columns (1)–(3). A notable result is that satisfaction with education is significant and positive in columns (1) and (2).

Table 7.14 Descriptive Statistics for Objective Indicators
and Control Variables

Indicator	Observations (n)	Mean	SD
Age of respondent (years)	604	42.76	14.24
Completed secondary education (%)	604	0.72	0.45
Children between 0 and 5 years (n)	604	0.11	0.15
Children between 6 and 18 years (n)	604	0.2	0.19
Respondent has a partner (%)	604	0.75	0.44
Family per capita income (US$ per month)	604	224.12	202.10
Rate of economic dependence	582	1.85	1.40
Roof is made of appropriate material (%)	604	0.40	0.49
Walls are made of appropriate material (%)	604	0.64	0.48
Attends health center in the district (%)	604	0.74	0.44
Children in public school (%)	604	0.87	1.14
Victim of attempted robbery (%)	604	0.21	0.40
Gangs exist in the neighborhood (%)	589	0.66	0.47
Streets are cleaned daily (%)	604	0.21	0.40
Green areas in good condition (observation) (%)	604	0.29	0.34
Roads in good condition (observation) (%)	604	0.39	0.49
Respondent goes to movie shows (%)	604	0.24	0.43
Municipality organizes sports activities (%)	540	0.36	0.48
Recreational activities with neighbors (%)	586	0.80	2.24
Trust in neighbors (%)	604	4.87	2.27

Source: Authors' calculations.
Note: SD = standard deviation.

In the urban sphere, the only dimension that appears to be statistically significant is predicted satisfaction with cleaning conditions of the streets. Where objective indicators are used as independent variables, the fact that other predicted dimensions under the control of local authorities are not correlated with self-declared QoL opens a debate about

Table 7.15 Self-Reported QoL with Objective Indicators

Explanatory variable	(1) Self-reported ordered logit (control variables only)	(2) Self-reported ordered logit	(3) Self-reported OLS	(4) Self-reported COLS
Sex of respondent	0.0180 (0.1545)	-0.1116 (0.1680)	-0.1597 (0.1911)	-0.0563 (0.0675)
Age of respondent	-0.0615** (0.0302)	-0.0730** (0.0338)	-0.0732** (0.0366)	-0.0272** (0.0129)
Age of respondent^2	0.0006* (0.0003)	0.0008** (0.0004)	0.0007* (0.0004)	0.0003* (0.0001)
Completed secondary education	0.1933 (0.1725)	-0.0363 (0.1889)	-0.0822 (0.2120)	-0.0647 (0.0749)
Children between 0 and 5 years	-0.3891 (0.6875)	-0.1110 (0.8429)	-0.3233 (0.9323)	-0.1194 (0.3292)
Children between 6 and 18 years	-0.6380 (0.5132)	-0.3576 (0.7357)	-0.3069 (0.8253)	-0.1317 (0.2914)
Respondent has a partner	0.4778*** (0.1722)	0.3470* (0.1855)	0.4017* (0.2098)	0.1186 (0.0741)

(continued)

Table 7.15 Self-Reported QoL with Objective Indicators *(continued)*

Explanatory variable	(1) Self-reported ordered logit (control variables only)	(2) Self-reported ordered logit	(3) Self-reported OLS	(4) Self-reported COLS
Family income per capita	0.2906** (0.1288)	0.0730 (0.1508)	0.0883 (0.1669)	0.0346 (0.0590)
Rate of economic dependence		0.2483 (0.1997)	0.2735 (0.2273)	0.1060 (0.0803)
Roof is made of appropriate material		0.2213 (0.2008)	0.2967 (0.2260)	0.0504 (0.0798)
Walls are made of appropriate material		0.1951 (0.2031)	0.1920 (0.2226)	0.0722 (0.0786)
Attends health center in the district		−0.0652 (0.1855)	−0.0992 (0.2130)	−0.0616 (0.0752)
Number of children in public school		−0.2561 (0.2075)	−0.2788 (0.2335)	−0.0901 (0.0825)
Victim of attempted robbery		−0.2048 (0.2714)	−0.2104 (0.3127)	−0.0986 (0.1104)

Gangs exist in the neighborhood	0.0268	-0.0071	-0.0153
	(0.2391)	(0.2672)	(0.0943)
Streets are cleaned on a daily basis	0.9283**	1.0211**	0.3707**
	(0.3642)	(0.4118)	(0.1454)
Green areas in good condition (observation)	0.2839	0.3289	0.1362
	(0.2579)	(0.2914)	(0.1029)
Roads are in good condition (observation)	0.0498	0.0488	0.0199
	(0.1720)	(0.1932)	(0.0682)
Respondent goes to movie shows	0.7205**	0.7112**	0.2549**
	(0.2827)	(0.3142)	(0.1110)
Municipality organizes sports activities	-0.0135	0.0298	-0.0206
	(0.2380)	(0.2668)	(0.0942)
Recreational activities with neighbors	0.4565***	0.4802***	0.1614***
	(0.1372)	(0.1482)	(0.0523)
Trust in neighbors	0.1011***	0.1050***	0.0297**
	(0.0377)	(0.0401)	-0.0142
La Victoria	—	—	—
Los Olivos	-0.0366	-0.0666	-0.0347
	(0.2470)	(0.2830)	(0.0999)

(continued)

Table 7.15 Self-Reported QoL with Objective Indicators *(continued)*

Explanatory variable	(1) Self-reported ordered logit (control variables only)	(2) Self-reported ordered logit	(3) Self-reported OLS	(4) Self-reported COLS
Villa El Salvador		0.7200*** (0.2597)	0.7204** (0.2862)	0.2770*** (0.1011)
Constant			5.6328*** (1.2560)	0.4817 (0.4435)
Observations (n)	602	548	548	548
R^2			0.14	0.13

Source: Authors' calculations.

Note: — = not available; COLS = cardinal ordinary least squares; OLS = ordinary least squares. Standard errors appear in parentheses. The following control variables were included in the regression, but their results are not reported: sex, age, age^2, educational level, whether respondent has a partner, proportion of children between 0 and 5 years and between 6 and 18 years, and whether the respondent is employed.

*p < .10 **p < .05 ***p < .01.

Table 7.16 Self-Reported QoL with Predicted Satisfaction, by Dimension

Dimension	(1) Self-reported ordered logit	(2) Self-reported OLS	(3) Self-reported COLS
Individual sphere			
Income (hat)	0.2200	0.2637	0.0970*
	(0.1486)	(0.1654)	(0.0585)
Dwelling characteristics (hat)	0.2464**	0.3034***	0.0923**
	(0.0990)	(0.1110)	(0.0392)
Health (hat)	0.0918	0.0674	−0.0031
	(0.1664)	(0.1917)	(0.0678)
Education (hat)	0.3617*	0.3862*	0.1172
	(0.1910)	(0.2316)	(0.0819)
Urban sphere			
Crime and safety (hat)	0.2328	0.2416	0.0974
	(0.1550)	(0.1792)	(0.0634)
Cleaning conditions (hat)	0.2033*	0.2524*	0.1144**
	(0.1150)	(0.1328)	(0.0469)
Parks and green areas (hat)	0.1852	0.2136	0.0776
	(0.1229)	(0.1420)	(0.0502)
Transportation system (hat)	0.1760	0.1348	0.0430
	(0.3400)	(0.3962)	(0.1401)
Civil society/trust sphere			
Recreational activities (hat)	0.2413	0.2814	0.0983
	(0.1560)	(0.1752)	(0.0619)
Civil society/trust (hat)	0.1770*	0.2006*	0.0510
	(0.1004)	(0.1114)	(0.0394)
District			
Los Olivos	−0.5612	−0.5354	−0.2084
	(0.7120)	(0.8234)	(0.2919)
Villa El Salvador	0.4886	0.6266	0.2816
	(0.6139)	(0.7058)	(0.2496)

(continued)

Table 7.16 Self-Reported QoL with Predicted Satisfaction, by Dimension *(continued)*

Dimension	(1) Self-reported ordered logit	(2) Self-reported OLS	(3) Self-reported COLS
Constant		−5.6188 (3.8195)	−3.2430** (1.3507)
Observations (n)	449	449	449
R^2		0.14	0.14

Source: Authors' calculations.

Note: COLS = cardinal ordinary least squares; hat = estimated dimension-specific predicted values as independent variables; OLS = ordinary least squares; QoL = quality of life. Standard errors appear in parentheses. The following control variables were included in the regression, but their results are not reported: sex, age, age^2, educational level, whether respondent has a partner, proportion of children between 0 and 5 years and between 6 and 18 years, and whether the respondent is employed.

*$p < .10$ **$p < .05$ ***$p < .01$.

the effectiveness of services provided by local government in improving people's living conditions.

Last, in columns (1)–(3) for the civil society/trust sphere, the predicted satisfaction with recreational activities is not statistically significant, but it is positive. The level of trust in neighbors is significant in all specifications except column (3).

Three main ideas emerge from these results. First, determinants of QoL are drawn from all three spheres considered. This result comports with the notion that QoL is a complex phenomenon related to areas of life beyond income. Second, policy makers with the capacity to intervene in the urban sphere may take a wide variety of actions. Safety conditions, the transportation system, and cleaning conditions of the streets, for example, are strongly correlated with residents' QoL. That most indicators in the urban sphere were not significant from a statistical point of view may mean that they are not being effectively provided at present. That possibility opens opportunities for constant improvement. Finally, the civil society/trust sphere proves very important for QoL. The number of recreational activities in which respondents are involved with nonrelative friends was significant in some specifications, and trust in neighbors shows a coefficient statistically different from zero.

QoL Indexes

Table 7.17 shows descriptive statistics for the two QoL indexes estimated using the two sets of indicators of the regressions presented in the previous

Table 7.17 QoL Indexes under Different Specifications

Specification	Observations (n)	Mean	SD	Minimum	Maximum
Self-reported, objective variables	550	6.09	0.77	4.01	8.97
Self-reported, predicted dimensions	461	6.15	0.81	4.15	8.33

Source: Authors' calculations.
Note: QoL = quality of life; SD = standard deviation.

section (objective indicators and predicted dimensions). Because not all the indicators are available for the whole sample, the resulting number of observations varies for each index. The mean values oscillate between 6.09 and 6.15, and the standard deviations are of the same magnitude (roughly 0.8). The mean estimates are of a similar magnitude to the mean of the self-reported QoL directly observed from the survey responses (6.05), as reported in the "QoL Regressions" section.

Each of the previous estimated indexes also can be computed on the bases of district of residence and socioeconomic level. Table 7.18 shows that the QoL index is higher in Villa El Salvador, followed first by La Victoria and then by Los Olivos. This order holds, regardless of the set of regressors, weights, and indicators used to compute the index. Table 7.19 shows a positive correlation between the QoL index and higher SELs.

Results of a different exercise are presented in figures 7.4, 7.5, and 7.6, which show the shares of the individual, urban, and civil society/trust spheres in the QoL index. To compute these shares, the predicted value of the self-reported QoL was computed from the regressions, using objective indicators as explanatory variables; then the contribution of the set of variables belonging to each sphere in explaining this predicted value was calculated.[5]

Figure 7.4, which presents the results for the overall sample, reveals that the individual sphere makes the greatest contribution (42.41 percent) to the QoL index. Second in importance are indicators in the civil society/trust sphere (37.75 percent). Dimensions in the urban sphere contribute only 19.84 percent. These shares are interesting because they show that social interaction, trust in neighbors, and recreational activities—indicators under the control of neither individuals nor policy makers—have a major influence on QoL. Nevertheless, the role of the urban sphere cannot be ignored.

Figure 7.5 presents the contributions of each sphere by district. An interesting result is that in each district, the rank of the contribution of the three spheres is different. In La Victoria, the most important share is

Table 7.18 QoL Indexes under Different Specifications,
by District

QoL Index	Observations (n)	Mean	SD	Minimum	Maximum
La Victoria					
Self-reported, objective variables	185	6.20	0.77	4.55	8.17
Self-reported, predicted dimensions	144	6.25	0.79	4.27	8.10
Los Olivos					
Self-reported, objective variables	184	5.75	0.79	4.01	8.97
Self-reported, predicted dimensions	144	5.79	0.83	4.15	7.85
Villa El Salvador					
Self-reported, objective variables	181	6.31	0.64	5.11	8.46
Self-reported, predicted dimensions	162	6.38	0.69	4.69	8.33

Source: Authors' calculations.
Note: QoL = quality of life; SD = standard deviation.

that of the individual sphere, followed by the urban sphere and then the civil society/trust sphere. In Los Olivos, the rank found for the overall sample holds (individual sphere, followed by the civil society/trust sphere, and finally the urban sphere). In Villa El Salvador, however, the greatest contribution comes from the civil society/trust sphere (48.64 percent), followed in order by the individual sphere (41.30 percent) and the urban sphere (10.06 percent). That finding is in line with Villa El Salvador's tradition of collective action. Also remarkable is the contribution of the urban sphere in the central district of La Victoria (31.73 percent), compared with that sphere's contributions in the peripheral districts of Los Olivos (13.69 percent) and Villa El Salvador (10.06 percent). Finally, the contribution of the individual sphere is slightly above 40 percent in all three districts, but is most important in Los Olivos—a result that is

Table 7.19 QoL Indexes under Different Specifications,
by Socioeconomic Level

QoL Index	Observations (n)	Mean	SD	Minimum	Maximum
Levels A/B					
Self-reported, objective variables	76	6.43	0.75	5.03	8.97
Self-reported, predicted dimensions	61	6.53	0.70	5.12	8.05
Level C					
Self-reported, objective variables	245	6.17	0.77	4.01	8.46
Self-reported, predicted dimensions	204	6.26	0.80	4.38	8.33
Level D					
Self-reported, objective variables	229	5.88	0.73	4.12	7.99
Self-reported, predicted dimensions	186	5.91	0.78	4.15	7.79

Source: Authors' calculations.
Note: QoL = quality of life; SD = standard deviation.

in line with the market-oriented development in that district. Finally, it may be the case that the low contribution of the urban sphere in the QoL index for Los Olivos and Villa El Salvador is compensated by higher contributions coming from the civil society/trust sphere and the individual sphere.

Figure 7.6 shows results of a similar exercise for SELs, with three main findings. First, the individual sphere is the most important contributor for SELs A/B and C, but the civil society/trust sphere is most important in SEL D. Second, although the shares of the individual and urban spheres are directly correlated with income, the opposite holds true for the contribution of the civil society/trust sphere. Third, the contribution of the urban sphere decreases from 26.07 percent in SEL A/B to almost 13.82 percent in SEL D.

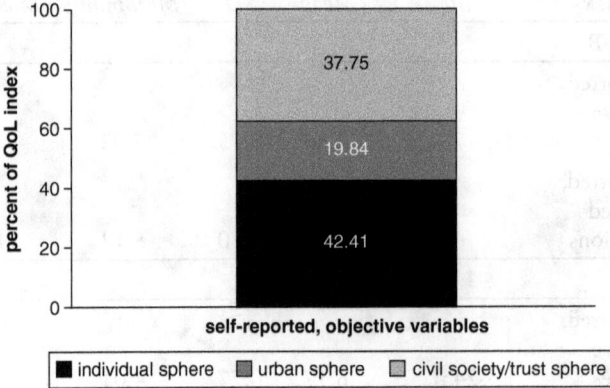

Figure 7.4 Shares of Individual, Urban, and Civil Society/Trust Spheres in the QoL Index

Source: Authors' estimations.
Note: QoL = quality of life.

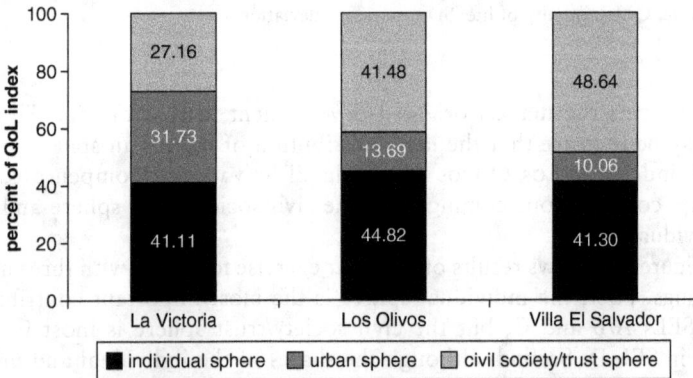

Figure 7.5 Shares of Individual, Urban, and Civil Society/Trust Spheres in the QoL Index, by District

Source: Authors' estimations.
Note: QoL = quality of life.

Figure 7.6 Shares of Individual, Urban, and Civil Society/
Trust Spheres in the QOL Index, by Socioeconomic Level

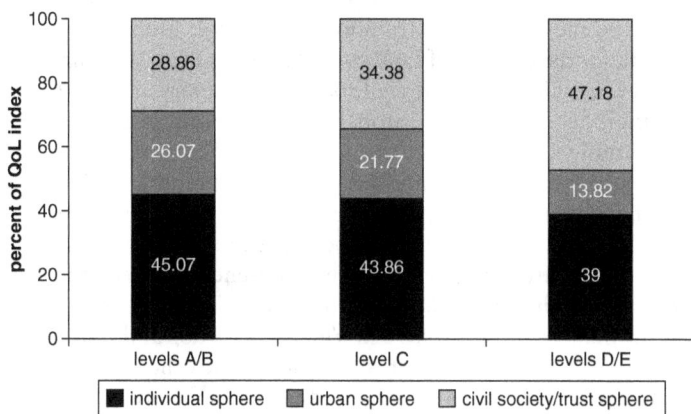

Source: Authors' estimations.
Note: QoL = quality of life.

Two general findings arise from this analysis of shares. The first finding concerns the importance of the individual sphere. Variables related to
income, dwelling characteristics, health, and education are very important contributors to QoL. The second finding involves the importance
of the civil society/trust sphere, particularly in districts on the periphery
and among lower SELs. Moreover, the civil society/trust sphere appears
to increase in importance as the role of the urban sphere decreases. This
result is seen clearly at the district level: Villa El Salvador's high levels of
QoL arise mainly from the civil society/trust sphere, given that its urban
sphere has a lower contribution than is true in the other two districts.

Conclusion

The findings presented in this chapter illustrate the importance to QoL
of indicators from the individual, urban, and civil society/trust spheres.
For example, an increase in income indicators, improvement of housing characteristics, availability of recreational activities, and frequency
of street cleaning are associated with increases in QoL. In contrast, some
specifications show that a reduction in the level of satisfaction with safety
conditions is significantly associated with a decrease in QoL. Regardless of
specification used, variables related to participation in civil society and trust
proved statistically significant.

With the use of the coefficients of the regression analysis, indexes of QoL were constructed for the whole sample and for each district. Then the contributions of the individual, urban, and civil society/trust spheres' indicators were estimated. Results show that indicators in the individual sphere make the greatest contribution to the QoL index for the whole sample and for the districts of La Victoria and Los Olivos. In Villa El Salvador, however, indicators in the civil society/trust sphere make the greatest contribution. In addition, indicators in the urban sphere are more important in centrally located La Victoria than in the other two districts, and the urban sphere is more important in Los Olivos than in Villa El Salvador. Finally, indicators in the individual sphere are very important: they contribute more than 40 percent in each of the three districts.

These results are consistent with the differences between the districts under analysis. First, the facts that the civil society/trust sphere is more important than the urban sphere in Villa El Salvador and that it is more important in that district than it is in either of the other districts may be associated with Villa El Salvador's tradition of collective action. Moreover, the greater importance of the individual sphere in Los Olivos, relative to the other components of the index within that district and relative to the other districts, is consistent with that district's entrepreneurial growth pattern. In older and centrally located La Victoria, the urban sphere is more important than it is in the other districts—a finding that is consistent with expected differences between central and peripheral development. It also should be noted that although the individual sphere is more important in Los Olivos than in the other districts, that difference is not highly pronounced. Greater differences occur in the relative contributions of the urban and civil society/trust spheres, suggesting that low levels of contribution from the urban sphere may be partly compensated for by the contribution of the civil society/trust sphere. In essence, in the presence of inadequate urban facilities or services, aspects of the civil society/trust sphere appear to be substitutes and to positively affect the index.

These results have several noteworthy policy implications. First, although the contribution of the urban sphere to the estimated QoL is not as important as the variables belonging to the individual sphere, urban variables still contribute close to 20 percent in the overall sample. This result suggests that urban policy makers have an important space for intervening to improve QoL. Citizens particularly value their neighborhoods' safety conditions and the cleaning of streets.

Second, the civil society/trust sphere clearly represents an important aspect of QoL. Although it is true that addressing urban problems such as crime and safety, transportation, and street cleanliness is undoubtedly important, those activities should not reduce municipalities' efforts to promote social interaction and trust. Providing sports and cultural facilities and events and organizing sports tournaments or other recreational activities should become an important part of the local government's plan and policies. Moreover, creating and promoting neighborhood organizations may promote trust among neighbors and increase social capital.

Finally, it is both important and feasible for municipalities to monitor residents' QoL. The monitoring system should include both baseline and follow-up surveys for a representative sample of district citizens. The indicators to be collected should consist mainly of two types, which can be used simultaneously and complementarily: (1) information on objective indicators, such as number and places of robberies and attempted robberies, frequency of street cleaning, and conditions of parks; and (2) subjective information, such as the level of satisfaction with municipally provided services. Given that QoL involves factors in addition to income and other socioeconomic indicators, the resulting data should be used to construct an urban and district-level QoL index that municipal officials may use to guide their activities and set priorities, as well as to monitor interventions. Furthermore, QoL estimations should be undertaken in all municipalities for benchmarking purposes.

Notes

1. See, for instance, Tiliouine, Cummins, and Davern (2006). Kahneman and Krueger (2006) present an extensive discussion on the measurement and determinants of subjective well-being.
2. Descriptive statistics for these 10 topics are provided in appendix 2 of Alcázar and Andrade (2008), the working paper on which this chapter is based.
3. Here and in the following discussion of methodology, orthogonality between the different dimensions is assumed.
4. Further regressions and discussion of methodology are found in Alcázar and Andrade (2008).
5. The methodology for this exercise is discussed in Alcázar and Andrade (2008).

References

Alcázar, Lorena, and Raúl Andrade. 2008. "Quality of Life in Urban Neighborhoods in Metropolitan Lima, Peru." RES Working Paper 3261, Research Department, Inter-American Development Bank, Washington, DC.

Baker, Dwayne A., and Robert J. Palmer. 2006. "Examining the Effects of Perceptions of Community and Recreation Participation on Quality of Life." *Social Indicators Research* 75 (3): 395–418.

CAPECO (Cámra Peruana de la Construcción). 2006. *El mercado de edificaciones urbanas en Lima Metropolitana y el Callao.* Lima, Peru: CAPECO.

Cattaneo, Matías D., Sebastián Galiani, Paul J. Gertler, Sebastián Martinez, and Rocío Titiunik. 2007. "Housing, Health and Happiness." Policy Research Working Paper 4214, World Bank, Washington, DC.

Di Tella, Rafael, and Robert MacCulloch. 2006. "Some Uses of Happiness Data in Economics." *Journal of Economic Perspectives* 20 (1): 25–46.

Easterlin, Richard. 1974. "Does Economic Growth Improve the Human Lot? Some Empirical Evidence." In *Nations and Households in Economic Growth: Essays in Honor of Moses Abramovitz*, ed. Paul A. David and Melvin W. Reder, 89–125. New York: Academic Press.

Frey, Bruno S., Simon Luechinger, and Alois Stutzer. 2004. "Valuing Public Goods: The Life Satisfaction Approach." Working Paper 1158, CESifo Group, Munich, Germany.

Frey, Bruno S., and Alois Stutzer. 2002. *Happiness and Economics: How the Economy and Institutions Affect Well-Being.* Princeton, NJ: Princeton University Press.

Gonzales de Olarte, Efraín. 1992. *La economía regional de Lima. Crecimiento, urbanización y clases populares.* Lima, Peru: Instituto de Estudios Peruanos and Consorcio de Investigaciónes Económica y Social.

Kahneman, Daniel, and Alan B. Krueger. 2006. "Developments in the Measurement of Subjective Well-Being." *Journal of Economic Perspectives* 20 (1): 3–24.

Oswald, Andrew J. 1997. "Happiness and Economic Performance." *Economic Journal* 107 (445): 1815–31.

Tiliouine, Habib, Robert A. Cummins, and Melanie Davern. 2006. "Measuring Well-Being in Developing Countries: The Case of Algeria." *Social Indicators Research* 75 (1): 1–30.

van Praag, Bernard M.S., and Barbara Baarsma. 2005. "Using Happiness Surveys to Value Intangibles: The Case of Airport Noise." *Economic Journal* 115 (500): 224–46.

van Praag, Bernard M.S., and Ada Ferrer-i-Carbonell. 2008. *Happiness Quantified: A Satisfaction Calculus Approach.* Rev. ed. New York: Oxford University Press.

van Praag, Bernard M.S., Paul Frijters, and Ada Ferrer-i-Carbonell. 2003. "The Anatomy of Subjective Well-Being." *Journal of Economic Behavior & Organization* 51 (1): 29–49.

8

Housing and Neighborhood Satisfaction in Montevideo, Uruguay

Zuleika Ferre, Néstor Gandelman,
and Giorgina Piani

Montevideo is Uruguay's capital, largest city, and main port. With a population currently estimated at 1,349,000 inhabitants, it is more than twice the size of the second-largest city (Canelones), and it comprises roughly 44 percent of the country's total population. Unlike many other capital cities in Latin America, however, Montevideo has grown slowly in the last five decades and has not struggled with massive inflows of poor immigrants from the countryside. Although by 1960 Uruguay had become one of Latin America's most urbanized countries,[1] it also had attained one of the region's highest per capita income levels.[2] Montevideo has preserved most of the European features it acquired in the first two decades of the 20th century, when it benefited from booming exports of beef and agricultural products, and attracted both ambitious entrepreneurs and relatively well-educated workers from Europe. The city's waterfront promenade along the Río de la Plata—currently the most popular rendezvous—has a distinct appeal that mixes the city's European tradition with a refined sense of modernity not often seen in other cities of the region.

This chapter discusses the extent to which the city's features and amenities influence the rental prices of dwellings and its inhabitants' satisfaction with their dwellings, neighborhoods, and lives as a whole. The main source of information is a special survey conducted in selected, representative neighborhoods.[3] Although housing prices and housing

The authors thank Martin Hahn for his assistance with the maps in this chapter.

satisfaction mainly reflect housing characteristics, they also are affected by location and other neighborhood-specific factors. Neighborhood satisfaction, in particular, is associated with factors ranging from the abundance of trees, public parks, and green areas to the presence of gangs and vandalism. The econometric analysis presented in this chapter indicates that, whereas housing influences life satisfaction, neighborhood characteristics and neighborhood satisfaction matter far less. Consequently, the life satisfaction (LS) approach cannot be used to value neighborhood-related public goods.

Brief Description of the Neighborhoods Selected

The city of Montevideo is divided into 62 neighborhoods. In half of these neighborhoods, more than 70 percent of households belong to only one of the four strata defined by the National Statistical Institute on the basis of household per capita income and unemployment. The highest stratum is the most highly concentrated, which reflects the tendency of the rich to isolate themselves from the rest of the population—a process facilitated by higher living costs in rich neighborhoods.

To assess the influence of individuals' housing and neighborhood characteristics on their quality of life (QoL), a detailed survey was carried out in selected neighborhoods.[4] Five neighborhoods were chosen to represent areas with different strata composition, and households were selected at random to ensure representativeness at the neighborhood level.[5] In addition, households from the rest of the city were randomly picked as comparators, with no expectation of representativeness.

Two of the five selected neighborhoods are low- or medium-low-stratum neighborhoods located on the southwest side of the city: Tres Ombúes-Pueblo Victoria and Cerro (figure 8.1). Approximately 90 percent of the households in those two neighborhoods are currently classified as low-or medium-low-stratum households (table 8.1). In the first half of the 20th century, the neighborhoods were shaped by European immigration as the meat-processing industry developed, creating an important local working class and contributing to the Uruguayan labor union movement. These factors, in turn, produced a strong sense of neighborhood identity and cohesion. The industrial crisis of the mid-1950s, however, greatly affected both neighborhoods as local employers closed their doors, leaving widespread unemployment and changing the neighborhoods' composition and lifestyle. A long period of declining industry, high unemployment rates, low salaries, social segregation, and environmental damage has produced striking effects in this area. For instance, the subneighborhood Cerro Norte (not included in the survey) is well known as a dangerous area that is rife with criminal activity, and

Figure 8.1 Stratum Composition of Montevideo Neighborhoods

Percentage of low-stratum households in neighborhoods having more than half their population within low and medium-low strata
- ☐ 0–27
- ▨ 28–54
- ■ 55–100

Percentage of high-stratum households in neighborhoods having more than half their population within high and medium-low strata
- ▦ 0–18
- ▦ 19–49
- ▨ 50–100

Source: Authors' illustration, based on 2007 Montevideo QoL Neighborhood Survey sample.
Note: The five neighborhoods indicated by name were selected for the in-depth survey used in this chapter.

Cerro as a whole is often portrayed as a marginal zone with its inhabitants stigmatized by high reported rates of crime and delinquency.

The other three neighborhoods selected are predominantly medium-high- to high-income residential neighborhoods with high population density: Buceo, Malvín, and Parque Batlle. The first two, located on the southeast side of the city along the waterfront promenade, formerly were resorts and were consolidated as residential neighborhoods during Montevideo's expansion. Parque Batlle (which takes its name from the main city park that it surrounds) is located in a central area close to downtown Montevideo. Virtually all the households of these three neighborhoods are classified as medium-high- or high-stratum neighborhoods.

Table 8.1 Stratum Composition of Neighborhoods and Number of Households Surveyed

	Neighborhood						
Stratum	Tres Ombúes-Pueblo Victoria	Cerro	Buceo	Malvín	Parque Batlle-Villa Dolores	Average of other surveyed neighborhoods	Average of all neighborhoods
Low (%)	73.15	21.34	0	0	0	23.83	13.43
Medium-low (%)	16.08	71.27	0	0	0	35.27	25.29
Medium-high (%)	10.77	7.40	62.11	15.14	59.20	29.17	27.70
High (%)	0	0	37.89	84.86	40.80	11.73	33.59
Number of households surveyed[a]	152	228	121	103	104	93	n.a.

Source: Authors' compilation, based on the National Statistical Institute's Household Survey of 2006.

Note: n.a. = not applicable.

a. The number of households surveyed refers to the survey carried out by the authors for this study (that is, Montevideo QoL Neighborhood Survey 2007).

Brief Description of the Survey Results

The survey collected information about the respondents, their dwellings, and their neighborhoods.

Individual Characteristics and Opinions

Information gathered about respondents consists of both subjective and objective variables. Among the subjective variables are respondents' opinions on their levels of satisfaction with different aspects of their lives, including their housing and neighborhoods. However, some objective variables also may be affected by a degree of subjectivity and may be subject to reporting bias. Table 8.2 presents summary statistics for objective individual characteristics.[6] The data are presented in three groupings: "low to medium-low" includes respondents in the two poorer neighborhoods surveyed, "high to medium-high" includes respondents in the three richer ones, and "other" is the comparison group (from surveys in the rest of Montevideo). As expected, people from the poorer neighborhoods fare worse in every area than do people from the more affluent neighborhoods.

Information gathered on individuals includes human capital dimensions. On average, people from richer areas have four more years of schooling and a much higher rate of having completed secondary and university education. In high-stratum areas, private health care coverage is 86 percent, compared with 50 percent in low-stratum areas. There are no significant differences across strata regarding whether the respondent felt ill in the last 30 days (30 percent in higher-income areas versus 27 percent in lower-income areas). Other questions in the survey permit a calculation of respondents' body mass index,[7] and results reveal that obesity rates are higher in lower-income neighborhoods (18.1 percent versus 13.3 percent).

With respect to the use of time and labor market activities, the survey indicates that, although a larger share of low-stratum individuals is unemployed (12.4 percent versus 9.6 percent), overwork is also more common among the poor. When overworked people are defined as those who work more than 60 hours a week, 21 percent of the population in low-stratum areas meets this criterion; by contrast, only 10 percent of people in high-stratum neighborhoods meets it. The opposite is found, however, in relation to a clearly less objective indicator of work addiction: whereas 38 percent of high-stratum respondents "often" and "very often" find themselves "thinking about work," only 32 percent of low-stratum respondents do so. As expected, incomes are lower in the low-stratum neighborhoods, with household incomes only about half of those in the richer areas; per capita income gaps are even wider because families in poorer areas are larger.

Individual variables include several (somewhat subjective) indicators of social capital. The responses of people in higher-income neighborhoods

Table 8.2 Objective Individual Characteristics: Summary Statistics

Individual characteristic	Characteristic	Indicator	Low to medium-low	High to medium-high	Other	Total
Demographics	Sex	Female (%)	56.3	62.8	57.0	59.1
	Age	Mean	46.9	47.4	45.9	47.0
		SD	18.4	19.0	17.8	18.6
	Partner (married)	%	34.3	40.4	33.3	36.9
	Partner (not married)	%	18.2	9.8	19.4	15.0
	Family size	Mean	3.2	2.7	2.9	3.0
		SD	1.9	1.3	1.7	1.7
Human capital: education	Years of schooling	Mean	8.2	12.4	9.2	10.1
		SD	3.5	3.6	3.6	4.1
	Completed secondary education	%	12.6	16.5	18.3	14.8
	Completed university education	%	2.9	27.8	8.6	13.7
Human capital: health	Private health care coverage	%	49.7	86.0	62.4	66.0
	Felt sick	%	26.8	29.6	19.4	27.1
	Physical activity	%	35.8	60.7	41.9	46.7
	Body mass index	Overweight (BMI > 25) (%)	47.6	40.6	52.3	45.3
		Obese (BMI >30) (%)	18.1	13.3	15.9	15.9

Labor market: use of time	Employed full-time	%	48.9	50.3	52.7	49.9
	Unemployed/underemployed	%	12.4	9.6	15.1	11.5
	Overworked	%	20.9	9.8	28.1	17.1
	Not in the labor force	%	31.6	30.8	28.0	30.8
	Hours of leisure in the last weekend	Mean	14.8	16.1	13.0	15.1
		SD	7.8	7.6	8.3	7.9
	Hours worked weekly	Mean	43.7	39.7	47.4	42.5
		SD	19.4	14.6	17.7	17.5
	Workaholic	%	32.1	37.8	37.6	35.1
Income	Household income (Ur$)	Mean	12,016	23,853	13,465	16,857
		SD	10,884	17,604	10,147	14,964
	Per capita family income (Ur$)	Mean	4,662	10,323	6,551	7,117
		SD	4,249	7,827	7,440	6,810
	Individual income (Ur$)	Mean	6,282	13,641	8,435	9,471
		SD	5,977	15,737	7,947	11,626
Social capital	Sociable	%	66.3	75.9	64.5	70.0
	Trustful	%	21.8	46.6	23.7	32.2
	Religious	%	11.3	11.9	7.5	11.1

Source: Authors' compilation, based on 2007 Montevideo QoL Neighborhood Survey.
Note: BMI = body mass index; SD = standard deviation.

indicate they are much more sociable and trusting than are people in poorer areas (76 percent versus 66 percent in the sociability dimension, and 47 percent versus 22 percent in the trust dimension). Religiosity is low (11–12 percent) in both groups of neighborhoods.

Respondents' opinions on different aspects of their lives are central to the approach taken in this book to assess the urban QoL. The survey included questions about overall happiness and satisfaction with the following life dimensions: economic situation, family, social life, current work, health, leisure, housing, and neighborhood. Table 8.3 presents summary statistics only for overall happiness, housing satisfaction, and neighborhood satisfaction because those aspects will be the focus of the rest of this chapter.

Respondents from higher-income neighborhoods tend to be happier and more satisfied with all life dimensions (including those not presented in the table). In particular, levels of satisfaction with housing and neighborhood display striking differences among strata.

Figures 8.2, 8.3, and 8.4 present the results by census tract. The intensity of the greys indicates the percentage of respondents in each census tract who describe themselves as "very happy" or "fairly happy" (figure 8.2), or as "very satisfied" or "satisfied" with their housing (figure 8.3) and their neighborhood (figure 8.4). In general, higher-strata neighborhoods present higher levels of happiness and satisfaction; but considerable heterogeneity is observed across census tracts within each neighborhood—which, in turn, reflects much greater heterogeneity among individuals.

Housing Characteristics

Information on housing, obtained from responses to the 2007 Montevideo QoL Neighborhood Survey, is summarized in table 8.4. The average monthly rent for dwellings in the survey is Ur$4,849 ($226), and rent in rich neighborhoods is 150 percent higher than in poor neighborhoods. The most important differences between the neighborhood and housing characteristics of the two types of neighborhoods considered are location (measured as distance to the promenade) and provision of services and appliances (measured by an index that adds 1 point for each service or appliance[8]). It is interesting to note that homes in the two types of neighborhoods do not differ substantially in their basic construction materials or number of rooms and bathrooms; and a surprising finding is that overcrowding is more common in the higher strata. With respect to housing tenure patterns, ownership rates are approximately 55 percent in both types of neighborhoods; but renting is more common among higher-income residents, and occupancy without payment is more extensive among lower-income residents.

Table 8.3 Happiness and Satisfaction: Summary Statistics

Aspect of life	Response	Low- and medium-low-strata neighborhoods selected	High- and medium-high-strata neighborhoods selected	Other neighborhoods (all strata)	Total
Overall happiness	Very happy	26.8	31.4	35.5	29.7
	Fairly happy	47.6	56.4	47.3	51.2
	Not very happy	20.5	11.0	12.9	15.7
	Not at all happy	4.5	0.6	4.3	2.9
	No answer	0.5	0.6	0	0.5
Housing	Very satisfied	24.7	39.6	31.2	31.6
	Satisfied	47.6	44.8	53.8	47.2
	Not very satisfied	21.3	12.5	9.7	16.4
	Not at all satisfied	6.1	3.0	5.4	4.7
	No answer	0.3	0	0	0.1
Neighborhood	Very satisfied	25.0	44.8	18.3	32.3
	Satisfied	48.9	46.6	51.6	48.3
	Not very satisfied	18.4	6.1	21.5	13.7
	Not at all satisfied	7.1	2.1	8.6	5.2
	No answer	0.5	0.3	0	0.4

Source: Authors' calculations, based on 2007 Montevideo QoL Neighborhood Survey.

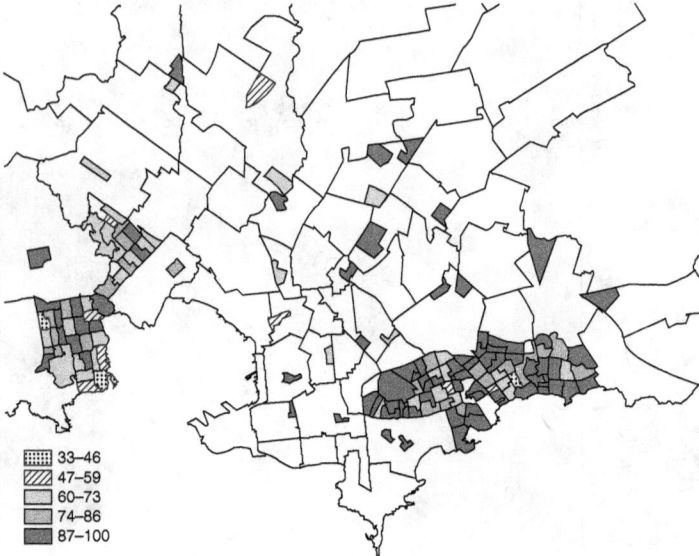

Figure 8.2 Overall Happiness, by Census Tract
Percentage who are "fairly happy" or "very happy"

33–46
47–59
60–73
74–86
87–100

Source: Authors' illustration, based on 2007 Montevideo QoL Neighborhood Survey.

Neighborhood Characteristics

Because this chapter considers how neighborhood amenities, services, and other characteristics influence urban QoL, the survey devoted a great deal of attention to their measurement. Answers obtained from the respondents were complemented with information provided by the interviewers, who received training to ensure that similar standards of measurement or qualitative evaluation were used. Table 8.5 summarizes information from both respondents and interviewers. Respondents in all strata consider their neighborhoods' most serious problems to be speeding and dangerous driving, the presence of people who make them feel unsafe, and drug trafficking. Respondents in lower-strata neighborhoods believe they are more affected by virtually every problem. The problems with the greatest differences between low- and high-stratum neighborhoods are drug trafficking, water pollution, rubbish in the streets, vandalism, the presence of gangs, and air pollution. Only noise pollution affects high-stratum

Figure 8.3 Satisfaction with Housing, by Census Tract
Percentage who are "satisfied" or "very satisfied"

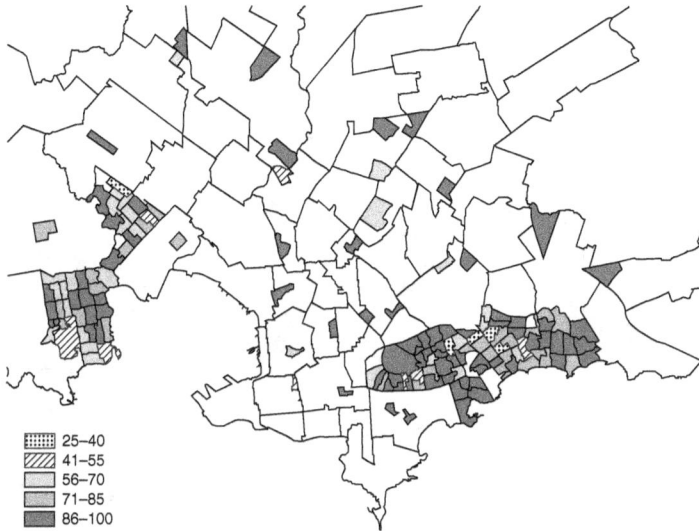

25–40
41–55
56–70
71–85
86–100

Source: Authors' illustration, based on 2007 Montevideo QoL Neighborhood Survey.

neighborhoods more severely, and the incidence rates of this problem are rather low.

The middle block of table 8.5 shows how respondents judge the provision of public goods. Questions could be answered only "yes" or "no,"[9] and the table presents percentages of affirmative answers. The only two dimensions where residents of low-stratum neighborhoods seem more satisfied are access to daily garbage collection and a feeling of security when walking at night. The provision of all other public goods, however, is seen as worse in those neighborhoods. The two areas with the greatest differences are satisfaction with public parks and green areas and satisfaction with the condition of sidewalks.

The bottom block of the table summarizes information based on interviewers' observations of conditions in the immediate vicinity of respondents' dwellings. Interviewers' observations tend to confirm respondents' opinions in some cases, but not in others. For instance, although respondents and interviewers offer essentially the same assessment of street lighting, interviewers see street paving and sidewalks as

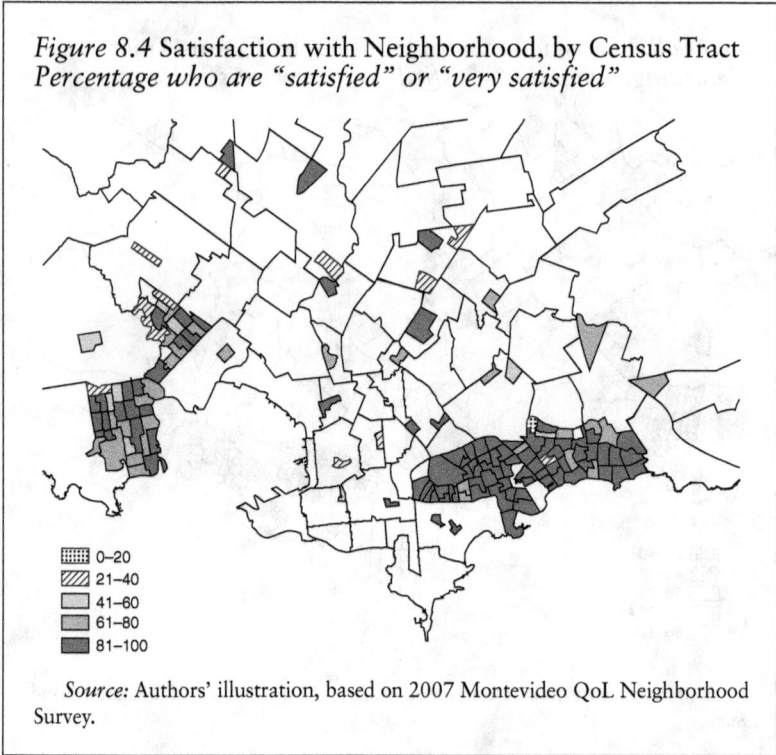

Figure 8.4 Satisfaction with Neighborhood, by Census Tract
Percentage who are "satisfied" or "very satisfied"

- 0–20
- 21–40
- 41–60
- 61–80
- 81–100

Source: Authors' illustration, based on 2007 Montevideo QoL Neighborhood Survey.

being in much worse condition than do respondents—especially in low- and medium-low-stratum neighborhoods.[10]

General Econometric Strategy

Given this rich data set, a strategy is needed to explore systematically how individual characteristics, housing characteristics, and neighborhood characteristics relate to urban QoL. As in other chapters, the hedonic and the LS approaches are combined.

The typical housing hedonic regression is

$$ln\ p_{ij} = \alpha + \beta'\ H_i + \gamma'\ Z_j + v_{ij}, \tag{8.1}$$

where p_{ij} is the rental price of house i located in neighborhood j; H_i is a vector of housing features; Z_j is a vector of neighborhood j characteristics; and v_{ij} is the composite error term, which is a combination of a neighborhood-specific error component and a house-specific error

Table 8.4 Housing Characteristics: Summary Statistics

Characteristic	Indicator	Low- and medium-low-strata neighborhoods selected	High- and medium-high-strata neighborhoods selected	Other neighborhoods (all strata)	Total
Distance to the promenade (minutes)	Mean	28.1	12.3	33.4	22.1
	SD	18.9	10.2	21.0	18.3
Overcrowding[a]	%	12.1	14.9	11.8	13.2
Housing tenure	Owners (%)	54.5	56.4	55.9	55.4
	Renters (%)	14.7	27.4	15.1	20.0
	Occupants (%)	30.8	16.2	29.0	24.6
Construction materials of bad quality	Walls (%)	6.3	0	4.3	3.5
	Roof (%)	10.8	1.5	7.5	6.6
	Floor (%)	7.1	0	5.4	4.1
Rooms	Mean	3.22	3.61	3.26	3.38
	SD	1.30	1.43	1.33	1.37
Bathrooms	Mean	1.08	1.41	1.19	1.23
	SD	0.34	0.70	0.42	0.55
Kitchen exclusive for the household	%	95.8	100.0	97.8	97.8

(continued)

Table 8.4 Housing Characteristics: Summary Statistics *(continued)*

Characteristic	Indicator	Low- and medium-low-strata neighborhoods selected	High- and medium-high-strata neighborhoods selected	Other neighborhoods (all strata)	Total
Utilities (comfort index)	Mean	9.1	12.5	9.9	10.6
	SD	4.1	4.1	3.3	4.3
Rental value (Ur$)[b]	Mean	2,956	7,237	3,972	4,849
	SD	2,268	4,542	2,491	3,975

Source: Authors' compilation, based on 2007 Montevideo QoL Neighborhood Survey.
Note: SD = standard deviation.
a. More than two people per room.
b. For owners or occupants, the rental value is the respondent's estimation of the rent he or she would have to pay if the dwelling were rented.

Table 8.5 Neighborhood Variables: Summary Statistics
Percentage of affirmative responses

Variable	Low- and medium-low-strata neighborhoods selected	High- and medium-high-strata neighborhoods selected	Other neighborhoods (all strata)	Total
Problems seen as serious or very serious by the respondent				
Speeding and dangerous driving	52.9	56.7	47.3	53.8
People who make you feel unsafe	55.3	50.0	58.1	53.4
Drug trafficking or drug sales	60.7	40.3	40.9	50.0
Vandalism	55.0	40.0	42.0	47.3
Car theft or damage	44.4	50.6	47.3	47.3
Presence of gangs	46.8	34.8	29.0	39.8
Rubbish in the streets	40.6	23.8	43.1	34.0
Air pollution	31.1	19.8	31.2	26.4
Noise pollution	18.4	28.0	18.3	22.3
Water pollution	29.2	10.4	14.0	19.8
Graffiti	15.0	10.0	12.9	12.7

(continued)

Table 8.5 Neighborhood Variables: Summary Statistics *(continued)*
Percentage of affirmative responses

Variable	Low- and medium-low-strata neighborhoods selected	High- and medium-high-strata neighborhoods selected	Other neighborhoods (all strata)	Total
Affirmative responses regarding characteristics of the neighborhood				
Access to running water?	98.6	99.7	98.9	99.1
Access to sewerage?	86.1	99.4	83.9	91.3
Street lighting?	85.5	97.6	89.2	90.9
Street pavement?	83.9	98.2	84.9	89.9
Access to waste disposal?	85.0	96.6	67.7	87.8
Access to drainage pipe?	75.0	96.0	86.0	84.9
Satisfied with public transportation?	74.2	75.6	75.3	74.9
Satisfied with public parks and green areas?	53.4	84.5	45.2	65.2
Sidewalks in good shape?	48.4	85.7	53.8	64.3

Feel safe and secure?	52.1	48.2	51.6	50.4
Satisfied with sports infrastructure?	38.2	57.3	38.7	46.1
Satisfied with police service?	31.1	44.2	43.0	37.8
Access to daily garbage collection?	20.3	19.2	40.9	22.2
Affirmative responses by interviewers				
Street lights?	87.6	99.7	83.9	92.1
Good, paved streets?	45.9	87.2	55.9	64.0
Many trees?	33.2	53.7	37.6	42.1
Good, paved sidewalks?	13.0	54.1	21.5	30.8
Constant traffic?	12.1	36.3	25.8	23.6
Garbage in the street?	15.0	9.5	26.9	14.1

Source: 2007 Montevideo QoL Neighborhood Survey.

component $v_{ij} = d_j + \eta_i$. Error component d_j is common to all houses in the neighborhood, and it may capture both uncontrolled differences in amenity characteristics across subcity areas and systematic uncontrolled differences in housing quality across neighborhoods. Either of those two factors would imply that the composite error term across houses within the same subcity area will be correlated, in turn implying a downward bias to the ordinary least squares (OLS)–based standard errors (Moulton 1987) that must be corrected using clustered standard errors. It is assumed that housing prices are independent of individuals' characteristics (such as marital status, income levels, or education of the respondents or their families).

The LS regression takes the following form:

$$QoL_{ij}^{d*} = constant + \beta'H_i + \gamma'Z_j + \delta'X_i + v_{ij}, \tag{8.2}$$

where QoL^{d*} is a QoL dimension indicator, and X_i is a vector of individual characteristics. The true valuation of the dimension cannot be observed because of the ordinal nature of the dependent variable. For instance, if the specific QoL variable used as the dependent variable is "happiness," it will take four values ("not happy at all," "somewhat not happy," "somewhat happy," and "very happy"). It is assumed implicitly that people whose happiness levels are below a certain threshold μ_1 will be "not happy at all," those between that value and a larger μ_2 will be "somewhat not happy," those between μ_2 and an even larger μ_3 will be "somewhat happy," and people with happiness levels above μ_3 will be "very happy":

$$QoL_i^d = 1 \text{ if } QoL_i^{d*} \leq \mu_1. \qquad \text{Not happy at all.} \tag{8.3}$$

$$QoL_i^d = 2 \text{ if } \mu_1 \, QoL_i^{d*} \leq \mu_2 \qquad \text{Somewhat not happy.} \tag{8.4}$$

$$QoL_i^d = 3 \text{ if } \mu_2 \, QoL_i^{d*} \leq \mu_3 \qquad \text{Somewhat happy.} \tag{8.5}$$

$$QoL_i^d = 4 \text{ if } QoL_i^{d*} \geq \mu_3 \qquad \text{Very happy.} \tag{8.6}$$

If one assumes that the error term is normally distributed across observations, an ordered probit model implies the following probabilities:

$$\text{Prob}(QoL_i^d = 1) = \Phi\,(\mu_1 - \beta'H_i + \gamma'Z_j + \delta'X_i), \tag{8.7}$$

$$\text{Prob}(QoL_i^d = 2) = \Phi\,(\mu_2 - \beta'H_i + \gamma'Z_j + \delta'X_i) \\ - \Phi\,(\mu_1 - \beta'H_i + \gamma'Z_j + \delta'X_i), \tag{8.8}$$

$$\text{Prob}(QoL_i^d = 3) = \Phi\,(\mu_3 - \beta'H_i + \gamma'Z_j + \delta'X_i) \\ - \Phi\,(\mu_2 - \beta'H_i + \gamma'Z_j + \delta'X_i), \tag{8.9}$$

$$\text{Prob}(QoL_i^d = 4) = 1 - \Phi(\mu_3 - \beta'H_i + \gamma'Z_j + \delta'X_i), \tag{8.10}$$

where $\Phi(\ )$ is the normal cumulative distribution function.

Van Praag and Ferrer-i-Carbonell (2008) argue that even in an ordered probit estimation, there is (to a certain extent) an implicit cardinalization of the variable under study. Expanding on that idea, they propose a probit-adapted OLS (POLS) method based on a transformation of the data that allows discrete variables to be treated as continuous variables. The transformation consists, first, of deriving the values of a standard normal distribution that corresponds to the cumulative frequencies of the ordinal dependent variable:

$$\Phi(\mu_1) = p_1, \tag{8.11}$$

$$\Phi(\mu_2) = p_1 + p_2, \tag{8.12}$$

$$\Phi(\mu_3) = p_1 + p_2 + p_3, \tag{8.13}$$

$$\Phi(\mu_3) = p_1 + p_2 + p_3 + p_4, \tag{8.14}$$

where p_i is the proportion whose dimension lays in the ith bracket. The final step in the POLS method is estimating the conditional means for the variables under study.

The main advantage of POLS is that it requires less computing time and allows the application of more complex methods (systems of equations, fixed effects, and so forth). Its drawback is that a harsher normality assumption is needed. The results reported in van Praag and Ferrer-i-Carbonell (2008) suggest that POLS and ordered probit yield very similar results, except for a scale factor.

To facilitate comparison with other chapters in this book, the POLS approach is followed for all discrete choice dimension satisfaction variables.

Results of the Regression

Regression results for the hedonic approach are presented in the "hedonic regressions" columns of table 8.6. The explanatory variable is the log of the rental value. The first hedonic regression takes into account only individual household characteristics. Whenever possible, the regressors also were included in logs so that the estimated coefficients could be interpreted as elasticities. For instance, the 0.355 coefficient for rooms implies that a house with twice the number of rooms commands rent that is 35.5 percent higher than another house similar in all other aspects. In the same way, a house with twice as many bathrooms as other houses similar in other aspects would command 85.4 percent higher rent. With respect

Table 8.6 Housing and Neighborhood Regressions

	Hedonic regressions (ln rent)				
Variable	House characteristics	Public goods/ neighborhood externalities	Total	Housing satisfaction	Neighborhood satisfaction
"Objective" individual characteristics					
Female				0.026 (0.035)	−0.002 (0.033)
ln(age)				−4.792 (2.348)**	−3.139 (1.681)*
ln(age)^2				0.639 (0.322)*	0.438 (0.229)*
Turning point				43	36
ln(family size)				−0.361 (0.077)***	0.046 (0.095)
ln(household income)				0.227 (0.029)***	0.038 (0.025)
Housing characteristics					
ln(distance to the promenade)	−0.097 (0.029)***		−0.106 (0.024)***	−0.075 (0.023)***	
Construction materials of bad condition (walls)	−0.311 (0.065)***		−0.447 (0.077)***	−0.432 (0.130)***	

Construction materials of bad condition (roof)	-0.149 (0.066)**	-0.103 (0.088)	-0.098 (0.154)	
Construction materials of bad condition (floor)	-0.378 (0.051)***	-0.367 (0.057)***	-0.202 (0.082)**	
ln(rooms)	0.355 (0.038)***	0.365 (0.035)***	0.315 (0.054)***	
ln(bathrooms)	0.854 (0.159)***	0.801 (0.177)***	0.217 (0.184)	
Kitchen exclusive for the household	0.206 (0.091)**	0.160 (0.056)***	0.156 (0.221)	
Problems seen as serious or very serious by the respondent				
Vandalism	0.050 (0.042)	0.044 (0.032)	-0.126 (0.114)	-0.119 (0.042)***
Presence of gangs	0.037 (0.047)	-0.021 (0.042)	0.046 (0.063)	-0.228 (0.087)**
Rubbish in the street	-0.075 (0.042)*	-0.048 (0.037)	0.087 (0.062)	-0.142 (0.064)**

(continued)

Table 8.6 Housing and Neighborhood Regressions (continued)

Variable	Hedonic regressions (ln rent)			Housing satisfaction	Neighborhood satisfaction
	House characteristics	Public goods/neighborhood externalities	Total		
Pollution (air, noise, or water)		0.014 (0.043)	0.004 (0.035)	-0.149 (0.052)***	-0.120 (0.061)*
Affirmative responses by interviewees to questions on neighborhood characteristics					
Access to running water system?		0.456 (0.254)*	0.042 (0.110)	0.130 (0.414)	0.198 (0.286)
Access to sewerage?		0.374 (0.056)***	0.030 (0.052)	-0.098 (0.124)	-0.122 (0.089)
Access to drainage pipe?		0.034 (0.052)	0.061 (0.050)	-0.026 (0.107)	0.124 (0.116)
Satisfied with public transportation?		-0.183 (0.058)***	-0.107 (0.050)**	0.151 (0.049)***	0.206 (0.076)**
Satisfied with public parks and green areas?		0.113 (0.069)	0.079 (0.055)	0.094 (0.056)*	0.239 (0.064)***
Satisfied with sports infrastructure?		-0.014 (0.052)	0.035 (0.025)	-0.019 (0.064)	0.123 (0.076)
Affirmative responses by interviewers to questions on neighborhood characteristics					
Street lights?		0.175 (0.070)**	0.008 (0.066)	-0.209 (0.115)*	-0.083 (0.090)

Many trees?		0.062 (0.043)	0.035 (0.030)	0.046 (0.057)	0.204 (0.062)***
Good, paved sidewalks?		0.156 (0.070)**	0.047 (0.032)	0.059 (0.100)	0.049 (0.059)
Area dummies					
High-medium- and high-strata area	0.583 (0.051)***	0.683 (0.077)***	0.491 (0.043)***	-0.150 (0.082)*	0.227 (0.120)*
Other areas	0.230 (0.068)***	0.275 (0.098)***	0.224 (0.063)***	0.076 (0.110)	-0.120 (0.183)
Constant	7.061 (0.092)***	6.910 (0.252)***	7.047 (0.204)***	6.798 (3.965)*	4.551 -3.093
Observations (n)	651	609	589	647	667
R^2	0.61	0.43	0.63	0.18	0.19

Source: Authors' calculations, based on 2007 Montevideo QoL Neighborhood Survey.

Note: QoL = quality of life. Clustered standard errors appear in parentheses.

*$p < .10$ **$p < .05$ ***$p < .01$.

to housing construction and conditions, houses with wall or floor problems have statistically significant lower rents. Finally, having a kitchen for the household's exclusive use (that is, one not shared with another household) is associated with higher rent. House location also was found to be statistically significant: the farther away from the promenade, the lower the rent; doubling the distance from the promenade reduces the rent of a house by approximately 10 percent.

The second hedonic regression explores the relationship between rents and block/neighborhood-level public goods and amenities, leaving aside housing characteristics. Some public goods, such as access to running water and to sewerage, increase real estate prices. Sidewalks in good condition and public street lighting also are associated with higher rent. It is not surprising to find that houses in neighborhoods with public transportation and garbage pickup problems command lower rents. The regression also considers neighborhood problems that may affect housing values, such as vandalism or pollution. No significant association is found between any of the problems considered and the rental values.

The third regression (reported in the "Totals" column) combines the two previous sets of regressors. Of the house characteristics that were previously found to be significant, roof condition is the only one that loses its statistical significance. In contrast, not one of the public goods and neighborhood externalities retains its significance. This does not imply, however, that neighborhood features are irrelevant for rental values. Further econometric analyses (not presented in detail here) indicate that a mix of all types of neighborhood characteristics (with and without variation in each neighborhood) is able to explain 20 percent of the variance of rental values in our sample.

The remaining two columns of table 8.6 explore the influence of housing and neighborhood characteristics on housing and neighborhood satisfaction. Individuals' characteristics must be controlled for, as explained in the previous section. Specifically, it is found that housing satisfaction and neighborhood satisfaction show a U-shape, with minimum satisfaction at ages 43 and 36, respectively. As expected, housing satisfaction is significantly associated with family size and family income, but neighborhood satisfaction is not. Family income is expected to affect housing satisfaction because it must be related to aspects of housing comfort that are not captured in the limited set of regressors. As in the hedonic regressions, people living in houses with more rooms and without construction problems are associated with greater housing satisfaction, and housing satisfaction is inversely associated with distance to the promenade.

Among public goods, public parks and public transportation have a positive effect on satisfaction with both housing and neighborhood. In contrast, the number of trees on the block has an effect on the neighborhood dimension, but not on housing satisfaction; and such neighborhood problems as vandalism, gangs, garbage, and pollution have a negative impact on neighborhood satisfaction. Pollution decreases housing satisfaction as well.

The dummies included to capture other neighborhood effects are significant. All other things being equal, people living in high-stratum and medium-high-stratum neighborhoods have higher neighborhood satisfaction, but lower housing satisfaction, than do people living in low- and medium-low-stratum neighborhoods.

Because housing and neighborhood satisfaction can be considered components of life satisfaction, it is worth exploring how housing and neighborhood characteristics directly impact life satisfaction. The regressions reported in table 8.7 confirm that several of those characteristics do affect life satisfaction. As in the previous satisfaction regressions, individuals' characteristics are controlled for. In this respect, life satisfaction declines with age[11]; it is lower for women, but higher for those women who have a stable partner and for those women with more education. Lifestyles also make a difference: whereas sociable people declare themselves happier, workaholics derive less satisfaction from life. Income also matters for life satisfaction.

Several housing characteristics are strongly associated with life satisfaction across the full sample. In particular, the number of rooms, the conditions of the walls and floors, and access to running water affect life satisfaction. Some of these variables, however, lose their significance when the sample is split between workers and nonworkers. Neighborhood features seem to be less relevant for life satisfaction. Among specific features, only public street lighting is significant.

Because life satisfaction depends on both income and a set of housing and neighborhood characteristics, the relative coefficients can be used to estimate the value of those characteristics. For example, an additional room is worth the equivalent of 70.0 percent of average household income, access to running water is worth 9.0 percent, and street lighting is worth 3.7 percent.

Further econometric analyses (not presented here) suggest that although housing satisfaction has some influence on life satisfaction under certain specifications, neighborhood satisfaction is never significant. Consequently, the LS approach cannot be reliably used to value neighborhood amenities or other neighborhood-related public goods.

Conclusion and Policy Implications

Based on a survey of 801 individuals in neighborhoods of different strata, this chapter has described housing and neighborhood conditions in Montevideo, Uruguay, at a level of detail never before attempted. This rich data set was used to explore the factors that influence housing prices, on the one hand; and housing, neighborhood, and life satisfactions on the other.

Table 8.7 Overall Satisfaction, by Employment Status

Variable	All	Workers	Nonworkers
"Objective" individual characteristics			
Female	−0.025	0.016	−0.057
	(0.040)	(0.055)	(0.144)
ln(age)	−0.506	−0.524	−0.710
	(0.106)***	(0.140)***	(0.151)***
Partner (married or not)	0.352	0.330	0.541
	(0.090)***	(0.099)***	(0.106)***
ln(family size)	−0.278	−0.190	−0.493
	(0.194)	(0.223)	(0.258)*
ln(years of schooling)	0.218	0.207	0.230
	(0.093)**	(0.125)	(0.136)
Private health care coverage	0.001	−0.122	0.288
	(0.048)	(0.085)	(0.120)**
Physical activity	0.118	0.106	0.130
	(0.076)	(0.089)	(0.117)
Body mass index	0.005	0.003	0.006
	(0.007)	(0.011)	(0.019)
ln(hours of leisure in the last weekend)	−0.026	0.024	−0.114
	(0.053)	(0.056)	(0.126)

Workaholic	-0.202 (0.052)***	-0.271 (0.056)***	0.051 (0.127)
ln(household income)	0.089 (0.042)**	0.092 (0.061)	0.052 (0.053)
Sociable	0.139 (0.078)*	0.137 (0.053)**	0.153 (0.131)
Housing characteristics			
ln(distance to promenade)	0 (0.049)	0.009 (0.049)	0.002 (0.085)
Construction materials of bad condition (walls)	-0.553 (0.218)**	-0.495 (0.319)	-0.931 (0.202)***
Construction materials of bad condition (roof)	0.087 (0.062)	0.046 (0.080)	0.303 (0.178)*
Construction materials of bad condition (floor)	-0.100 (0.047)**	-0.009 (0.059)	-0.472 (0.130)***
ln(rooms)	0.215 (0.105)**	0.205 (0.118)*	0.195 (0.137)
ln(bathrooms)	0.006 (0.216)	-0.144 (0.171)	0.377 (0.335)

(continued)

Table 8.7 Overall Satisfaction, by Employment Status *(continued)*

Variable	All	Workers	Nonworkers
Kitchen exclusive for the household	−0.423 (0.490)	−0.352 (0.480)	0 (0)
Problems seen as serious or very serious by the respondent			
Vandalism	0.113 (0.060)*	0.045 (0.073)	0.327 (0.146)**
Presence of gangs	0.026 (0.066)	−0.022 (0.075)	0.072 (0.125)
Rubbish in the street	−0.039 (0.066)	−0.023 (0.064)	−0.081 (0.173)
Pollution (air, noise, or water)	−0.063 (0.071)	−0.030 (0.072)	−0.137 (0.121)
Affirmative responses by interviewees to questions on neighborhood characteristics			
Access to running water system?	0.830 (0.407)**	0.961 (0.632)	0.298 (0.417)
Access to sewerage?	−0.171 (0.171)	−0.076 (0.220)	−0.651 (0.173)***
Access to drainage pipe?	−0.010 (0.093)	−0.225 (0.119)*	0.371 (0.128)***
Satisfied with public transportation?	0.094 (0.065)	−0.092 (0.068)	0.576 (0.120)***

Satisfied with public parks and green areas?	-0.034 (0.075)	-0.070 (0.084)	0.118 (0.209)
Satisfied with sports infrastructure?	0.087 (0.070)	0.088 (0.076)	-0.003 (0.125)
Affirmative responses by interviewers on neighborhood characteristics			
Street lights?	0.330 (0.148)**	0.321 (0.162)*	0.242 (0.387)
Many trees?	-0.120 (0.106)	-0.097 (0.127)	-0.056 (0.100)
Good, paved sidewalks?	-0.058 (0.091)	0.008 (0.135)	-0.154 (0.110)
Area dummies			
High-medium- and high-strata area	0.025 (0.075)	0.026 (0.058)	-0.055 (0.173)
Other areas	0.166 (0.095)*	0.291 (0.117)**	0.003 (0.164)
Constant	-0.199 (0.771)	-0.099 (0.656)	0.766 -1.249
Observations (n)	608	414	194
R^2	0.19	0.19	0.31

Source: Authors' calculations, based on 2007 Montevideo QoL Neighborhood Survey.
Note: Clustered standard errors appear in parentheses.
$*p < .10 **p < .05 ***p < .01$.

Housing prices tend to reflect mainly housing characteristics, although they also are affected by location and by unspecified factors that are common to each group of neighborhoods selected. Whereas housing satisfaction is strongly associated with a similar set of factors, neighborhood satisfaction reflects variables ranging from the abundance of trees, public parks, and green areas to the presence of gangs and acts of vandalism. Life satisfaction depends on housing, but little or not at all on neighborhood characteristics or satisfaction; and, therefore, the LS approach cannot be used to value neighborhood-related public goods.

Even though neighborhood variables play almost no role in the hedonic regressions or in individuals' overall well-being, significant differences in rent levels and in overall satisfaction between poor and rich neighborhoods suggest that neighborhood-related factors are at work. Because the provision of specific public amenities is not reflected in housing rents or in people's satisfaction with their own lives, at first glance there appears to be no justification for financing those amenities through housing taxes. However, both housing rents and satisfaction may respond to bundles of neighborhood amenities and characteristics (which would be consistent with the neighborhood-dummy effects found in this study). This response would justify taxation to finance urban amenities, based on the location of dwellings.

Notes

1. According to data from the Economic Commission of Latin America and the Caribbean, 82 percent of the Uruguayan population lived in urban areas in 1970, compared with an average of 57 percent for Latin America and the Caribbean.
2. The Economic Commission of Latin America and the Caribbean reports that in 1960, with a per capita GDP of $3,602 (in 2000 dollars), Uruguay was the third-richest country in Latin America (below Argentina and República Bolivariana de Venezuela). In 2007, with a per capita GDP of $7,255 (in 2000 dollars), Uruguay was the second-richest country (surpassed only by Argentina).
3. More details on the survey methodology and results can be found in Ferre, Gandelman, and Piani (2008) and Ferre et al. (2008).
4. The survey was conducted as a module of the 2007 International Social Survey Program, an annual program of cross-national collaboration on surveys covering topics important for social science research.
5. The sampling design combined the International Social Survey Program methodological requisites for a survey representative of the general population with a representative sample of the neighborhoods selected. The survey is representative of the population aged 18 and over. To avoid a self-selection bias, the questionnaire was answered by a randomly selected member of the household. The interviews were conducted using a face-to-face, paper-and-pencil method. The fieldwork took place from October 2007 to March 2008. The effective number of interviews obtained was 801. (See table 8.1 for distribution by neighborhood.) The overall response rate was 64.9 percent.
6. The table does not attempt to be comprehensive. In particular, the survey included an extensive list of questions on free-time activities.

7. Body mass index is a measure of the weight of a person, scaled according to height. It is defined as the body weight (in kilograms) divided by the square of the person's height (in meters). According to the World Health Organization, a body mass index above 25 is considered overweight and above 30 is considered obese.

8. This index refers to a number of electrical appliances, communication devices, and transportation facilities owned by the surveyed dwellings. The appliances considered are water heater, instant water heater, refrigerator, television, cable television, video player, washing machine, dishwasher, microwave oven, personal computer, motorcycle, automobile, land-line phone, and cell phone.

9. There was one exception. The question on satisfaction with police service offered these response options: "very satisfied," "satisfied," "not very satisfied," and "not at all satisfied." In the table, the information for this item is the sum of "very satisfied" and "satisfied" responses.

10. This type of bias, especially where the poor and those with low levels of education have overly optimistic views of their own lives and living conditions, is not unique to our survey. For an extensive analysis, see IDB (2008).

11. The inclusion of age-squared eliminates the significance of both age variables, without altering significantly the rest of the coefficients.

References

Ferre, Zuleika, Néstor Gandelman, and Giorgina Piani. 2008. "Quality of Life in Montevideo." Research Network Working Paper R-561, Research Department, Inter-American Development Bank, Washington, DC.

Ferre, Zuleika, Néstor Gandelman, Giorgina Piani, and Sven Schaffrath. 2008. "Calidad de vida, tiempo libre y actividad física de los uruguayos: Presentación de resultados empíricos." Working Paper 40, School of Management and Social Sciences, Universidad ORT, Uruguay, Montevideo.

IDB (Inter-American Development Bank). 2008. *Beyond Facts: Understanding Quality of Life*. Development in the Americas: 2009 Report. Washington, DC: IDB.

Moulton, Brent. 1987. "Diagnosis for Group Effects in Regression Analysis." *Journal of Business and Economic Statistics* 5 (2): 275–82.

van Praag, Bernard M.S., and Ada Ferrer-i-Carbonell. 2008. *Happiness Quantified: A Satisfaction Calculus Approach*. Rev. ed. New York: Oxford University Press.

Index

Figures, notes, and tables are indicated by f, n, and t following page numbers.

A

Acosta, Olga, 33
Administrative Department of
    National Statistics
    (Colombia), 118, 156
African Americans, 56
Agustin Codazzi Geographic
    Institute, 156
Alcázar, Lorena, 187
AMBA. *See* Buenos Aires
    Metropolitan Area
amenities pricing (Costa Rica),
    161–86
    data and statistics, 162–67,
        164–65t
    in different urban areas,
        175–79, 176–78t
    using hedonic analysis, 167–75,
        184–85
Amorin, Érica, 32–33
AMSJO. *See* San José, metropolitan
    area of
Amsterdam Airport, noise at, 38
Andrade, Raúl, 187

B

Baarsma, Barbara, 37, 38, 53, 73
Bayer, Patrick, 155

Benabou, Roland, 155
Berger, Mark C., 32, 161, 167, 168
Blacks in U.S., 56
Blanco, Mauricio, 32–33
Blomquist, Glenn, 32, 101,
    161, 167, 168
body mass index (BMI), 227, 253
Bogotá and Medellín (Colombia),
    xxiii, 117–60
    crime and crime rates
        in, 118, 155
    data used in study, 118–20,
        119f, 148
    educational levels and schools
        in, 118, 127–28,
        134, 148, 155
    hedonic approach, 118,
        120–34, 122–26t,
        129–33t, 148, 153–54f
    LS approach, 118, 134–42, 136f,
        137–40t, 142f, 143–45t,
        148, 153–54f, 155
    neighborhood amenities in, 48
    public transportation in, 45,
        121, 127, 128, 134
    QoL indexes, 142–48, 146–47f,
        149–52t, 153–54f, 155
    QoL variables, 119f, 120
    safety in, 41
    segregation in, 55, 56

Bogotá Cómo Vamos
    (QoL monitoring
    scheme), xx, 58
Borjas, George J., 155
British Household Panel Survey, 82
budgeting, participatory, 203
Buenos Aires (Argentina), xxiii,
    91–115
    AMBA description, 91,
        92–93, 94, 97
    city, defined, 35
    crime and crime rates in, 99
    educational levels and schools
        in, 93, 101
    hedonic approach, 50–53,
        52t, 92, 95t, 101–4,
        102–4t, 110
    homes in, 8
    LS approach, 92, 105–10, 113
    methodological issues, 105–6
    neighborhood characteristics
        of, 42, 42t
    NQLS description, 92, 93–101,
        95t, 97–100t
    public transportation in, 45, 103
    QoL indexes, 92, 109–10,
        110–12t, 113
    regression results, 106–9, 107–8t
    segregation in, 55
    title deeds in, 18
    traffic in, 41
Buenos Aires Agglomerate
    (Gran Buenos Aires),
    92, 93, 94
Buenos Aires Metropolitan Area
    (AMBA), 91, 92–93, 94, 97

C

Canada, QoL monitoring in, 58
Caracas, Venezuela, 7, 8
cardinal ordinary least squares
    (COLS) method, 195
car purchases, 70
Cattaneo, Matías, 38
Cavallieri, Fernando, 33
census data for Costa Rica,
    162, 163

Centro Nacional de Consultoría
    (Colombia), 141
Chaparro, Juan Camilo, 18
city, defined, 34–35
civil society/trust sphere variables
    in Lima, 188, 192,
        202–3, 206–7, 206–7t,
        214, 215–21, 218–19f
Clark, Andrew E., 70
Codazzi Institute, 156
COLS (cardinal ordinary least
    squares) method, 195
Commission for Formalization
    of Informal Ownership
    (Peru), 5
Conley, Timothy G., 155
contingent valuation approach, 67
corruption, 28n12
Cortés, Darwin, 33, 117
Costa Rica, xxiii, 161–86.
    See also San José
    amenities pricing
        in different urban areas,
            175–79, 176–78t
        using hedonic analysis,
            167–75, 184–85
    AMSJO
        amenities pricing for, 168–72,
            169–71t, 175, 176t, 182
        neighborhood rankings for,
            172–75, 173–74t
    data and descriptive statistics,
        162–67
    educational levels and schools,
        166, 171
    Housing and Population Census
        data (2000), 162–63,
        164–65t
    LS approach, 161, 179–82,
        180f, 181–84t, 185
    Multipurpose Household Survey
        data (2003), 162, 163–67
credit, access to, 18
crime and crime rates. See also
        specific types of crime
        (e.g., drug dealing)
    in Bogotá and Medellín, 118, 155
    in Buenos Aires, 99

happiness and, 136
as indicator, 35
in Latin American cities, 20,
24f, 28nn13–14, 33
in Lima, 189, 192, 220, 221
in Montevideo, 224–25, 252
policy and, 91
safety and, 58
segregation and, 57, 59
Cristini, Marcela, 12
Cruces, Guillermo, 91, 93, 113n2
Cutler, David M., 155

D

deeds, title, 5, 18
deficits in housing.
See housing deficits
De Soto, Hernando, 18
Di Tella, Rafael, 32
Dolan, Paul, 67
Dominican Republic, public
services quality in, 22
drug dealing, 25, 99, 103, 232

E

earthquakes, 179
Easterlin, Richard, 20, 70
Echeverry, Juan Carlos, 157n12
econometric methods, 76–80
Economic Commission for Latin
America and the Caribbean
(UN), 12, 252nn1–2
educational levels and schools
in Bogotá and Medellín, 118,
127–28, 134, 148, 155
in Buenos Aires, 93, 101
in Costa Rica, 166, 171
as indicator, 35
in Latin American cities, 25
in Lima, 189
in Montevideo, 227
segregation and, 55, 56
electricity, access to, 8
employment status, 247, 248–51t
Encuesta de Calidad de
Vida-Bogotá, 118, 156

Encuesta de Calidad de
Vida-Medellín, 118, 156
environmental (dis)amenities,
166, 184
European Social Survey, 157n19
European Union, Urban Audit
program in, 58
Eurostat, xx, 83

F

Fang, Hanming, 155
Fay, Marianne, 27n7
Ferre, Zuleika, 223
Ferrer-i-Carbonell, Ada, 65, 77, 78,
80, 82, 135, 180, 195, 241
fertility rates, 2
fire departments, 162, 167, 171
flood risks, 175, 179, 184–85
Foreign Policy magazine Global
Cities Index, xix, 82
Formalization of Informal
Ownership, Commission
for (Peru), 5
Frey, Bruno, 32, 60n11
Frijters, Paul, 135
"full implicit prices," 101

G

Gallup polls, 22, 25, 27n5, 156
Gallup World Poll (2007), 13,
16, 20, 27n4
GAM. *See* San José, greater
metropolitan area of
Gamboa, Luis Fernando, 33, 117
Gandelman, Néstor, 223
gangs, 41
Gardner, Jonathan, 32
Gaviria, Alejandro, 20
GDP (gross domestic product),
13, 27n6
gentrification, 36
geographic information systems,
161, 162
German Socio-Economic
Panel, 158n19
Glaeser, Edward L., 155

Global Cities Index, xix, 82
González, Jorge I., 33, 117
Gran Buenos Aires. *See* Buenos
   Aires Agglomerate
green areas. *See also* recreation
      and recreation areas
   hedonic approach and, 73–74
   as indicators, 35
   in Latin American cities, 23, 25
   in Lima, 192, 201–2, 204*t*, 221
   in Montevideo, 224, 233,
      246, 252
   neighborhood characteristics
      and, 43
gross domestic product (GDP),
      13, 27*n*6
Guatemala, home satisfaction
      in, 16
Guerra, José Alberto, 33
Guyana, public services quality
      in, 22
Gyourko, Joseph, 161

H

Haiti
   home satisfaction in, 16
   public services quality in, 22
Hall, Luis J., 161, 163, 179, 180
Ham, Andrés, 91, 93, 113*n*2
happiness
   crime and, 136
   happiness economics, 70–71
   hedonic approach and, 75
   household heads and, 135
   income levels and, 141
   LS approach and, 96, 105, 106,
      134, 157*n*18
   microeconometric function
      for, 38
   in Montevideo, 230,
      231*t*, 232–34*f*, 247
   QoL and, 65–66
health and health facilities, 103,
      167, 199, 200*t*, 227
Heckman, James J., 168
hedonic price approach
   for Bogotá and Medellín, 118,
      120–34, 122–26*t*,
      129–33*t*, 148, 153–54*f*
   for Buenos Aires, 50–53,
      52*t*, 92, 95*t*, 101–4,
      102–4*t*, 110
   for Costa Rica, 167–75, 184–85
   for Montevideo, 234, 240, 241,
      242–45*t*, 246, 252
   QoL index, 67–70, 73–76, 83–84
   QoL measurement, xxii,
      31–32, 33, 35–37,
      43–59, 46–47*t*, 49–52*t*
Helliwell, John F., 155
Hoehn, John P., 32, 161, 167, 168
homicide rates, 20, 28*nn*13–14
hospitals. *See* health and
      health facilities
house prices. *See* real estate prices
Housing and Population Census
      (Costa Rica, 2000),
      162–63, 164–65*t*
housing characteristics. *See
      also* neighborhood
      characteristics
   in hedonic and LS approaches,
      36–37, 41, 46–47*t*, 49–51*t*
   household size in
      Costa Rica, 163
   as indicator, 35
   in Montevideo, 230–32,
      235–36*t*, 252
   ownership data, 4–8,
      5–6*t*, 11*f*, 199
housing deficits, 2, 8–13, 14–15*t*
human development index, 60*n*4

I

income levels
   in Costa Rica, 163, 165, 167,
      175, 182, 184
   happiness and, 141
   home and city satisfaction and,
      16–17, 18–19
   in Lima, 189, 197, 198*t*, 199
   LS approach and, 85, 105

in Montevideo, 246, 247
neighborhood characteristics
and, 43–44
segregation and, 54–55
Índice de Calidad de Vida, 55, 120
individual sphere variables
in Lima, 188, 197,
198–200*t,* 199,
215–20, 218–19*f*
infrastructure, 1, 91, 199, 199*t,* 207
Inter-American Development
Bank, 32, 67
International Social Survey Program
(2007), 252*nn*4–5

J

job satisfaction, 82

K

Kahn, Matthew, 161
Kahneman, Daniel, 75
Kremer, Michael, 155

L

labor force characteristics,
164–65*t,* 166
Latin American cities, xxiii, 1–29.
See also individual cities
home ownership and
services, 4–8, 5–6*t,*
7*f,* 11–12*f*
housing deficits, 2, 8–13, 14–15*t*
satisfaction with cities, 13–17,
16–17*t,* 20–27, 21*t,*
22–24*f,* 26*f*
satisfaction with homes, 13–20,
16–17*t,* 19*t*
urban expansion, 2–4, 3*f*
Latin American Demographic
Center, 12
Latinobarómetro, 20
Layard, Richard, 134
leisure-related venues, 103–4
Leyden School, 70

life satisfaction (LS) approach
for Bogotá and Medellín, 118,
134–42, 136*f,* 137–40*t,*
142*f,* 143–45*t,* 148,
153–54*f,* 155
for Buenos Aires, 92,
105–10, 113
for Costa Rica, 161, 179–82,
180*f,* 181–84*t,* 185
happiness and, 105, 106,
134, 157*n*18
for Montevideo, 224, 234,
240, 247, 252
QoL index, 67, 70–76, 83–84
QoL measurement, xxi–xxii,
31–32, 33, 35, 36–43,
39–40*t,* 53–59
Lima (Peru), xxiii, 187–222
city, defined, 34–35
civil society/trust sphere
variables in, 188, 192,
202–3, 206–7, 206–7*t,*
214, 215–21, 218–19*f*
context for, 188–92, 190*f,* 191*t*
crime and crime rates in, 189,
192, 220, 221
educational levels and schools
in, 189
green areas in, 192, 201–2,
204*t,* 221
home ownership in, 8
income levels in, 189, 197,
198*t,* 199
methodology, 193–95
public services in, 55–56
public transportation in, 202,
205*t,* 214, 220
QoL indexes, 188, 214–20,
215–17*t,* 218–19*f*
QoL indicators, 188, 197–204,
198–207*t,* 219–21
QoL regressions, 195–214,
196–97*f,* 208–14*t,* 215
safety in, 41
segregation in, 54–55
self-built homes in, 7
survey overview, 192–93, 193*t*

Linneman, Peter, 162, 171
Living Standards Measurement
      Surveys, 156
London (U.K.), QoL monitoring
      in, 58
Lopes, Gustavo Peres, 33
Lora, Eduardo, 1, 18
LS. *See* life satisfaction approach
Luechinger, Simon, 32, 60n11

M

MacCulloch, Robert, 32
Madrigal, Róger, 161, 163, 179, 180
McMillan, Robert, 155
Medellín. *See* Bogotá and Medellín
Medina, Carlos, 117, 120, 141
Mendieta, Juan Carlos, 157n11
Mercer (survey company), xix, 82
Metcalfe, Robert, 67
Metro-Plus station (Medellín),
      134, 157n17
Mexico City (Mexico)
   home ownership in, 8
   self-built houses in, 7
migration, 2–4, 188
Montevideo (Uruguay),
      xxiii, 223–53
   crime and crime rates in,
      224–25, 252
   educational levels and schools
      in, 227
   general econometric strategy,
      224, 234–41
   green areas in, 224, 233,
      246, 252
   hedonic approach, 234, 240,
      241, 242–45t, 246, 252
   house prices in, 45
   housing characteristics, 230–32,
      235–36t, 252
   income levels in, 246, 247
   individual characteristics
      and opinions, 227–30,
      228–29t, 231t, 232–34f
   LS approach, 224, 234, 240,
      247, 252

neighborhoods
   characteristics, 232–34,
      237–39t, 252
   description of, 224–26,
      225f, 226t
   policy implications, 247–52
   public transportation in, 246
   regression results, 241–47,
      242–45t, 248–51t, 252
   safety in, 41
   segregation in, 54, 55
   survey results, 227–34
Montevideo QoL Neighborhood
      Survey (2007), 230
Morales, Leonardo, 117, 120, 141
mortality rates, 2
Moya, Ramiro, 12
Multipurpose Household Survey
      (Costa Rica), 162, 163–67

N

National Institute of Statistics and
      Census (Argentina), 92
National Statistical Institute
      (Uruguay), 224
National Survey on Quality of Life
      (Colombia), 33
Necesidades Básicas Insatisfechas
      (Unsatisfied Basic
      Needs), 55
neighborhood characteristics.
      See also housing
      characteristics
   in Montevideo, 232–34,
      237–39t, 252
   description of, 224–26,
      225f, 226t
   QoL measurements, 41–55, 42t,
      46–47t, 49–52t, 84–85
Neighborhood Quality of Life
      Survey (NQLS), 92,
      93–101, 95t, 97–100t
neighborhood rankings, 172–75,
      173–74t
noise, 38, 104, 232–33
Núñez, Jairo, 117, 120, 141

O

obesity rates, 227, 253
Odría, Manuel A., 5
Oswald, Andrew J., 32, 70

P

"paradox of unhappy growth," 17
Pareto, Vilfredo, 65–66
parks. *See* green areas
participatory budgeting, 203
Perdomo, Jorge Andrés, 157n11
Piani, Giorgina, 223
police force, confidence in,
    20, 23f, 25
political participation, 166
pollution, 104, 232–33, 246–47
poverty, 3
Powell, Andrew, 31
pro-bit adapted ordinary least
    squares, 241
property prices. *See* real
    estate prices
prostitution, 99
public goods
    hedonic approach to valuation
        of, xxii, 32, 43
    in Lima, 192
    LS approach to valuation of,
        xxii, 37–38, 86–87
    in Montevideo, 233, 246, 252
    Multipurpose Household Survey
        data on, 166–67
public policy
    LS and hedonic approaches used
        to drive, 59
    in Montevideo, 247–52
    recommendations, 155–56
    to reduce segregation, 57
public transportation
    in Bogotá and Medellín, 45,
        121, 127, 128, 134
    in Buenos Aires, 45, 103
    hedonic approach and, 54, 84
    as indicator, 35
    in Latin American cities, 2, 25

in Lima, 202, 205t, 214, 220
in Montevideo, 246
Putnam, Robert D., 155

Q

quality of life (QoL), xxiii, 31–64.
    See also quality of life
    (QoL) index
    in Bogotá and Medellín, 117–60
    in Buenos Aires, 91–115
    choice of indicators, 35–36, 60n5
    city, defined, 34–35
    in Costa Rica, 161–86
    definition of, 65–66
    hedonic approach to, 31–32,
        33, 35–37, 43–59,
        46–47t, 49–52t
    in Latin America, 1–29
    in Lima, 187–222
    LS approach to, 31–32,
        33, 35, 36–43,
        39–40t, 53–59
    in Montevideo, 223–53
    segregation and, 45, 53–57, 59
quality of life (QoL) index,
    xxiii, 65–90
    econometric methods, 76–80
    hedonic price approach, 67–70,
        73–76, 83–84
    LS approach, 67, 70–76, 83–84
    two-layer and multilayer
        models, 80–82
    urban life index, 82–87
Quality of Life Project
    (New Zealand), xx, 83
Quality of Living survey
    (Mercer), xix, 82

R

real estate prices. *See also* rent and
    rental prices
    in Bogotá and Medellín, 118,
        120, 121, 127–28
    in Buenos Aires, 93, 113
    in Montevideo, 246

recreation and recreation areas.
    See also green areas
    in Latin American cities, 2
    leisure-related venues, 103–4
    in Lima, 202–3, 206*t*,
        214, 215, 220–21
    Multipurpose Household
        Survey data on, 167
rent and rental prices. *See also* real
        estate prices
    in Bogotá and Medellín,
        128–29, 134
    in Buenos Aires, 96, 101,
        102–3*t*, 103–4, 113
    in Costa Rica, 163, 167–68,
        171–72, 179, 182
    hedonic approach and, xxi,
        xxiii, 68–69, 73–75, 84
    in Montevideo, 223–24, 230,
        241, 246, 252
    in San José, 48, 162
Rivera, David, 33
roads, 70, 166, 175, 179, 184
Roback, Jennifer, 32
Robalino, Juan, 161,
        163, 179, 180
Robbins, Lionel, 65–66

S

Sabana Park (San José), 175
safety considerations. *See also*
        crime and crime rates
    in Costa Rica, 167, 171, 175, 182
    hedonic approach to, 68
    house prices and, 54
    as indicator, 35
    in Latin American cities, 20,
        22*f*, 24*f*, 25, 28*nn*12–13
    in Lima, 200–201, 202*t*,
        214, 220
    in Montevideo, 232
    neighborhood characteristics
        and, 41, 58
Sanguinetti, Pablo, 31
sanitation. *See* sewerage
        and sanitation

San José (Costa Rica)
    city, defined, 35
    gangs in, 41
    greater metropolitan
        area of (GAM)
        amenity prices for, 175,
            176*t*, 179, 182
        Housing and Population
            Census data for, 163
        unemployment rates in,
            165–66
    metropolitan area of (AMSJO)
        amenity prices for,
            168–72, 169–71*t*,
            175, 176*t*
        house prices in, 45
        Housing and Population
            Census data for, 163
        neighborhood and housing
            characteristics in,
            48, 49–51*t*
        neighborhood rankings for,
            172–75, 173–74*t*
        unemployment rates in, 166
    rental prices in, 162
Santiago de Chile, infrastructure
        in, xix–xx
São Paulo (Brazil), home
        ownership in, 8
Sarin, Rakesh, 75
satisfaction indifference curves,
        71–73, 72*f*
Schelling, Thomas C., 155
schools. *See* educational levels
        and schools
security. *See* safety considerations
segregation, 45, 53–57, 59
service delivery, 91
sewerage and sanitation, 8, 13,
        27*n*7, 168, 171, 246
shadow costs, 75
sidewalk conditions, 25, 41, 104
socioeconomic levels and status,
        164–65*t*, 166, 189,
        190*f*, 191*t*, 215, 217,
        217*t*, 219*f*, 221
Stein, Ernesto H., 20

street cleanliness, 201, 203*t*, 206, 214, 220, 221
street posts, 103
Stutzer, Alois, 32, 60*n*11

T

taxes, 53, 67
telephone services, 8, 27*n*5
Tetaz, Martín, 91, 93, 113*n*2
Tiebout, Charles, 54, 56, 57
title deeds, 5, 18
Topa, Giorgio, 155
Tracy, Joseph, 161
trade-off ratios, 74, 79
traffic, 41
TransMilenio station (Bogotá), 45, 121, 127, 157*nn*11–12
transportation. *See* public transportation
trees. *See* green areas
Trinidad and Tobago, home satisfaction in, 16
trust. *See* civil society/trust sphere variables in Lima
two-layer satisfaction model, 80–82, 81*f*

U

unemployment rates, 165–66, 224, 227
unhappy growth paradox, 17
United Nations
    Development Programme, 167
    Economic Commission for Latin America and the Caribbean, 12, 252*nn*1–2
    urban population statistics, 1
United States, segregation in, 54, 56
University of Antioquia, 118
Unsatisfied Basic Needs (Necesidades Básicas Insatisfechas), 55
Urban Audit system (Eurostat), xx, xxi, 58, 83

urban expansion, 2–4, 3*f*
urban sphere variables in Lima, 188, 200–202, 202–5*t*, 208, 214, 215–20, 218–19*f*

V

Vandell, Kerry, 54, 61*n*19
van Praag, Bernard M.S.
    cardinal ordinary least squares method, 195
    econometric method, 77, 78, 80
    happiness economics, 70
    hedonic and LS approaches, relationship between, 37, 53, 73
    job satisfaction, 82
    LS approach, 180
    noise nuisance, 38
    pro-bit adapted ordinary least squares, 241
    QoL index, 65
Vienna (Austria), QoL in, xix
volcanic eruptions, 45, 48, 175, 182

W

wages. *See* income levels
Wakker, Peter, 75
water sources
    housing satisfaction and, 18
    in Latin American cities, 8, 13, 23, 27*n*7
    in Montevideo, 246
    public health and, 199
    rental prices and, 168, 171
Winkelmann, Liliana, 32
Winkelmann, Rainer, 32
women
    life satisfaction for, 247
    safety for, 25

Z

zoning, 57, 69
Zurich (Switzerland), QoL in, xix